LIFE STANDS EXPLAINED

When we remember we are all mad, the
mysteries disappear and life stands explained.

-Mark Twain

LIFE STANDS EXPLAINED

The Simple Fun Book That's All About You

and why

SOMETHING like NOTHING is EVERYTHING!

C.J. CAREW

HEATHEN ORIGINALS
THEIR BOOKS. THEIR WAY.

Published in the good ole United States of America
by Heathen Originals, an imprint of
Heathen Creative
P.O. Box 588
Point Pleasant, WV 25550-0588

Heathen Originals are available at quantity discounts.
Bear witness to the yackety-yak and tomfoolery at:

heathenoriginals.com | heatheneditions.com

Social? Tag us! @heatheneditions
Photo? Tag it! #heathenedition #heathenoriginal

***Life Stands Explained**: The Simple Fun Book That's All About You — and why Something like Nothing is Everything!*

Caution: This book may alter your mind.

eBook ISBN: 9798900759012
Hardcover ISBN: 9798900758015
Paperback ISBN: 9798900757018

Library of Congress Control Number: 2026933494

Book and cover design by Sheridan Cleland
Set in 10.5pt New Century Schoolbook
Titles in Seuss & Constructive Buddy

HEATHEN ORIGINAL #1
FIRST EDITION
May 15, 2026

To the Family

THE PARTS

HEATHENRY
The Preface

One hundred and one . . . 101.

That's how many months separate the official publication dates of the first **Heathen Edition** (December 15, 2017) and this first **Heathen Original** (May 15, 2026).

I wish I could say that we planned it that way from the beginning, but I can't. And I do not subscribe to coincidence, so — rightfully so — the universe has made it so, with its seemingly random yet strategic alignment of varying schedules and contractual deadlines.

But it's perfect. It's *so perfect*.

So utterly perfectly-perfect that I have tears filling my eyes as I type this.

Why?

Because of what that number can mean when you choose to peer beyond its surface. Yes, many college introductory courses begin at 101, and that is, in itself, perfectly fitting for a book entitled **LIFE STANDS EXPLAINED**. But, at its root, in basic terms, 101 represents: form, void, form.

In Jungian psychology, it is the ego confronting the unconscious and returning changed, or the self returning after passing through emptiness, representing a cycle of initiation, void, and re-initiation. A wilderness between two identities; exile and return; death and rebirth; the moment when a person steps into something new, passes through uncertainty, and re-emerges still themselves, but changed.

In short, 101 is the Hero's Journey in numeric form.

And why it's perfect is because, as you will soon learn, the Hero's Journey is, in part, why **LIFE STANDS EXPLAINED** exists. (One could argue it's the reason any book exists, but let's stay focused.) However, it's also perfect because, in many ways, it mirrors the journey of **Heathen** itself: borne of uncertainty and death (both figurative and literal), unsure of its literary destiny as its creator wrestled with his own destiny, he who has somehow managed, in eight short years, to begin and conclude two wholly and vastly different careers, all while engineering, sustaining, and maintaining a burgeoning **Heathen** catalog.

We launched **Heathen Editions** with one book, and now, after eight years, we're launching **Heathen Originals** with one book, which brings to mind another way to say 101 — one-oh-one — because a definition of "oh" most assuredly underpins this *form-void-form* journey of ours—

> oh, ***exclamation.*** — used to express a range of emotions including surprise, anger, disappointment, or joy.

—because "a void of uncertainty in which a range of emotions has been experienced" is the exact right way, and perhaps the only way, to describe the journey that has taken place between the publication of the first **Heathen Edition** and this first **Heathen Original**.

So, how did we arrive at this **Original**?

In the words of David Foster Wallace, the "screen gets all fuzzy now as the [reader]'s invited to imagine this . . ."

In late 2023, my friend Justin[1] contacted me and said (paraphrased), "Hey, I met this guy at a leadership event, he lives in Charleston, he's spent a decade writing a book of philosophy, and now he's looking for a publisher."

I replied (paraphrased), "I'm not sure we're ready to publish original works, yet — but I absolutely have to meet this West Virginian who's spent a decade writing a book of philosophy!"

If you're not from or in any way familiar with West Virginia, I'm not sure any words exist to accurately express the absurd-rarity of this exchange. Had Justin said, "Hey, check out this video I shot of a real-life, honest-to-God unicorn in Kanawha State Forest," the immediate, staggering effect would have been the exact same. If I were made to choose a word, though, gun-to-head, then "incredulous" surely nears the bullseye.

And so, on December 22, 2023, we three convened, naturally, at the central and unofficial meeting place of West Virginia creatives: Taylor Books, 226 Capitol St., Charleston.

And since I've dug a little into number meanings already, I will say that, in hindsight, that 22 date is not lost on me. In numerology,[2] the number 22 is considered the "Master Builder" number, symbolizing the ability to turn ambitious dreams into reality through balance, discipline, and practical action. Certainly an auspicious number for this meeting!

I remember I arrived early, got my usual latte, and parked myself near a corner, still incredulous but now a little anxious, and awaited the arrival of "the philosopher."

[1] Justin Litton is (and will perhaps go down in the history books as) the best cinematographer currently working in and to ever hail from West Virginia. Check him out online https://backporch.pictures and hire him!

[2] For the record, I don't wholly subscribe to numerology, but I do love the "lookit, that's neat!" meaning it ascribes to numbers.

ends p. xviii

Justin arrived next, which I was thankful for because I didn't actually know what "the philosopher" looked like, although, if I'm being honest, I was hoping for a wild-man hybrid-fusion of full-beard Walt Whitman and crazy-hair Tom Waits.

Then, a gentleman rounded the corner, and my first impression upon seeing him was, "unassuming, soccer dad, probably golfs — this must be our guy," and, sure enough, Justin introduced me to C.J. Carew.

Next, we ordered a round of coffees, then promptly got down to the business of chitchat. Turns out I was correct about the soccer-dad and golf-playing impressions, but, according to the Myers-Briggs Type Indicator, I'm an INFJ, so that means I know you better than you know you.[3] And life experience, married with twenty years of filmmaking know-how, has taught me that unless you're auditioning an actor for Bozo the Clown, "unassuming" is *always* the best first impression. If someone arrives to a first meeting "assuming" and strutting like a peacock, good luck!

Another impression I perceived about C.J. after a couple minutes of conversation was that he seemed a little cocky — not a lot, just a little (certainly not enough to render the "unassuming" impression null) — which made me curious, "Were you born here?" I asked.

"No, I was born and raised in New Jersey. I've only lived in West Virginia for a decade."

Aha! Jersey: where cockiness is ingrained like attitude in a rooster. But, I mean, to be fair, living next door to an assemblage of entitled New Yorkers is enough to make any persons cocky — *generationally*. *insert rooster crow here*

After a few more minutes of general meet-and-greet appetizer-talk, then came the main course: "So, tell me about this book of philosophy that you've written."

[3] Technically, if it matters, I'm a Sigma INFJ, so if anyone is curious why I'm a hermit who rarely leaves his hermitage and cares not what you think about it — *voila!*

And that's when I noticed a discernible change in C.J.'s demeanor: down came the Jersey-borne defenses and he locked in to that "thing" I've begun to notice is present in all bona fide writers: an inimitable authenticity . . .

Imagine, if you will (re: DFW's fuzzy screen), that, as C.J. began telling his story, all of the background actors quietly gathered their things and slowly exited, just as the background soundtrack volume gradually decreased, lowering in tandem with the background lighting, leaving C.J. spotlit in a chair, articulating a soliloquy so moving that your eyes could only ever do one thing: leak.

Artistic expression spewed forth like soldiers storming a beach, the cannons of inspiration sounded, booming names: Jung, Campbell, Twain, Seuss, Emerson, Frankl, Updike. In one moment, C.J. was recounting life when he was at his lowest, when life itself was at its darkest, then the next moment was accented with a hard-won, golden-rayed, silver-lined cosmic revelation disguised as a *ba-dum-tss* joke. I was moved, engrossed, I wanted — no, *I needed* — to know more, so the very first thing I did was attempt to convince C.J. that we were *not* the publisher for him, "We've never published an original work before, and if we were to, then you'd be the first, and that ride might be turbulent and a whole lotta not-fun as we discover that process."

A wide grin tore across his face, "I like the idea of being the first **Heathen Original**. There's something novel about that!"

I then spent the next several minutes trying to convince him otherwise, but he was undeterred. If I zigged, he zagged; if I lunged, he parried. Justin's head moved back and forth as if he were watching a ping-pong match. I began to get the impression that C.J. showed up to the meeting *knowing* that we were the publisher for him, no matter what, come hell or high water, and that's when I remembered: Jersey.

insert rooster crow here

ends p. xviii

"Okay, okay," I said, "Send me your manuscript, and we'll go from there."

A couple weeks later, I got my first look at **LIFE STANDS EXPLAINED** — all 350 pages of it.

A couple weeks later, I received a revised copy.

A week later, I received another revised copy.

A week after that, another revision.

Two weeks later: yep, another.

"We've got a tinkerer!" I exclaimed.

It seems to me that writers generally fall into one of two categories: one-and-dones or tinkerers. Both can be maddening in their own way: one-and-done's generally believe that they've already said best that which they needed to say and must be wholly convinced that revisions will improve their work, whereas tinkerer's generally believe that they can say better that which they've already said and must be wholly convinced that revisions must end (soon; very soon; no — *now*) or the work will never get published.

I'm chuckling as I type this because I'm a tinkerer myself, so I know the struggle well. It's taken me six days to arrive at this point of this **Heathenry** as I write and rewrite and revise, then revise some more, while I'm simultaneously waiting on C.J., ever the tinkerer, to send me his last and final-*final*-no-really-I-promise-these-are-the-*final* revisions for this book. But, I digress! Back to our timeline:

At the time, I honestly wasn't sure what to make of C.J.'s 350-page manuscript. If I were made to choose a word, though, "unwieldy" nears the mark. Within it, there was a book, but I didn't feel qualified to start hacking away at it to discover it. Part of that unqualified feeling was wrestling with the possibility that this *might* be our first **Original**, which meant our first time working with a living, breathing author, which meant that I didn't know what our process for doing that was, exactly, because I wasn't sure how to look a living, breathing author in the eyes and tell them that they needed to cut a hundred pages out of something they had poured their heart and soul into for a decade (re: turbulent discovery).

And then I got busy working full-time for the second of my two aforementioned eight-year-spanning careers, and *all* **Heathen** work went (mostly) quiet for a year.

During that time, in a moment of contention with my boss, I was reminded of the proverb — *if you don't have a plan for yourself, you'll become a part of someone else's* — and I realized that I had allowed myself to get sidetracked from my **Heathen** plan. Here I was experiencing the exile and return, the death and rebirth — I had stepped into something new, passed through uncertainty, and was now re-emerging changed. My **Heathen** resolve re-forged in a fire of reaffirming realization. *insert rooster crow here*

And, within what seemed like hours of that realization, as if on some grand cosmic, celestial cue, C.J. sent me a revised copy of his manuscript (again) — all 250 pages of it.

He had, unprompted yet somehow knowingly, taken it upon himself to fiercely eliminate one hundred pages.

I read it immediately.

And within the macro of C.J.'s manuscript — the personal story he tells, the universal wisdom he shares — I recognized the micro journey of my own reaffirming realization, and that's when I knew that the universe was doing that seemingly random yet strategic alignment of circumstances, and *that's* when I knew:

This was *the book*.

Its time *was now*.

This would be *the first* **Heathen Original**.

A little over a week later, after I had quickly gotten all of our preliminaries in order, I sent C.J. the first ever **Heathen Originals** publishing agreement.

Then, seven weeks later, after some negotiation, it was signed and made official on May 19, 2025 — and here we are.

ends p. xviii

For the record, I will say that I greatly admire C.J. for having the courage to cut one hundred pages out of his manuscript. I know how attached he was to those words, so I don't even have to confirm with him to know that *that* was his own micro *form-void-form* Hero's Journey.

And in that personal act there is a universal lesson . . .

Joseph Campbell taught "the cave you fear to enter holds the treasure you seek" and "choose your sacrifice, or it will be chosen for you."

Those one hundred pages meant all the difference in C.J.'s book getting published. He feared losing those words — that was the cave he feared to enter — but he willingly chose to sacrifice them, and in that act he found the treasure he sought — for you now hold that treasure in your hands.

And, I will say, C.J. has set a high bar for all **Heathen** authors to follow because now I will never hesitate to look a living, breathing author in the eyes and say, "C.J. Carew cut one hundred pages out of his manuscript, and his book was all the better for it. Are you willing to do the same?"

Finally, I want to bring your attention to a recurring undercurrent that you will soon discover in the pages ahead: it was only on my fourth read-through of this book that I became aware that **water** is present in nearly all of the turning points of C.J.'s life story — crossing a river led to the discovery of the book that inspired him to become an author, then, later, staring into a bathtub of water induced the realization that his life had to change. He even quotes a line from Ralph Waldo Emerson's essay "Spiritual Laws" concerning a river, but I want to present the full passage here because there is much wisdom to be gleaned from it:

"Each man has his own vocation. The talent is the call. There is one direction in which all space is open to him. He has faculties silently inviting him thither to endless exertion. He is like a ship in a river; he runs against obstructions on every side but one; on that side all obstruction is taken away, and he sweeps serenely over a deepening channel into an infinite sea. This talent and this call depend on his organization, or the mode in which the general soul incarnates itself in him. He inclines to do something which is easy to him and good when it is done, but which no other man can do. He has no rival. For the more truly he consults his own powers, the more difference will his work exhibit from the work of any other. His ambition is exactly proportioned to his powers. The height of the pinnacle is determined by the breadth of the base. Every man has this call of the power to do somewhat unique, and no man has any other call."

I have ruminated on that passage for weeks now because I am fascinated by the series of circumstances and events that have led to the existence of this book — how C.J. and I are like ships in Emerson's river, where our obstruction-less sides have brought us together. To bring meaning full circle in this **Heathenry**, it's not lost on me that the 2014 *water* cri–er, uh, *ahem* *kerfuffle* (occurring in a river, no less) is what brought C.J. to West Virginia; a kerfuffle without which C.J. likely would never have written this book, likely would never have met Justin, and Justin would never have introduced us.

Water is the oldest language the world speaks: the first darkness before creation, the mirror of the soul, the border between life and death, the womb and the grave, the flood that erases and the spring that renews. It is the unconscious rising in dreams, the baptism that drowns the false self, the river that remembers, the sea that forgets, the force that moves mountains, and the threshold every pilgrim must cross. In every tradition it is origin, danger, purification, desire, oblivion, and return — an element that holds both chaos and clarity, both dissolution and rebirth. To speak of water is to speak of the human condition itself: fluid, perilous, transformative, necessary, always seeking its level.

In short, water is the Hero's Journey in elemental form.

ends next p.

Knowing all of this, I now ask you, dear reader:

What is the cave that you currently fear to enter?

What is the sacrifice that you are afraid to make?

If those questions stirred something in you, then that stirring is precisely why this book has found its way into your hands . . . no matter *who* you are, *where* you are, or *when* you are, you must know that it was *not* coincidence or chance that brought you into possession of this book — it was, of course, a seemingly random yet strategic alignment of circumstances — *because how could it be otherwise?*

That stirring is your threshold-moment — the point where the river claims you, the path before you clears, and the Hero's Journey refuses to let you turn back. So unfurl your ship's sails, catch these winds of change, and let's move downriver as C.J. teaches us that **PLAY** is **the way**!

Sheridan Cleland
Co-Heathen
March 2026

P.S. If you're new to **Heathen** books, then you're probably wondering what that *thing* is at the bottom right of our two-page spreads. We call it the "rectometer" and it denotes on which page the current chapter ends.

At the beginning of each chapter, we note how many pages are in that chapter, so you can decide at-a-glance if you're ready to commit. Then, once you've started a chapter, every recto (right-hand page) in the chapter will state on which page the current chapter ends so you'll always know how many pages are left. On the chapter's next-to-last page, we signal that the chapter is ending, then it starts all over again with the next chapter.

The Prologue

The real tragedy of life is when
men are afraid of the light.
-Plato

Same goes for the ladies!
-Universalus

You're about to learn about *everything*. And you may learn a thing or two! Because this is about life, and how it all works. Which means that it's all about you. Learning 'it all' may seem complex and difficult, but we try to keep it all simple and fun. It's all to help open you to all you are, so you live all life has to give before it's all done.

So you know: As you learn more and more about everything, you may see things nothing like how you do now. And who knows? You may grow to know you *are* everything — a 'something' like 'nothing' — once we explain how. This 'something' like 'nothing' that is 'everything' is Life itself — or, as physics would say, *energy*. And although our five senses can't notice this 'something,' without it, nothing can happen, or be.

Awareness you *are* Life itself — which *is* everything — brings to life all you think, feel, and do. And although you may not, now, believe that you're everything, our wisdom and science both teach us it's true. The problem is, changing belief (about anything) requires a mind that is open to light.

For a closed mind reacts to hard facts as attacks, and will hide in the dark out of fear it's not 'right.'

The closed mind — our shared, self-created insanity — denies, and divides, and destroys our humanity. By barring all truth that presents contradiction, its phobic defensiveness causes constriction. And because it shuns Light, the closed mind doesn't know that it dims and it darkens when it hinders Life's flow. But it's physics, and karma, and simple deduction: The mind closed to Life brings about its destruction.

Those who hunger for power prey on closed minds, and they do it by seeding, and breeding, division. 'We're right, and they're wrong, and that means they're bad' is the misleading, fear-feeding core of their vision. These wolves pledge protection from the fears they inspire. It's why 'true believers' believe, falsely, they're needed. Blind, sheep-like abidance is what they desire. And once they, alone, define truth, they've succeeded.

We see this sometimes in religion and politics, when dogma is built up in minds like a wall of bricks. And those who expose false beliefs with a fact get ignored, shunned, resented, condemned, and attacked. This has happened forever, and it's happening now. We blind ourselves with our own worldviews, somehow. And it's something that all of us, in some way, do. Which brings us back around to the subject of you.

You believe your beliefs, and that's all well and good — that is, when belief is, itself, understood. Therefore please understand: The true measure of 'true' all amounts to how much a belief *opens* you. For your heart opens up when you open your mind, and that's how a truth beyond words you will find. The light that *is* Life itself — love! — lives in you. And the more you are open, the more it shines through.

And so it's with hope in your mind being open, enough to let in what we know to be 'known,' that we share all our knowledge about everything — because, by you knowing, your mind will be blown. Which is a good thing! Because you'll free the real you with a blown-open mind — a 'you' that's much more than your 'self,' you will find. And your whole life will change, changing how you see you. You'll become something more. And you'll save the world, too!

Of course, there is more to what we've been explaining. Although more means less if your attention is waning. Which is why, in the interest of interest-maintaining, and our need to succeed at attention-retaining (not to mention, to limit potential complaining — or worse, a reaction that requires restraining), as we explain more of what we've been explaining, we'll try to make what we explain entertaining. What we're sharing is meant, after all, to help you. But we understand people ignore what is true. Which is why our intention is the gain and retention of that vital extension of you: Your attention.

Oh! And on a related note: As for the rhyming, it's all about timing, which means that we won't try to rhyme all the time. There will, though, be times when we do try some rhymes, although most times we don't. Like now, for example.

Speaking of 'times,' generally, and this particular time, now, now is a particularly good time to mention that, generally speaking, these times we now live in, also known as the present, present some pretty big problems — and it's not pretty. We always have big problems, of course. And it's always, of course, the present. The big problem is, we're not always *being* present — that being why big problems are always present.

The seemingly endless list of harmful, hurtful, and often hateful things we do to ourselves, each other, and other life forms on our planet are the painfully plain and plentiful evidence that humans are the most destructive life form to ever live. Not to sound critical! But the facts are empirical.

pt. ends next p.

And the revolting and appalling things we've done to our own children are the jolting and most galling form of evidence of all.

The good news (it being the reason we're here, to present this good news in a new way to hear) is that we can reverse the downward spiral of our self-destruction, and solve every problem every person ever created, by understanding, and resolving, one big problem. If you were paying attention, we gave our problem a mention. And if you weren't paying attention, our problem is: We don't pay attention. We live *in* the present; it's where Life exists. But no one *is* present. One's own mind resists.

Here we have the irony of our big problem — the paradox, if you will (as well as if you won't, because it's what it is, whether you see it or you don't): We don't see our biggest problem in the world because our biggest problem is that we don't see the world. This life is our Eden, and yet we reject it. Instead of accepting *what is*, we project it. And the problem, the cause, of our senseless resistance is that 'bad apple' — ego — that feeds our existence. With the lures of temptation, it obscures Life's creation. Thus, with *everything*, ego destroys our relation.

How, then, do we see Life — and live in connection? 'The way' is to look in an inward direction. After all, we all see life, each moment that passes, through a thick pair of self-centered, personal glasses. You see everything in life through you. And I see everything in life through me. So . . . unless we can see *what* we see through, what, then, can we really see?

Seeing this problem is hard for us to do. Especially when my problem is me, his problem is him, her problem is her, and your problem is you. And what makes our big problem ever more problematic is that we don't know how to look at ourselves, or even what to look at, because we ignore what we really are, and how we really work. 'Know thyself,' is what Socrates said. Though most of us are occupied with other stuff, instead.

But we *can* know ourselves, thanks to wisdom and science — humanity's great self-awareness alliance. We just need to make all that is known more relatable — and by showing they say the same thing, less debatable. Which is why we are here: To help explain you. In a way that will help you believe in what's true. And beyond all of that, what we're trying to do is to help save the world, helping you be more . . . you.

Keep in mind what this means is you'll have to let go — of the world, and the life, that you think that you know. It takes suffering, sacrifice — death! — of ego. It's the timeless and storied way of . . . *the hero*. The reward, in the end — to transcend, and renew, the world once created, and negated, by you — will allow you to see, and to be, something new. And you'll brighten the world with the Light found in you.

Though it may be hard to believe it, it's true: The hero our world needs to save it is *you*. And you'll find that you're able, the Light will shine through, when you open yourself to what you love to do. When you do for the world through what you love to do, love will then grow within you, and throughout the world, too. And while saving the world may not be 'child's play,' it's our children, and play, that can show us the way.

So it's time to go, now. And we need to go, then. For unless we go now, then the question is, when? There is no better time, for there's no time at all — except for the present. There's now — and that's all! So it's time to break free of your self-subjugation. Which is really the point of this whole explanation. Please, then, check that your mind isn't closed, to be sure.

Now let's help you *believe*, so you'll *be* and *live* more!

PART ONE

The Point

We can't point to awareness
And say it's 'here' or 'there'
But as our point of everything
It must be everywhere

The highest expression of life is art with jokes.
-Neil Peart

Life goes in circles. We live in a circle of life. Physicists and metaphysicians will tell you the circle is the defining shape of life. If one of them tells you otherwise, and insists that, say, the rhombus is the defining shape of life, you are talking with an imposter — and who knows what else! You want to get out of this conversation as soon as possible, and one effective way is to move backward in quick little shuffle steps toward the nearest exit while acting surprised, as if you have no idea what your feet are doing. The important thing, here, is to do something out of the ordinary, because, usually, no one will follow you — unless, of course, you're well-known for doing something out of the ordinary, in which case you probably have a following, and may get followed by nearby followers.

The point is, or at this point, it was: The circle is everywhere in our lives. And you don't need a scientist, or philosopher, or even your favorite celebrity to point it out. Look a-*round*, and there it is: In the symbols of our religions, the cogs of our machinery, the circuitry of our technology, and the patterns and shapes of nature on every scale. Even if you are no longer a young child and therefore don't often pay open-minded attention to the world around you, too preoccupied by what circulates in your own mind, or your cellphone, it's hard to ignore all the circles in life — especially if you're driving one of those motorized cages collecting golf balls at a crowded driving range, and everyone is aiming at you.

Everything in life is relatable to circles. On a related note (to what we just related), some people say golf is life. This idea may be hard to relate to if you've never played, or only tried it at a public course where they let people out dressed for the state fair. But there's no denying that a round of hitting round balls into round holes has its circular aspects. And there are universal lessons about our unique human lives we can all learn from playing. For example, how sometimes you have it, and sometimes you don't. And how sometimes it goes your way, and sometimes it doesn't. Playing can even make you wonder what 'it' really is. When you think about it, we hardly think about 'it.' Yet 'it' is all there is to life. 'It' being Life itself — the energy that enlivens all life. Which is everything in life, if you think about it.

Of course, the main life lesson to be learned on the course is that golf is a journey, an adventure, a *game* to be *played*, in which the main objective is to overcome your 'self.' And every experience of playing — the joyful celebration, holing out from off the green; the deep regret from heaving your whole bag down a ravine; and all the satisfaction, and frustration, in between — can open your mind and expand your perspective, no matter what your golf handicap is. Even if you're handicapped beyond golf by an unconscious fear of opening your mind and expanding your perspective (which, most likely, like most people, you mostly are), playing golf can help!

The enlightenment that comes from golfing, as it happens from living (that is, when circular thinking doesn't prevent it from happening, which often happens), is typically achieved gradually, almost unnoticeably, through the 'ups and downs' of playing — including but not limited to when you're trying to get up and down. Sometimes, though, it arrives all at once, and strikes you with the proverbial thunderbolt of revelation. The great writer John Updike, who golfed a great deal but apparently wasn't so great at it, wrote that, while golfing, he could experience 'a momentary amplification of myself within a realm larger than life.' I'm a big Updike fan, but you figure it had to be a little weird being in his foursome when *that* happened. And imagine accidentally putting your golf cart in reverse when it did.

In any case, even if you never get to play a round of golf in your life, if you get to play around in life, in a way that opens you to Life, you're living the life you're meant to live. We should point out that this (or is it that?) is an important point of our book — even if at this point, that point, and this book, may seem pointless. Which brings us back around to a point we made earlier: Life is circular. And our book about life is circular, too. We'll point out circular forms and patterns, and circle back to discuss certain ideas — some of which may not obviously relate to circles, but undoubtedly somehow, in some way, do.

We'll talk more about how circularity permeates life and keeps it going. But because it's so integral to everything, it also necessarily gives shape to life's many burdens. Take cannon balls, for example. Or please at least consider taking mine. It was left behind by the previous homeowner, public works won't take it (not even with a 'donation' accompanied by a friendly note), and it's impossible to blend in with our home décor because we don't live on a pirate ship. If it's not the most useless and inconvenient encumbrance of our modern existence, I don't know what is. (But if you want one, let me know.)

Then there's 'the little things in life' among its roundish burdens, like the hurtling hailstone that dimples one's car; the bothersome pebble that hinders one's step; the haphazard BB that threatens one's eye (according to warnings issued by one's mom). On a larger scale, you have those amusement park rides that spin you around in circles, all of which should be limited to unconstitutional interrogation purposes only, yet they allow young children on them, force an adult with them to pay for it, and sometimes even require that you get on with the kids. And let's not forget traffic circles — or 'roundabouts,' as they're also called. While they're supposed to be helpful (this is implied, being funded by taxes), all they really do is invite indecision and incite panic, for some reason especially among people who drive Buicks. Even the circular food chain has its hazards — although humans, generally, (pun alert) 'fare well' in it, as long as we remain in so-called civilized areas, and therein avoid the buffet at family restaurants.

Rounding out our point, here, round-shaped perils lurk everywhere. But for most human beings, the most dangerous circles we most often encounter in life — by far, and it's not even close! — are our own bad habits, those circular patterns of thought that cause our circular patterns of behavior that cause our mental, emotional, and physical self-destruction. While the destruction is obvious if you're paying attention, our bad habits often provide temporary relief from an otherwise constant, gnawing sense of emptiness in our hearts that we manage to ignore with superfluous fixations — including, but not limited to, those bad habits.

Later we'll expound on the metaphysical nature of this hole inside, and how it gets bigger the more we try to cover it up rather than bring awareness to it, accept it, and open ourselves to allow it to be filled with the love for life that *is* Life itself. But for now, beware that their insidious allure, combined with their self-perpetuating circular nature, make our own bad habits the most dangerous of life's circles. They're even more burdensome than the ponderous presence of a cannon ball — by a lot! Unless, perhaps, one shows up as a projectile while you're tidying up around the house.

Related to the problem of our circular thinking, there's something humanity bewilderingly imposes on itself with a straight face called 'circular logic,' which enables and abets circular thinking that is typically proven untrue by science, the legal system, legitimate journalism, and/or other institutions built on objective evidence, and invariably wreaks societal havoc when consumed *en masse* and in large doses over an extended period of time. By way of quick refresher on the term, or in case you never heard of it, 'circular logic' is what people use to ignore facts and the sensible (let's call it *linear*) logic that aligns facts into knowledge, insight, and understanding of 'what is' — that is, objective reality. Enclosed by its circularity, circular logic is, by definition, illogical, because it is closed off to all facts and physical evidence that dispute it. People will even disregard their own personal observations, experiences, and values — not to mention math — when it contradicts the circular logic that circulates in their minds. Thus insulated, circular logic allows for unfounded and usually confounding beliefs such as, 'the universe revolves around the earth,' or 'Jesus loves guns,' or 'Bigfoot is too smart to be caught on camera.' Importantly, and the reason we're bringing this up, is that we use circular logic, unburdened by facts and other measures of objective reality, to justify our own self-destructive habits.

In this book, facts are frequently related, as they're appreciated, and even venerated; whereas we'd like to see circular logic, and *all* destructive circular thinking, get eliminated. Which is possible (and we'll explain why and how later on) through the extraordinarily simple and yet endlessly challenging process of bringing awareness to it, and then letting it go, while it's happening in real time. 'Real time' being the present moment, which is the only time reality exists. Which is, of course, all the time — while at the same time, only now.

Having, now, mentioned the subject of 'now' — a truly mind-blowing dimension; at least it is when it's the timeless space absorbing your attention — here's a fact (with many more to come) we should presently mention: Simply 'being' in the present moment, we can overcome all the untrue and otherwise obstructive — and, therefore, destructive — circular thinking that circulates within our minds. 'Being' — just *being*, without our thoughts in the way of it — empowers us to observe and identify what is self-destructive among our thoughts, to unburden ourselves of them. Our ability to simply be, and thereby broaden what we see, is our greatest human power which, alone, can set us free — from the self-created prison of our own negative circular thinking. The importance of this ability, and our awareness that we possess it, cannot be overstated (and we'll spare you an attempt to do so), given how nearly all of our thinking is circular: Ninety-five percent of our tens of thousands of daily thoughts are pretty much the same, according to science-based studies that more than ninety-five percent of us aren't aware of and don't think about. Think about that! And if you're not inclined to think about it, having never thought about it before, think about *that*.

We repeat the same basic thoughts over and over and over again. Some of us do it our entire lives! It's like a merry-go-round, going around in the mind. Unless, of course, your thoughts aren't merry. And for most of us, most are not. Not to be negative, but the same studies about all of us that none of us are aware of or think about say that about eighty-five percent of most people's thoughts are mostly negative. These 'negative' thoughts invariably reflect our fears, desires, or judgments related to what we perceive to be going on around us, most of which create emotions that cause bodily stress. Self-oriented, and self-generated, all of this thinking is a rejection of, and so disconnects us from, life — and Life itself. Which inhibits how Life flows into and through our lives, and so limits how Life works for us.

If all of that sounds overly dramatic, deeply confusing, or like something someone selling power crystals at a street fair would say to you, we'll explain this relation between life and Life itself, in terms of physics — that's right, *physics*; the physical science of how everything in the universe works! — because it's necessary to understand and, more necessarily, believe: We close ourselves off from life — wherein Life itself exists — with our own, continuous, compulsive, self-centered, circular thoughts. And when we are closed to Life itself, we are in some way destroying our own lives. We may not be aware of the destruction as it happens; and often, we are not. But eventually it becomes impossible not to notice when it keeps happening over time. By which time it's too often too late to do anything about it.

Now, there's a caveat here: If you're a student of nature, and/or operate a wrecking ball for a living, you know that sometimes destruction necessarily precedes creation. (Or we could say *re*-creation, although they're really the same thing.) In the context of a person's perspective on life (which, essentially, *is* your life), it's what we refer to as 'learning the hard way.' While necessary for some (and perhaps for all of us, in some way), learning the hard way is generally unpleasant, and specifically involves a lot of unpleasantness. It's also risky, because some people, as many of us have learned (usually, the hard way), never learn. And when self-destructive people never learn, because their own circular thinking and logic obstructs the plain truth of their self-destructiveness, the self-destruction continues until they get the job done for good. Which obviously isn't good. And it's, really, too bad.

Circling back to the circularity that keeps life going: We see circles in the forms and actions of everything in the universe, from the hydrogen atom to our planet earth, both of which are round, spin around, and go around, all at once and always. It's dizzying to think about, and probably nauseating if you were for some reason pirouetting at the same time. Human life systems are very much circular, too, the way we circulate blood through the heart, air through the lungs, and sustenance through the body. In and out, in and out — over, and over, and over again. This applies to certain sexual activity as well, although sometimes it can be more like 'in and out — and over,' especially for guys who lack experience with another person in the room. Of course, if this keeps up later in life — and okay, maybe 'keeps up' isn't the best way to put it — there are pharmaceutical solutions to the problem one can learn about from television commercials that can be embarrassing to watch with certain family members.

Bringing this back around to our book: Like life itself, human and otherwise, there's a circular aspect to **LIFE STANDS EXPLAINED**. This happens to be the case with many of the greatest books ever written; in particular, those describing the archetypal hero's journey — which, as comparative mythologist Joseph Campbell explained, represents the circular path of universal human experiences necessary for the psychological transformation required to optimize the manifestation of Life itself within us, and to therefore realize our life's full potential so we are able to save the living world around us. If all of that sounds unimportant and boring, these stories often involve things like magic, monsters, mystics, and miracles. And if *that* stuff doesn't float your boat either, there are hero stories like *Moby Dick*, *Huckleberry Finn*, and *The Old Man and the Sea* that prominently feature floating boats.

While we're on the subject of the book itself, and off the book's subject, we should acknowledge that, although **LIFE STANDS EXPLAINED** has its circular aspects (as we mentioned is the case with many great literary works), there will no doubt be some serious-minded readers who find this particular assemblage of words to be less of the 'classic philosophical' or 'epic artistic' variety and more reminiscent of, say, the experience of watching one's own underwear flop around in the dryer. Hey, you can't make everyone happy! And you can hardly ever make *anyone* happy among the many, unfortunate, misguided people out there who take themselves and therefore most of life too seriously. This book can transform how you look at everything, though! Though it all depends on how you look at everything.

Reflecting on this reflection, 'how you look at everything' is what this book about life is all about. And it's not only about how you look at everything, which really is everything in life, but as we pointed out earlier, it's also about everything, and how it all relates to nothing — which, in turn, explains why life is all about how you look at everything.

How, then, should we begin explaining everything — and for that matter, the point of it all? After all, the circle is an endless line, likewise with no starting point. You could well say it's pointless, like the intangible essence of Life itself — which is, of course, the point of everything, even if we can't know why, or how. This starts us off with a paradoxical problem, which is typically unsolvable, or at least seems that way. Though at least we're not getting involved in, say, splitting an atom, or calculating the source of dark energy, or explaining to someone we hardly know why their haircut looks *hilarious*.

We should always look for the positive in life because it's somehow always there. It's called 'the bright side' for a reason, after all, even if many of us have a hard time seeing it. It's where 'the Light' that *is* Life sheds light for the life that's there. It's also helpful when the electricity is out and you're looking for your car keys. Although, to clarify an earlier comment, no one's suggesting you should seek illumination in your underwear. Especially if you're wearing it and other people are around.

Well . . . we've got to start somewhere, or else we'll go nowhere, in which case there's no point in either of us being here. So let's begin here, and get to the point — or at least it's *a* point, related to *the* point, to get us pointed in the right direction:

The point of your life is to save the world.

Hooray for you — and thank you very much!

Or . . .

The point of your life is to destroy the world.

[HEAR: *wan-waah* sound effect
for failure on a TV game show.]

The point, here, being, there's a point to you being here. There's a purpose, a reason, that you exist. One big reason, to be exact! That is, unless you're like most of us 'normally' insane people, and you spend your life destroying the world sometimes, and saving it from destruction other times, in which case there's *two* big reasons for you being here.

You may think, 'There must be more to life than just *that*.' Or you may instead think, 'There can't be *that* much to life.' More likely you don't think about life at all because you're busy and have things to do. But whatever it is you may think, feel, or do, your experience of life is one of the two — because saving or destroying the world is all we ever do. And which of the two *you* happen to do is always, each moment, entirely up to you. The choice is yours — for you, alone, to make! Although you're not alone in having the choice to make. And you often have to make the choice while you're not alone — especially if you have artistic sensibilities and work weekends at a New Jersey Walmart during the holidays.

This is something to keep in mind, which (perhaps paradoxically) requires that you keep an open one: You're *always* helping to save the world or contributing to its destruction. It applies to everything and anything you do, even when you're doing nothing and are alone with your thoughts. If you're wondering, at this point, what the heck we're talking about, that's okay! We obviously have a lot of explaining to do. Which is probably what you'd expect from a book with this title. Although whatever may be your expectations regarding this book's explanations, we're going to explain everything later, and how it all relates to your mind right now. But the important thing to keep in mind for right now is that, however you do it, in ways large or small, saving the world is the most important thing of all. It's more important than anything. Nothing is more important. Because it's everything, to everyone — including and especially you. And this includes the people in the world around you, too.

And here's another thing, or perhaps a thing or two, about what you most likely think, as it all relates to you: While you probably think what you think is important, and likely have a high opinion of your own opinion (which is not unusual if you lack perspective on your perspective, which is typical if you never think about it — and it's typical to never think about it), it's important to understand that saving the world is more important than whatever you were thinking about before, are thinking about now, or will think about later. No matter what you're thinking about — *ever*, saving the world is more important. Unless, perhaps, you're thinking about something that will help you save the world. (Or unless, of course, you're reading or listening to something intended to help you save the world.) The *one* exception — and really, the *only* exception; and it's an *exceptionally* important exception, as exceptional exceptions go — would be if, instead of saving the world, you were thinking about . . .

pt. ends p. 56

[PLACE YOUR AD HERE]

Just kidding about the advertising space! That is, unless this book's brilliant, visionary, and overall terrific publisher — who doesn't mind publishing unpublished writers no one has ever heard of before, no matter how unpublished or unknown the writer may be — thinks it's a good idea to help the bottom line. In any case, here's the bottom line: Saving the world really *is* everything. Which we mention because this is a book about everything. And as much as I'm necessarily involved, it's especially about you. In fact, more than anything, it's really all about you. And this is related to the fact that you are everything.

Admittedly, there's an altogether reasonable reason you don't likely believe you are everything. Using the standard definition of 'everything,' we'd be saying that you comprise over two hundred billion galaxies, span thirty billion cubic light years, and are constantly expanding in a way that may require a new form of physics to calculate. I have no idea what any of that means either, but some physicists now believe 'everything' may comprise *two trillion* galaxies. Try to imagine *that* the next time you have time to imagine something you'd never imagine spending time on! A universe with two trillion galaxies is nearly *ten times larger* than physicists thought it was, which you have to figure was a big surprise to the person who discovered it. If it was anything like meeting a blind date ten times larger than expected, I can tell you from personal experience that it's the kind of shocker that makes you look at existence differently.

The point here being, you see yourself as a separate being, and so you don't see yourself as being everything. Your worldview — informed by your own senses, and the worldview of others who have shared their worldview with you (whether you asked them to or not; and most likely, you did not) — tells you the opposite. As you perceive 'everything' right now, the world, indeed the universe, is all circumstantial to the being or system that is you. In other words, you see yourself as part of, and yet separate from, everything. This perspective makes some sense, in a sense, because it's what you sense with your physical senses. But what you sense, or are conditioned to sense, is, in a sense, nonsense. Because physics has proven that your so-called 'sensible' worldview is wrong. It's the diametric opposite of what, really, is.

This is not only ironic, and quite possibly paradoxical, but it's also the basic problem of the human condition. Most everyone sees themselves as singular; and it's a singular problem — in more ways than one! — that threatens the end of human existence. So, to be clear: How you see everything is a problem. A big one, at that. But again, you're not separate and alone in the world, seeing yourself as separate and alone in the world. In fact, the opposite is true: Pretty much all of us see ourselves as singular, separate beings. Though I know it's not true, I mostly do, too.

People feel comfortable with this uncomfortable worldview because most everyone else sees everything the same way. It's reassuring when most everyone believes what you do. Although believing what most everyone believes does not, of course, make it true — unless, that is, you have facts, objective evidence, and linear logic to back it up. This is not to be confused with — as it often is, most often by close-minded people who are too close-minded to acknowledge their minds are closed — false speculations, subjective characterizations, and circular logic.

Consider how there were times in human history when pretty much everyone believed the earth was shaped like a tortilla, human sacrifice was a viable community service, and the generous application of human poop to the human body was a cure-all for human maladies. The people who were the first to challenge these beliefs, because they became aware of *facts* to the contrary, were characterized in negative ways — even 'evil' and therefore deserving of demonization and severe punishment. It has forever been the case, and still is today, that if you contradict someone's non-factual, evidence-free, and otherwise illogical beliefs, you are characterized in a negative light. *You* are the problem. Well, of course you are! Because people can't or won't believe that their own beliefs, no matter how unbelievable they may be, are *objectively* false and therefore . . . hm, what's the word? Oh, that's right — *wrong!*

Over time, the popular view on the aforementioned matters — the shape and dimension of the earth, the group benefits of human sacrifice, and the curative powers of poop — were proven wrong (and the product of ignorance posing as confident understanding), thanks to humans broadening their knowledge with scientifically and otherwise proven facts. Popular acceptance of those facts occurred too late for those who used them to argue for the truth *before* they were popularly accepted, especially the ones who were impaled, set on fire, or pushed off a cliff because they did. But such is the tragedy of ignorance, of people who live afraid of the light. Especially for those who aren't afraid, but have to deal with those who are.

You would think we'd learn our lesson. But unfortunately, we have not. Quite the opposite. Ignorance remains, in fact, a vicious cycle — more accurately, it's *the* vicious cycle — of our humanity. People still believe made-up ideas that are unproven, and even disproven — with contradictory facts that are easily accessible and in vast supply. False beliefs, rooted in ignorance, continue to get advanced in cultures all over the world. It's become a major domestic product here in America! (Although, admittedly, some of it is imported.) And these falsehoods are not soft-peddled or politely suggested to be truth. Oh, no! Ignorance is promoted with not only confidence, and even bravado, but usually it's a package deal that comes with self-righteous conviction, dizzying hypocrisy, and eventually, when all else fails, aggression in the form of violence. This phenomenon remains particularly problematic when a person of significant societal stature tells people lies that they want to hear because those lies are aligned to, and therefore somehow validate in their own minds, their current beliefs; specifically, beliefs that contradict, ignore, and are even hostile to facts. And it doesn't matter how incredible the lies are, or how un-credible is the liar who's telling them, because people are so desperate to reaffirm their own beliefs, they'll believe anyone or anything that in any way supports them. Believers will even ignore the plain truth of what's happening before their own eyes! They will instead seek out and consume more lies, contradicting that plain truth, as if their lives depended on it. Because, in a real way, their lives *do* depend on it.

If you find this hard to understand, it's really not. It's simply our human condition. Belief is the lens through which we all experience every moment of our lives. Belief shapes our lives. It defines our lives. *Belief* — in a very real sense; and as the word clearly suggests — *be*-comes one's *life*. And because people can't, or won't — in any case, they don't — dissociate between life and their own view of it, they will fight for their lives to reinforce and, therefore, defend their beliefs, no matter how unbelievable they may be. This is even the case when false beliefs are destructive to the believers, themselves — which, unbeknownst to them, they often are. All of which is to say that we have to be careful about believing something because everyone else we know, or listen to, or read, or watch on TV believes (or at least *claims* to believe) it. For example, that we are all separate from the universe, and not each the whole of it.

Directly related, it also means we have a lot more

evolving to do, because we're still a species of so-called 'intelligent beings' applying a bunch of poop to people, nowadays of the 'bull' variety, who are ignorant of their own ignorance, making things worse for them, when they need more substantive help. This is what happens when we ignore or dismiss facts simply because they're not aligned to our own current beliefs. We run the risk of getting pooped on, and then having to deal with the unpleasant consequences. This is why we all benefit from acknowledging and accepting what is — including what are facts. It's *especially* beneficial to consider the facts when they contradict our own beliefs — at least it is if we want to make our own lives better, and help save the world instead of participating in its destruction.

It's important to understand and accept facts, because the truth is the only thing that will, truly, set us free. To be clear, we're talking, here, about a metaphysical kind of human freedom. The kind that psychiatrist Victor Frankl talked about in his extraordinary little book, *Man's Search for Meaning*. Not freedom from some literal, physical captivity — which Frankl, having been a Nazi concentration camp prisoner, experienced in an unimaginably horrible way — but from the bondage of our own perspective, one rooted in a false sense of separation from everything. This deeply held but factually disproven and false belief — again, shared by most everyone in the world — is the root cause of all human forms of destruction. It's what inhibits our creative ability to save the world — from ourselves, and for ourselves.

The fact is, because the scientific evidence says so (and wisdom from sources *you* may believe in says so, too), you *are* everything! But the important question is, do you believe it? And even if you don't, the equally important question is, *can* you believe it, if you don't believe it now? And by that, we mean this: Is it possible for you to believe that your beliefs about 'everything' are wrong? For that matter, are you capable of believing that your current beliefs about *anything* are wrong? Because the thing is, if you can't believe your beliefs can be wrong regarding the various lesser matters of anything, it's not likely you'll ever believe you're wrong about the singular broader matter of everything. Especially given how your beliefs *are* everything. That is, your beliefs are everything to *you*. Because a belief — as the word suggests (as we suggested earlier, and will suggest again, so you don't forget) — *be*-comes your *life*.

Your beliefs *are* everything to your experience of life — and it's a fact of your human nature, whether you believe it or not. Which brings us back around, yet again, to the point of this book, which is to explain what's happening with everything, generally; and in particular, to help you become aware that you *are* everything — by explaining why and how, so you'll *believe* you are everything. Which is important, so you'll believe you can save the world. Which is important because the world needs saving, and you're the one to do it.

In case you're doubtful (and likely, you are — because isn't 'saving the world' the job of a *hero*?), the wisest and most impactful thinkers and writers and leaders in the history of humanity agree on this point, regarding the point of your life. Consider the words of this wise artist and writer — the renowned path-lighter, profound dream-inciter, and 'your-own-worst-enemy' fighter — Dr. Seuss:

> "Unless someone like you cares a whole awful lot,
> nothing is going to get better. It's not."[1]

[1] Welcome to our first footnote! Maybe you're thinking, 'The words are so small - how important can they be?' Horton the Elephant taught us that size doesn't always matter. On a related note, we have a Dr. Seuss quote here. And by that, I mean that we quoted him there. Up above, in the main text, about why it's important to care. Hopefully you do care about saving the world. But if you don't care, our job here is to get you there. 'There' being 'here' — wherever you are out there.

And you *can* save the world; you can make everything better — including and especially for you. *If* you believe you can do it. Which you *will* believe, if you understand *why* and *how* you can do it. Which you *will* understand, if you're aware of everything — and how it all works. And you will be aware of it all, if you choose to keep on reading this simple fun book that's all about you. Because **LIFE STANDS EXPLAINED** is the book that explains everything — in a way, by the way, that is both childishly scientific *and* scientifically childish. All of which is to say, in a slightly different way: This is a book about saving the world, which most people would agree is a serious matter. And it's about simple fun, which hardly anyone takes seriously. It's also scientific, and about science — a serious subject of the serious-minded. And it's about childishness, and is childish — which is the opposite of 'serious' to serious people, and often quite seriously annoys them.

All of this may well seem like a paradox because . . . well, it *is* all a paradox. Which makes sense, in a sense, because even though a paradox doesn't make sense, this is meant to be a sensible book while at the same time all about paradox. Make sense? Probably not! Although *everything* is a paradox — if you look at it all in a certain way. And this is paradoxical book about everything, and looking at it all a certain way.

To be clear, this is not a book about everything, individually, because I don't know much about anything in particular. Rather, it's about everything, generally, and how it all relates to nothing (that is, something that *resembles* nothing, but *is* everything), specifically. This, being a paradox, brings us back to the subject of paradox, and at the same time — paradoxically, come to think of it — it brings us forward to the subject of you. Because you, my good reader, are a paradox. You may or may not look like a soap opera star. You may or may not have a genius-level IQ. You may or may not even be a good reader! For all we know, you may be someone who walks around your neighborhood wearing pajamas, welding goggles, and a skateboard helmet that's too small for your head. Or maybe you spin around like a tornado all day to ward off invisible aliens who keep asking to use your bathroom. Maybe you do both, and were formally employed as the director of research for *InfoWars*.

But here's the point: No matter who you are, or what you're like, or what you like to do, one thing's for sure: You *are* a paradox. This is related to the fact that *everything* is a paradox. And the related fact that *you* are *everything*. Which is the main reason why you are very much able to save our world. You may well be wondering at this point if the subject of 'you' will get lost in the subject of 'everything.' Especially if it all comes down to 'nothing.' You may also still be wondering what the heck we're talking about. But not to worry! Which you will be frequently encouraged to do — or rather, *not* to do. Because there's never a need to worry. In fact, there's no need for any form of stress in the system that is you. Not ever!

Okay, sure, stress-induced adrenaline can sometimes be helpful in an *actual* life-threatening situation. For example, if you are being chased by a hungry bear, or a pack of angry parents after refereeing a middle school soccer game. But the problem is that people get stressed by any and all perceived threats, and that's always counterproductive. We'll discuss this more later, but for now, please remember, there's never any need, because it never helps, to worry and get stressed about the past or future — or for that matter what you're going to wear to a social gathering. That said, you probably shouldn't show up uninvited at a motorcycle gang initiation ceremony wearing a spinning bowtie and a beanie with a little propeller on top, especially if you're one of those people who can't stop giggling when you shouldn't.

The main point here is that, if the system that is you — that is, ***unique you*** — is going to work properly (that is, if it's going to work positively, constructively, and creatively), then what's 'needed' is *reduction* of stress in the system that is you.

Simply put, we need to reduce your stress to nothing, because stress does nothing to help you work better, in whatever work you do.

It just gets in the way of everything, generally. And in particular, it gets in the way of you being you. You being, of course, everything. (And a paradox, too.)

And by the way, none of what we're saying here is anything new. Science and wisdom, the twin pillars of our human knowledge and understanding when it comes to pretty much everything, are aligned on this idea that you *are* everything. Albert Einstein described as an 'optical delusion of consciousness' the human experience of thinking and feeling we are separate from the universe. The theoretical physicists who followed Einstein have been saying the same thing. Just as our sources of wisdom have been saying it for millennia, and still do. As spiritual teacher Eckhart Tolle reminds us: 'You *are* the universe.' And consider that more than two thousand years ago, the Chinese philosopher Lao Tzu wrote in the 13th verse of the *Tao Te Ching*:

> "One who sees himself as everything
> is fit to be guardian of the world."

Now *that's* what we're talking about!

And it's why the point of this book is to get you to see 'everything' with a more open mind, by bringing your awareness to, so you'll therefore believe in, the facts of who and what you really are — which is everything. Why? So that you can and will change everything in your life, starting with you, in a positive way. Which is, by the way, the way you save the world.

Now then. (Have you ever thought about that phrase?

Go ahead and give it a moment.) We have arrived at the point where we need to relate some rules, because there are three rules relating to you, if you're going to relate to this book. Before relating these three rules — which we're calling, '**The Big Three Rules**,' because they're big, in terms of their general magnitude, and because there's three of them, in terms of their specific magnitude — it's important to understand and distinguish between two basic types of rules that relate to human life. Because the two basic *types* of rules relating to human life relate to and help explain **The Big Three Rules** of you relating to this book. Which, of course, intends to relate to you an understanding of 'everything,' and how you relate to it all — including what may now seem unrelatable.

The Two Basic Kinds of Rules of Human Life

As the stand-alone and un-punctuated line above attempts to highlight, sans highlighter, there are two basic kinds of rules that relate to all aspects of human life and our experience of it. One kind of rule of human life *prescribes what should be*. The other kind of rule of human life *describes what is*. They're somewhat similar, but mostly different. And unfortunately the former often ignores the latter, which contributes to the dysfunction contributed by the former, and we'll explain why later.

Rules that *prescribe what should be* basically organize organizations into the organization they are, be it religious, government, political, social, academic, business, athletic, or whatever you call people who wear costumes to pretend battle in large outdoor spaces. These rules stipulate what you should and shouldn't do; they usually define consequences for doing what you shouldn't do *and* not doing what you should do; and, thankfully for the rest of us, they mostly only apply to organization members, although you have to follow at least some of them if you're visiting, sometimes with the additional requirement that you sign in and wear a nametag.

The other kind of rule, the kind that *describes what is*, are the rules you find in the universe. At least you do if you're a scientist or mathematician and you're looking for them. The rules that *describe what is* universally apply to everything and everyone, no matter what organizations you are part of, and irrespective if you're wearing a nametag, because they apply to the entire universe, to which you need not sign in — not even if you have an inflated opinion of the rhombus and are compelled to let others know about it. As a part of nature, every aspect of the system that is 'you' works within the rules *describing what is*, even if you have no idea what they are, and that you follow them.

As we mentioned, they're different, these two basic types of rules — fundamentally, so — but they're also the same, in this fundamental way: All rules relate to how systems work. And 'how systems work' is what this book is all about. How else could we explain everything, unless we did it in a systematic way — or at the very least, talked about systems? Because everything *is* a system. And so this book about 'everything' is about systems, and how they all work. Or rather, it's about how *we* all work, all of us being systems. The noted astrophysicist and turtleneck icon Carl Sagan said, 'Our species needs and deserves a citizenry with minds wide awake and a basic understanding of how the world works.' Some might argue we don't deserve it, given our destructiveness extends well beyond ourselves, but let's agree that we certainly do need it, because without it, *billions* and *billions* of people will be former members of an extinct species that proved our human ignorance to be as destructive as an asteroid the size of Brooklyn.

So let's please be clear about this important fact: *You* are a system. Also, while we're on the topic: You *are* a system.

And to put a fine point on it: You are a *system*. You're a system comprised of smaller systems. And you're a system comprising larger systems. All of which comprises the one big system of the universe — which may in fact be a system within an unfathomable and infinite system of a multiverse, a literally limitless multitude of universes in which every possible outcome of everything that *could* happen, *does* happen.

Have you heard about this? There are theoretical physicists who believe this theory is not only possible, but probable! The possibilities (or probabilities?) are mind-boggling, especially if your mind hasn't been boggled lately. Imagine, for example, a Spanish Inquisition conducted by multiple choice survey. Or an Age of Enlightenment in which philosophers advanced 'higher truth' with hand puppets in the public square. Or how about an era called 'Art-O-Rama' because a papal edict declared the word Renaissance 'too Frenchy and confusing to spell.' If my understanding of the multiverse is correct, which is highly unlikely (certainly in *this* universe), all of that crazy stuff *had* to happen in some universe, in some dimension! That said, I think we can all agree that there were never any airport battles during the American Revolution — not in any universe, ever — because that just doesn't make sense.

Where were we, then? Because we should be there now. Rules! Ah, yes — *rules*. Rules relate to how systems work. And we have three big rules about how the system of this book will (or will not) work for the system that is you. Which we're calling, as you may recall (having called it out earlier), **The Big Three Rules**.

While **The Big Three Rules** that apply to this book are very much the '*prescribe what should be*' kind of rules (created by me, the writer, reflecting what I believe is necessary for the system of communication between you and me — that is, this book — to work for you, the reader), they are, more importantly, the '*describing what is*' kind of rules, because they reflect scientific insights and observations about how all books — and for that matter, all forms of human communication — work. These rules describe what *is* in terms of human nature, generally, and how and why we pay attention to what we do, and don't pay attention to what we don't, specifically.

Oh, one more thing, before we get to **The Big Three Rules**: Don't worry if you're not a 'rules person.' Remember, there's never any need to worry, or to experience any form of stress. 'Worry,' Eckhart Tolle points out, 'pretends to be important.' And as the Dalai Lama said, 'There is no benefit to worrying whatsoever.' Except — and on this point, I think the Dalai Lama would agree (not that we've had the chance to discuss it yet, as one of us has a very busy schedule and has no idea the other person exists) — when you choose to use the stress from worrying as a signal to bring your attention to your stress, so you're able to make the choice to observe and let go of the stress, and/or the worrisome thoughts creating your stress. All of which is to say *please* don't worry about these rules. Because, as rules go, they leave a lot of room for unruliness.

So here we go: **The Big Three Rules** that apply to you, if this book is going to 'work.' Which means 'help you save our world (and get more Life out of life while you're at it).' Feel free to imagine a chorus of singing angels. If that seems a bit much, maybe a kazoo playing the 'Charge' song feels more appropriate. Go ahead and imagine anything you like (or, for that matter, nothing at all) as prelude to our presentation of the book's **Big Three Rules**:

Big Rule One: You have to like simple fun.

Big Rule Two: You can't be a complete wee-wee.

Big Rule Three: You have to be open to being more open.

Let's clarify what we mean by these rules, and let's begin at the top by saying I am confident that you like simple fun. Not that *everyone* likes simple fun. As we all well know, perhaps all too well, there are unwell people out there, ranging from the flat-out deliberately hateful and hurtful, to those poor souls who just don't know how to enjoy *anything* in life — even, and sometimes especially, simple fun.

These invariably serious people hold the invariably serious view that serious matters should be considered seriously, and then seriously addressed with additional seriousness. Life is serious — and these serious people are, too! And for the serious people who are seriously skeptical about the value and purpose of simple fun, generally, I figure it could and likely would manifest in skepticism about the value and purpose of a simple fun book — particularly one on the serious subjects of life, and Life, and saving the world. Oscar Wilde tried to help us understand that 'some things are too important to be taken seriously.' But people who dismiss or dislike simple fun — sadly; really, *tragically* — just can't seem to grasp the idea.

All of which is to say that not *everyone* likes simple fun. However! If marketing strategies for business giants are any indication, simple fun is *very* popular among the economically relevant demographic of people between the ages of 'socially acceptable binky user' and your typical grain of beach sand. In other words, *most people* like simple fun. And in this particular instance, I think the majority has got it right — because, when you think about it, what's not to like? If you have a ready answer, because you *don't* like simple fun, this is not the book for you, and rather than read it, you may want to suck on a binky or pound beach sand.

So **Big Rule One** for this book to work is that you have to like simple fun. And I have confidence that you do! Mostly because you're still reading this. We'll explain in a moment exactly *why* we like simple fun, and why it's constructive that we do. But let's now talk about **Big Rule Two**, which is that you can't be a complete wee-wee. A 'wee-wee' being the childish term for the somewhat less childish term — inappropriate for children to use, although frequently used by grownups — to describe someone who thinks and therefore feels and therefore acts entirely within the prison-like walls of the ego; someone whose existence is predominantly characterized by the mental state of selfishness in their mental form of being, and therefore the emotional state of fear in their emotional form of being; someone whose perspective is deeply grounded in the habitual and false belief that they are separate from the world 'around' them, rather than being a part of and connected to it all; someone whose experience of life reflects the all-too-human condition that is destroying our world — a condition well-documented and increasingly understood in the fields of psychology and neurology, and long well-established and understood in the fields of philosophy and spirituality, not to mention regularly addressed in the world's great religions, and ultimately reflecting the basic laws of physics related to the nature and flow of energy: We're talking, here, about being a *complete dick*. You just can't be one, if this book is going to work for you — that is, if it's going to help you save the world. It's just the way things work — scientifically speaking, in a childish way.

Simply put, if you're a *complete* wee-wee, you can't save the world, because you won't change yourself. Because you can't — or, rather, won't — see yourself and the world around you differently than you see it right now. Why? Because you think you know it all. And why is that? Because you *need to believe* you know it all. And why is that? Because you're too afraid to believe otherwise. Even though, deep down, you *know* otherwise.

Making your problem more intractable (which is our problem, too, because *you* are *our* problem as well as your own), if you're a complete wee-wee, you have convinced yourself that your hard-headedness is a 'strength of character.' After all, 'strength' and 'hard' go together — right? Actually, no, it's the opposite of right, because it's wrong, and it means that you are, unfortunately for everyone in your orbit of engagement, a wee-wee. The mountain of facts documenting the history of life on our planet, some of which literally come from the mountains, prove that *adaptability* makes a system stronger and more likely to survive — and better yet, to thrive. Whether we're talking about an organism or an organization, it's how systems work. And as a human system, that means you need to be able to change how you look at yourself and the world around you — to adapt, and survive, and moreover, to thrive. But if you're hard-headed, you need to put up a hard shell around you, to protect you, because you're afraid. The foundation of your own worldview is that you should look out only for yourself because you have to, and you have to because you believe you're separate and alone in the universe. Which is a lonely and terrifying existence, indeed.

This is why hard-headedness, *closed-mindedness*, is called a 'bunker mentality.' If you're familiar with the TV character Archie Bunker, it's like *his* mentality, though usually not as funny to observe. Being hard-headed, closed to 'what is,' is a mindset for people who need a place to hide. You're afraid — especially and in particular — to be wrong about your sense of reality, your own beliefs. (Again, this is likely because you sense, deep down, where your connection to everything exists, you *are* wrong about your beliefs.) And so you're too afraid to change how you think. As a human system, you're broken. Even though you tell yourself, and act as if, you have it all together.

Okay, so maybe you hold down a job — even a good one; and maybe you have a home — even a nice one; and maybe you've got a family, and some friends, or at least a few neighbors and colleagues who don't seem to mind talking with you, or politely wait for you to stop talking and leave. You somehow manage to maintain a façade of 'normalcy' in your own mind, regarding your own life. But on the inside, beneath all the thinking, you know it's not really going your way. This 'knowledge' exists in the continuous, if inconspicuous, but nevertheless real sense of discontent that comes from feeling completely disconnected from the world within and around you. You feel empty inside, always trying to cover the hole in ways that only make it bigger. And although you don't see it, or won't see it, it's obvious to others.

And no matter how helpful this book or any other source of information and intended assistance may be, you can't be a complete wee-wee and make anything — and for that matter, everything — better than it is right now. You can't positively change you, and what's going on within you, and so you don't positively change what's going on around you. And because there's only two basic forms of change in the universe — positive (constructive, creative) change or negative (destructive, dissipative) change, if you're not a source, and manifestation, of positive change, you're therefore — inevitably, invariably, and let's throw in 'indubitably' before the word goes extinct from disuse — a source, and manifestation, of destruction. (Technically, you're *first* a manifestation of change, and *then* you're a source of it — having manifested yourself as that source.)

But here's the thing: It's okay to be a wee-wee *sometimes*. It's alright. Nothing to worry about. Remember, worrying is unhelpful. Besides that, we're all wee-wees sometimes. And it's okay to be a wee-wee sometimes. You just can't be a *complete* wee-wee. At least not if this book is going to work for you. It's a rule. A rule of nature. The scientific kind of rule describing what is, albeit in a childish way. The childish rendering of scientific facts (including some scientific facts about childishness) being, by the way, an important point of this book.

Speaking of science, and childishness: among the many remarkable things I learned while researching this book (yes, there *was* research involved: there was reading, lots of reading; and Googling, lots of Googling; and life experience, *lots* of trials and an unfortunately disproportionate number of errors) — basic things, in basic terms, about how the universe works, how energy works, how Ohm's Law works, how the human brain works, and how it all works out that metaphysical insights of ancient wisdom align to physical facts of modern science — is just how many synonymous terms there are for 'wee-wee.' Oh sure, it was amazing to learn about the first second of the Big Bang, and how more change happened in the universe within that first single second than has happened in all of the 13.4 billion years since. It still amazes me, and always will amaze me, to think about the first second of the Big Bang.[2] But I may have been even more amazed — astonished, even — to learn that there are over a hundred synonymous terms for wee-wee. The aforementioned term 'dick' is perhaps the most popular one of all — at least here in the United States, among people in my general age group. Although it should be pointed

---

[2] Fundamentalists on both sides of the idea of God do not believe the Big Bang is evidence of God. Believers say the biblical story of creation happened, therefore the Big Bang didn't happen — so the Big Bang is *not* evidence of God. Non-believers say the Big Bang happened, which contradicts the Bible — so the Big Bang is evidence there is *not* a God. 'Believers' avoid facts in their argument; non-believers dismiss as 'coincidence' the miracle of the universe's existence. Both sides have high opinions of their own opinions, and try to elevate their opinions above the facts by increasing the number and/or volume of the words they use to argue. This tactic often works in politics, proselytizing, professional wrestling, and other forms of public bullying, but it's conspicuously idiotic in the context of physics.

out to broaden our worldview — which is, of course, the point of this book — that the term 'wanker' is generally preferred and comparably popular in Great Britain and Australia. The words tinker, dinky, and winky are three of my personal favorites (and it's also the name of a Pittsburgh law firm that would like to help you if you've been in an accident). Some synonymous terms for wee-wee evoke images of pyrotechnics. Others refer to weapons of war. A few for some reason rhyme with the word 'gong.' And some even refer to famous literary figures, such as 'Shakespeare,' 'Longfellow,' and 'John Kennedy Toole.' Oh, and of course there is 'Johnson,' which is probably related to the number of Johnsons around. The list goes on. And on. And on. The point being there are many alternatives to 'wee-wee' that we could have used to describe **Big Rule Two**.

Having shared this seemingly irrelevant (and perhaps irreverent) point, you may at this point wonder — although it's unlikely that you would (but in case you do): Why 'wee-wee' to describe **Big Rule Two**? The reason is simple: It's childish. And childishness is something we hope and strive to manifest in this book. As a rule (the kind describing what is), childishness will help us save the world. A very well-known expert on the subject tried to teach us this important truth: 'Unless you change and become like little children, you will never enter the kingdom of heaven.' That's a quote from Jesus, in case you didn't know. And interestingly, methinks, many serious people who say they believe in Jesus don't seem to believe that statement is worth taking seriously enough to be less serious — which is, of course, a necessary prerequisite to being more childlike.

So going with 'wee-wee' to describe **Big Rule Two** was, on purpose, childish. But it was also a bit of an homage to my Scottish heritage,[3] as the literal Scottish translation of 'wee-wee' is 'small-small.' And a wee-wee *is* a small, small person. Small in character, that is. Which is the same thing as a person with a big, big ego. Which is the same thing as a wee-wee.

So, there you have it: The 'why' of 'wee-wee.'

It bears repeating, to avoid forgetting, that we all think, and therefore feel, and therefore act like a wee-wee sometimes. Because we all see or perceive reality, and we therefore *experience* reality, through the lens, the delusion, and indeed the illusion, that we are separate from one another and the world around us. We've all done it. We all do it. And we all most certainly will do it again. It's our human condition. And it's important to be aware of it so that we can work around it, or work through it, and hopefully at some point get ourselves, at least more often than not, beyond it.

Before we get to **Big Rule Three**, let's add one more thing about complete wee-wees. Because complete wee-wees are the reason the world needs saving.

We hear about complete wee-wees in the news all too often. Complete wee-wees hold powerful positions in the institutions and organizations that significantly shape our human cultures and societies. They stand on cultural pedestals as great athletes, artists, or reality television

---

[3] My Gingee (pronounced 'GHING-ghee') — the name I gave to my maternal grandmother when I first began talking, and which she forever after insisted on keeping — was from the Scottish city of Dundee, located on something called the 'Firth of Tay,' near towns with fun and bouncy names like Kingoodie, Picketillum, and Newbigging. She will always be one of my favorite people, ever. She paid attention to and loved me a lot; she made sure we always had chocolate milk and Cheez Whiz at our weekend pajama parties; and she otherwise brought a lot of simple fun into my life. I sure do miss my Gingee! She would not have been at all surprised that I wrote a book to try to help save the world. In fact, she would have been absolutely certain of its success! And for all you parents and child caretakers out there, I strongly believe that her belief in me still exists — exactly where it needs to be, which is, of course, within me.

pt. ends p. 56

stars. They raise kids, as parents or guardians. They teach children at schools. They are in charge of entire nations. They lead global businesses that are larger than many nations. And in addition to the more prominent examples cited, many other complete wee-wees roam our planet, anonymous to most except to those of us who encounter them directly — sometimes temporarily, and in some cases, on a regular basis. The point, here, being that there are many complete wee-wees out there; we all know, and know of, more than a few of them; and if you happen to be one of them, this book isn't for you. Though I wish it were. And if you are one, and can find it in yourself to open up, just a little bit, it is entirely and especially for you.

This last point, at last, brings us to **Big Rule Three** — in some regards, the most important one of all, because it reflects and embodies the other two big rules, wrapping them up into one big rule, which we'll put in the middle of the page, to emphasize its importance:

You have to be open to being more open.

This has nothing to do with your store hours or willingness to express feelings. At least not necessarily. The point of this rule is to keep an open mind; and at this point we ought to also point out that being open to being more open requires being more aware of your awareness, paying more attention to your attention, and believing more in the power of your belief. All of which relates to your perspective and having more perspective on it. Which relates back to your awareness and being more aware of it. Opening your mind is necessary to open your heart, which is necessary to open you to your universal ability to do the unique work you do to make the world better for others. This rule is most of all intended to remind us that it all begins, and ends, with awareness.

Here we arrive, yet again, at more paradox, because awareness, which is the point of everything, is, as a point of fact, pointless. There is no 'point' in space or time of or for your awareness. If I'm wrong, please place your awareness in a box and send it to me. Ah, but of course you can't send me your awareness in a box! For one thing, they cut back Saturday hours at the Post Office — and who can get there during the week? More importantly, and relevantly, it's impossible to literally box your awareness (even if you figuratively do it all the time) because your awareness is pointless. It is 'nothing' — or at least it shares all the qualities of nothing. But it's really everything, because you can't experience anything in your life without it. You can't experience anything in your life, except *within* or *through* your awareness. This is why it's so empowering, and necessary, to be more aware — that is, more open — than you already are. Which requires that you are open to being more open.

With that, good reader, we have established our **Big Three Rules** for this book to work. To recap:

First, you have to like simple fun.

Second, you can't be a complete wee-wee.

And third, you have to be open to being more open.

Likely, your adherence to these three rules varies from moment to moment, so it's a good idea to check yourself. Which requires that you be more aware of what's going on inside. Which requires . . . well, you know.

The Simple Fun Part About Simple Fun

We skipped over our more in-depth reflections on simple fun to delve into what it means to be a complete wee-wee and open to being more open. Those two rules seemed to warrant more immediate clarification, but we need to pay more attention to the importance of simple fun because it's our guiding principle to get you to pay attention to what you otherwise may not want to pay attention to. Simple fun is always and in a lot of ways important, but it's uniquely important in the context of this book because 'saving the world' means 'sacrificing your life, as you know it.' And if you're like most people, 'sacrificing life as you know it' is probably not on the top of your 'to do' list. When asked what you want to do on the weekend, you don't respond by saying, 'Well, there's a new restaurant I'd like to check out; also there's a movie I've been wanting to see — but what I'd *really* like to do is sacrifice my life, as I know it.' Yeah, no one says that. Because no one wants to do it. Which is why we want to address, in a simple fun way, a simple fun way for you to save the world. Saving the world is challenging — not to mention inconvenient, uncomfortable, and sometimes, flat-out terrifying. But it can *also* be simple and fun! It all depends on how you look at everything. Which is the point of this book, after all. So let's give due attention to simple fun, and the scientific basis, based on childishness, for its remarkable inherent power. There's a point to simple fun, and we ought to point it out because, as we made the point earlier, there's a lot of people out there who find it pointless.

Have you ever heard of Coke and Pepsi? How about Burger King and McDonalds? Perhaps Budweiser and Miller sound familiar? And maybe Bank of America and Morgan Stanley, Verizon and AT&T, and Geico and Progressive all ring a bell? Assuming you are familiar with all of these corporations, you may have noticed that they make a lot of money. Maybe some of it is yours. Or at least it *was* yours, at some point. You also may have noticed that none of these powerful multi-billion-dollar profit machines ever attempt to sell you their products or services by presenting detailed, fact-based business cases. When they invest money to sell you something through advertising, they don't communicate with a dry page of bullet points. Why? Because they know how to engage your attention and encourage your action — specifically, to buy stuff. They know what works, or hire people who do, to leverage our human nature to manipulate our consumer choices; sometimes, even, against our own best interests. And what works, as they know quite well, is communication that's simple and fun.

Marketing messages and images are *always* simple — and often, if not typically, they are fun. And not only are the messages and images simple and fun, but they try to convince you that if you buy what they're selling, you'll *experience* simple fun. That's why we've seen the guy who plays Aquaman doing a backflip over his T-Mobile service, and what appears to be a physically and emotionally healthy person beaming with delight while eating a chicken tender from Popeye's. Now, one could argue that using your cellphone or eating a chicken tender are common and for that matter perfectly legitimate forms of simple fun — and that may well be true. Not so much that you're naturally propelled into a backflip, or for that matter, a wan smile. But marketers take the idea to absurd extremes because they know it works — that is, they know that simple fun *attracts your attention* and *motivates your action*.

And what about those companies that offer stuff that clearly *isn't* simple or fun? Because they also try to use simple fun to sell you what they do — even trying to associate what they're selling with the experience of simple fun. Take insurance and financial management companies, for example. If you ever dealt with one of them, you know there's not much about it that's simple or fun. You wait on phones, you realize you're not covered enough, or you're not saving enough, and you deal with people who are supposed to help you but seem to want to hang up the phone and go home. Where's the simple fun in that? And yet, watch the commercials for these businesses, and they're all trying to get you to believe that dealing with an insurance claim or planning your financial future is somehow simple and fun. Maybe some people like that kind of thing, but I think most of us would prefer having to look for a wedding ring in a port-o-potty toilet at a Mexican food festival.

Okay, so *why* is simple fun communication so powerful? It begins with the power of 'simple,' and in particular, the power of symbols. Because a symbol *is* simple — it's the simplest visual form of human communication. Symbols engage us. Because symbols *are* connections — to ideas, objects, and relationships. They *create* connections — to those who engage them. And we *do* engage them — because they naturally attract our attention. And they naturally attract our attention because they're simple. It's really as simple as that.

Symbols are a veritable manifestation of simplicity. Perhaps that's why the words 'simple' and 'symbol' sound the same. And the simpler the symbol, the more powerful it is. It's the ultimate example of 'less' being 'more.' Take our favorite shape, the circle, for example — the simplest, commonest, and most enduring of all symbols. It's a literal one-liner, about which we don't have a one-liner — unless, that is, you think 'round' is funny.[4]

Funny or not, depending on how you look at things, the circle is the most powerful symbol in the history of humanity. In its perfect, balanced, singular simplicity, the circle has, for many thousands of years, symbolized some of our most complex human concepts, implicitly or explicitly conveying the concept of power itself. The circle symbolizes *totality, wholeness, nature — all of life*. It symbolizes the

[4] This is a nod to the Coen Brothers movie, *Raising Arizona*. If, separate from that reference and its context, you happen to think round is funny, in some inherent and visceral way, it is likely you are either blessed with genius or eligible for government training in the assembly of paper hats.

incomprehensible concepts of *infinity, timelessness, and eternity*. It symbolizes *God*, and Life itself. What it does *not* symbolize, unfortunately, is the location of a facility where you can legally dispose of your cannon ball, because such a place evidently does not exist — not anywhere within the totality of the seemingly infinite universe.

While the symbolic meaning of a circle is often shared and common across cultures and historical timelines, even when connoting the profound, sometimes it can be unclear and a matter for debate, usually among people who wear corduroy sports jackets and appear unconcerned with their hair. For example, a circle in a cave painting may represent the transcendent (the life-nourishing power of a sun god), the practical (the interconnectedness of the clan), or even the prophetic (the inspired vision of an above-ground swimming pool). The point is, the circle has been around a long time, symbolically communicating a lot of ideas that reflect our endless quest to better understand our own existence.

All symbols connect us, on the inside, to ideas, objects, or relationships that exist and are happening on the outside. Symbols *engage* us. They attract our attention and emotion. And that means they energize us. And *that* means they evoke and manifest who we really are. It's no wonder, then, that humans have been using symbols to advance our wondering about ideas, objects, and ourselves for over 100,000 years — long before the written word and probably fashion existed. It's also no wonder they remain popular and powerful today. Pay attention and you'll see them everywhere — especially the form of symbol we call 'logos.'

Imagine life without logos. Professional team sports could hardly exist without them! Fans would lose interest, without a simple way to identify them — and to identify *with* them. (This would be especially disorienting for Philadelphia Eagles fans who used to sit in the 700 level of the Vet.) Logos are important to the auto industry as well

pt. ends p. 56

— because they're important to the people who buy cars. They're important to fast food restaurants, oil companies, and pretty much any business that employs two or more people.

It's important to use logos because it's logical to use them. And it's logical to use them because it's an effective, efficient, and therefore powerful way to communicate. Perhaps that's why the English word 'logic' is based on the Greek word, 'logo.' Which we, then, called 'symbol.' Which looks and sounds like 'simple.' The simple logic of it is hard to ignore. And if you still don't believe in the power of simplicity as a way to communicate and connect, we should point out that some of the greatest minds, ever, are of a different mind.

Leonardo Da Vinci said simplicity is the ultimate form of sophistication. This, from one of the all-time symbols of intelligence — a person who, as a brilliant and visionary artist *and* scientist, was a genius with both sides of his brain. Former Apple CEO Steve Jobs, a modern icon of genius, said simplifying the complex enables us to move mountains. And Albert Einstein said *everything* should be as simple as possible, but not simpler. Everything! These symbols of genius well understood that simplification of the complex, or for that matter, the not-so-complex, isn't easy to do — quite the opposite: It's why the French physicist Blaise Pascal once said, 'I would have written a shorter letter if I had had more time.'

Making things simple isn't easy, but it's worth the effort because, again, simplicity is understandable. It's *relatable*. And it's powerful. Because it engages the attention and emotion of people in a way that can get them to act. This is why we can and most certainly should use simplicity to *un-complicate* the complicated challenge of understanding, recovering, and redeveloping our amazing creative ability (yes, it's there, still inside you — and, in fact, it really *is* you) to make life better and save the world.

Relating this back to the point of our simple fun book: We can, and should — and so, we will — relate the scientific facts about how each one of us can, in our own unique way, make it happen. And yes, science *can* be simple! As Einstein put it: 'Most of the fundamental ideas of science are essentially simple, and may, as a rule, be expressed in a language comprehensible to everyone.'

So much for our simple talk about simple. Hopefully, it was fun. Now let's talk about fun!

Fun is good, Dr. Seuss said simply. And a lot of other doctors have since come around to agree. And we're talking about doctors, some of them of the medical variety, who understand, in terms of the scientific facts, how the human brain and body work, and how human behavior works. These are experts in aspects of the human system who have addressed the matter of 'fun' with medical, biological, and psychological data, the volume of which is growing all the time. And the data confirms that we not only enjoy fun, but it improves the systems that we are, and the work that we do. More simply put: Fun improves our 'being' and 'doing.' We'll explain later why positive change in our being and doing is the same thing as creativity, which we mention now because it gets to the importance of fun. 'Creativity,' Einstein said, 'is intelligence having *fun*.'

Fortune magazine conducted a survey involving tens of thousands of people who work for companies with successful bottom lines, and more than eighty percent of employees who described their company as 'great' said they were working in a *fun* environment. Other studies show that having fun on the job enhances motivation, increases productivity, improves task performance, and promotes creativity. And the data aligns to experience-based wisdom we've heard for a long time. The great inventor Thomas Edison said he never did a day of work in his life 'because it was all fun.' And leadership expert Dale Carnegie similarly observed,

'People rarely succeed unless they have fun in what they are doing.' There is even neurological science to explain the nexus between fun and success in your work. Having fun releases dopamine, which leads to memory stimulation, which enhances learning, which is fundamental to success — in everything. 'Leadership *is* learning,' John F. Kennedy once said. Although we all see people in leadership positions who apparently haven't learned that yet.

Most importantly, we know from our own personal experience that we feel better and become healthier when we enjoy what we're doing, when we're having fun. We perform better and produce better outcomes when we enjoy what we're doing, when we're having fun. And we're more engaged and retain information better when we enjoy how information is delivered, when it's fun to receive it. Humor is especially and uniquely powerful in this way because it can help convey ideas we otherwise don't want to consider, and prefer to avoid.

Humor brings on laughter, which is an enjoyable experience (it may well be the ultimate form of fun). And because it does, humor has a singular ability to overcome the ego's defense system, which ignores, repels, and attacks what it doesn't want to acknowledge. It's why the ancients considered comedy a higher form of writing than tragedy: It more effectively conveys truth.

A famous advertising pioneer named Leo Burnett, who created Tony the Tiger and the Marlboro Man, and counted Coca-Cola and McDonalds among his many clients, observed how advertising 'isn't just about circulating information; it's about *penetrating the public mind with desires and belief*.' Burnett was talking about changing people at their core being. And there isn't a form of communication that can do this in the way humor does. Satirists have always understood the power of humor, from Shakespeare, Cervantes, and Voltaire to the writers of *Saturday Night Live*, *The*

Simpsons, and *Family Guy*. Satirists communicate truth about the society and culture of which they are a part. And even though that truth challenges existing beliefs, they communicate it effectively — that is, they get people to open their minds and pay attention to it — because, as Mark Twain understood, 'Against the assault of laughter, nothing can stand.' There's even data-based proof that it works.

In 2012, Fairleigh Dickinson University conducted a survey in an attempt to identify the most well-informed American viewers on the subject of politics, based on their primary source of information. (It should be noted that Unfairly Dickinson also conducted the same survey the same year, but the results were immediately discounted for obvious reasons.) No matter what side you're on, one thing we can hopefully agree on is that political news is full of unpleasantness. It's about big problems, negatively impacting our lives, not getting solved by people with big egos 'in charge' of solving them, big problems which are mostly not getting solved *because* of those big egos, whose big priority is staying 'in charge' — not to solve the problems, but to remain in charge of solving them. Who wants to watch the news about that?

Well, some of us do. Silly as it may sound, some of us even consider it patriotic to be aware of the *facts* about our political goings-on, as opposed to pledging allegiance to our favorite talking head. And it turns out that the people who were the most factually well-informed about politics, and all of its unpleasantness and stupidity and egomania that is destroying our quality of life in America and the world, were the people who primarily got their news from National Public Radio and the network Sunday talk shows. This makes sense because, notwithstanding unsubstantiated claims to the contrary (specifically, by the people whose unsubstantiated claims are revealed by them), these sources of information present, to an interested audience

pt. ends p. 56

seeking objective facts, a balanced account of those facts, with representatives from both major parties and political points of view given equal opportunity to share their respective perspective on issues. Balanced, fact-based reporting, for those interested in balanced, fact-based reporting, yielded the most well-informed people on political matters. Not a surprise, and nothing to see, here.

But here's the thing, and it gets to the power of fun: The *next* most well-informed viewers on political matters, after NPR and the Sunday morning talk shows, primarily got their information from *The Daily Show with Jon Stewart* — a show that spent at least as much time every show getting laughs as it did providing political news. A *comedy* show did a better job informing their viewers on the facts of domestic and international political issues than the country's three largest news networks — CNN, MSNBC, and Fox News. Turns out, in case you were wondering, the *least* well-informed viewers were the people who watched Fox News; and in fact, people who watched 'no news at all' were better informed on domestic and international news than Fox News viewers. Again, this was in 2012, more than a decade before Fox News was settling $800 million defamation lawsuits for advancing a big lie. Which we're sharing not as a political statement, but to merely relay a couple of facts.

And the facts also tell us that through humor, Jon Stewart was able to engage people in the otherwise unpalatable facts of American politics. This was not an aberration. A Pew Research Foundation study from around the same time showed that viewers of *The Colbert Report with Stephen Colbert* were better informed about politics than people who got their information from all the right- and left-leaning news channels. Comedian John Oliver's show, *Last Week Tonight*, has more recently been identified as having among the most well-informed viewers of a political show, a fact attributed to the show's remarkable ability to maintain the attention of its viewers on in-depth reporting. Why were these shows successful in keeping their viewers well-informed on the facts of politics? For one thing, they informed their viewers of actual *facts*. That always helps! And, as importantly, they delivered those facts with humor. While bias is inherent in all comedy, if not all forms of human communication, humor is a uniquely powerful way of imparting truth that people don't want to hear.

It's notable, and so we'll note it, in case you never noticed: Comedians and scientists share a critical objective in helping to save the world, that being, both seek to convey truth by observing, analyzing, and communicating 'what is.' Their respective forms of analysis are conducted and communicated in different ways, but these differences could — and one could argue, as it is being argued here, *should* — be used to help one another, conveying 'what is' to people who need to be more aware. In his book about the science of human motivation, author Daniel Pink points out what he diplomatically refers to as 'the curious gap' between what science *knows* and what people — so-called leaders, especially — *do*. Science knows so much, and readily shares it. The information they uncover isn't hidden in a vault, unless perhaps it involves uranium. Otherwise, it's as easy to access as a recipe for lasagna. And yet leaders of people ignore what is known regarding things they should know about — either thinking they already know it all, or not caring to know what is known that is presently, to them, unknown.

To ignore or dismiss what is proven to be 'true,' or at least 'supported by factual evidence,' is completely counterproductive at best, and disastrously destructive at worst. But the fact of the matter is that leaders in all walks of life don't engage in the facts of what matters. Leaders who don't like the facts, usually because they make them look bad or otherwise threatens their position of leadership, will make decisions that often ignore the facts, and therefore often contradict them. But it doesn't change the fact that they're going against the facts. 'It is the easiest thing in the world to deny a fact,' said the writer Isaac Asimov. 'People do it all the time. Yet it remains a fact just the same.'

And while it may, in fact, be easy for people to deny facts, the fact is, it's *not* so easy to ignore fun. Which is why it's important to try to make the facts fun, even if they aren't in and of themselves fun — including and especially the un-fun facts related to you being the source of destruction in your world. As the French satirist Moliere put it, 'The duty of humor is to correct people by amusing us.' The point, here, being that humor is not only important to our ability to connect through communication, but it may well be necessary to save humanity from the self-destruction of our genetic, culturally reinforced self-orientation. It may, in fact, be our one and only hope! Mark Twain certainly believed it to be the case. 'The human race has only one effective weapon,' he said, 'and that is laughter.'

And so we are dutifully attempting to use the unique and special form of simple fun that is humor, successfully or not (no doubt, sometimes not), in our related dutiful attempt to engage you in a subject you otherwise might not want to engage in: The problem of you being your own worst enemy, and the related problem of how that 'worst enemy' part of you is destroying you, and the world around you. As my mom reminded me one day while visiting from New Jersey, as I was working on this manuscript:

'There's a lot of books out there about this subject, you know. The self-help stuff.'

'I know,' I said. 'But none of them are funny.'

'Well,' Mom replied, 'I hope *yours* is funny.' Then she shrugged and walked off to make the boys pancakes while I went back to work on a line that wasn't particularly funny.

So now we understand, in more or less childishly scientific terms, why **LIFE STANDS EXPLAINED** is meant to be simple and fun: It's to manifest the energy necessary for you to pay attention to some facts about everything (generally), and nothing (in particular), for the purpose of constructively changing how you see yourself, your world, and your relation to the world, so that you're able to positively change everything — about you, for you, and around you.

Now let's get to the scientific childishness of it all. The scientific part is easy to explain, and in case you missed it, we have already explained it. This book is meant to explain, in scientific terms — that is, in terms of the rules describing what is (aka *facts*) — what it means for you to save the world, and why and how you can do it. This is important because if we don't figure out how to take better care of ourselves and each other, we're going to end up, as George Carlin put it, 'another closed-end biological mistake that leaves behind some Styrofoam.'

And so you don't have to figure it out all on your own, this book explains the ability to save the world, and why and how we can all develop and manifest it. And in keeping with the paradigm of simple fun, the science here related is rendered in childishly simple terms. Which is why this book is childishly scientific. Also, my ability to understand and relate science at a more complex level is noticeably exposed in my regular use of terms like 'doohickey' and 'hoozeewhatzit.'

But this book is also, more importantly, scientifically childish — because science tells us that it's a fact, a law of nature, a rule *describing what is*, and so let's call it something we know to be true: 'Childishness' is something we should emulate, because children are a lot better at positively changing than grownups. Kids are just plain better at getting better than we are. They learn more — and learn more easily. They use their imagination a lot more. And

pt. ends p. 56

they're generally more creative. All because their minds are a lot more open to what is.

Ask yourself: Do you typically experience the level of learning, imagination, creativity, and open-mindedness that a child does? (Here's a hint: If you think the answer is 'yes,' you are wrong.) Learning, imagination, creativity, and open-mindedness are vitally important and necessary attributes of people who have made, and continue to make, positive change happen — in their own lives, and in the world around them. They are the qualities that make a scientist, teacher, artist, businessperson, political leader, and childhood guardian a person who makes a positive difference and a better world for the rest of us. They are the qualities of effective and successful leadership. And while uncommon for adults, they are qualities common in young children.

If you're not inclined to think that it's children who can best show us, by the example of their own behaviors and states of being, how to save this world which grownups — and grownups, alone — have imperiled with destruction, let's consider what actual geniuses think about the worldview of a child. Pablo Picasso said, 'We are all artists as children; the challenge is to remain one as an adult.' The French poet Charles Baudelaire said pretty much the same thing: 'Genius is nothing more or less than a childhood recovered by will.' And the great German writer Goethe wrote, 'If children grew up according to early indications, we should have nothing but geniuses.' Still not convinced? Then we have Walt Disney: 'Our greatest natural resource is the mind of a child.' Sigmund Freud: 'What a distressing contrast there is between the radiant intelligence of a child and the feeble mentality of the average adult.' And, of course, Einstein had something to say on the subject: 'The pursuit of truth and beauty is the sphere in which we are allowed to remain a child all our lives.' These observations are from people who are, themselves, widely regarded as geniuses.

We smile bemusedly at the way a child sees the world. We think, 'ah, they have so much to learn.' We verily brim with feelings of intellectual superiority when we watch a kid play T-ball, or order a hot dog at a good Italian restaurant. But as is often the case with the way we grownups see things, we have it all backward, upside down, and inside out. The diametric opposite of 'what is.' Because there is something special about the way a child sees the world. Not 'special' in a way to only mean 'cute' or 'innocent,' but 'special' as in 'powerful' and 'capable of positively changing the world.'

If we're going to open ourselves to all life has to offer, and in turn offer back to life all that we are, we must laugh, have fun, enjoy what we do — we have to remember to open our minds, and hearts, to *play*. We grownups vastly underestimate the value and necessity of play. Well, at least a lot of us do. Those who have fun for a living know better, as do those who seek it out and enjoy it as much as possible. And there's been a lot of wise and intelligent people who have well understood its value and our need for it. Freud's greatest student, the psychiatrist Carl Jung, noted, 'The creation of something new is not accomplished by the intellect but by the play instinct.' The psychologist Jean Piaget, renowned for his work in cognitive development in children, pointed out, 'Play is the answer to the question, how does anything new come about?' Staying in the field, Abraham Maslow, the pioneer in positive psychology who famously identified the highest form of human need as 'self-actualization,' asserted, 'Almost all creativity involves purposeful play.'

Many great thinkers have similarly noted the benefit and power of play. Plato wrote, 'Do not keep children to their studies by compulsion, but by play.' Writer George Bernard Shaw pointed out, 'We don't stop playing because we grow old. We grow old because we stop playing.' Einstein

pt. ends next p.

observed, 'To stimulate creativity, one must have the child-like inclination for play.' And lastly, because it so poignantly points to the point of our simple fun book: 'Humanity is won,' said the writer Ralph Ellison, 'by continuing to play.'

And so I ask you, good reader: If we're going to save the world by seeing it differently, and our problem is seeing it differently, why, then, shouldn't we try saving the world by seeing it through a child's eyes? Jesus seemed to think it was a good idea. So did Plato. And Goethe. And Walt Disney. And Albert Einstein. I'm just saying, in case you're not inclined to believe *me*. Which, believe me, I would understand. Belief being the key to you saving the world. The main problem being you may not believe it.

With that being the case, let's now try to change your belief about belief. And let's solve the problem of changing your belief by defining it. Which means it is time, now, to define everything. Having pointed out the point of this book, while at the same time pointing out the point of your life, and making a few other points along the way, let's now get to the problem with everything, so we can help you save the world. That being the point of it all.

PART TWO

The Problem

Awareness is the problem
And it's the answer, too
It is our key to everything
It's what we live life through

You wanna fly, you got to give up
the shit that weighs you down.
-Toni Morrison

To address any problem, however big or small — 'how to save the world' being the biggest one of all — the first thing you have to do is define it. It's often been said that Einstein once said that if he had an hour to save the world, he'd spend fifty-five minutes defining the problem, and the last five minutes solving it. It's unclear if Einstein actually said this, and perhaps doubtful that he did; although you have to figure it's even less likely he said: 'If you want to travel through time, all you have to do is stick your tongue out — *like this!*' Sure, we have the iconic photo. But if it were true Einstein *did* say it, and then he *didn't* travel through time — which he undoubtedly didn't, or we'd have heard that he did — you'd have to wonder why he ever said it, and why no one ever said that he did.

Whatever Einstein may or may not have said about problem-solving, we all well understand that he well understood, as every problem-solver does, that in order to fix a system that isn't working, you need to first figure out *why* it's not working — that is, you need to define the problem. And to understand why a system is not working, you need to understand how the broken system is supposed to work, so you're able to define what's not working, so you can fix it and make it work.

There are many examples of how this works. Your doctor must understand the system of the human body to solve your medical problem. Your mechanic must understand the system of the automobile to solve your car problem. And your lawyer must understand the justice system and its laws to solve your legal problem — for example, if you want to sue your doctor for your medical problem, or your mechanic for your car problem. A lawyer who *really* understands how the system works will therefore know how to work the system, and can somehow successfully sue your doctor for your car problem and your mechanic for your medical problem. This, of course, would create a problem for your doctor and mechanic. And so they, of course, would have a problem with you. In which case you would need a new doctor and mechanic, and so you'd have a couple of new problems, too.

All of which is to say that to address our general problem of saving the world, and our particular problem of helping you to save it, we need to take a systematic approach to explain you, the world around you, and how you relate to it all. In other words, we need to explain how it all works. To do that, we're going to explain everything, in a more or less systematic way, in terms of systems. Systems matter to everything in the universe because everything made of 'matter' in the universe is a system. And all matter is created, animated, informed, organized, connected, sustained, and ultimately enabled by energy. 'Enabled' being the key word because energy *is* ability. It's *the ability to do work*, according to physics. Work being everything that happens in the universe, including what happens for everything to be.

Pretty simple, right? It's how everything basically works, and is. It also speaks to the importance of nothing. Because energy has all the qualities of what we think of as nothing.

And yet, as Einstein put it, nothing is, and nothing happens, without energy. All of which means that energy is, as a matter of fact, everything, as it matters more than anything when it comes to the matter of matter. And for that matter, it's why it matters that we understand the basics of all systems — what they basically are, what they basically do, how they basically work, and how they relate to energy (which, remember, is Life itself).

Once we cover the basics of all systems, then we'll get to the particulars of the unique system that is you, all the unique systems in and around you, why there is a universal aspect to all of it, and how you uniquely relate to it all. Understanding all of this will help you understand how and why you fundamentally change everything by changing your perspective, which will likely require a change to some fundamental beliefs. This is especially true if some of your fundamental beliefs are *fundamentalist* beliefs, which reject a lot of fundamental facts, and fundamentally reject a lot of fun. The most destructive fundamentalist beliefs reject the people who don't believe them, even believing it's holy and righteous to do it with a bomb or a gun.

Remember, dear reader, and otherwise try to never forget: Belief defines your reality. A *belief be*-comes your *life*. That's how you work. It's how your life works. And by explaining life's work in terms of systems, hopefully our systematic approach to explaining life will work by helping you believe in the power of belief, generally, and of your own beliefs, specifically; become more aware of the beliefs that help you, and those that do not; and actively choose beliefs aligned to the constructive, positive life you want, enabling you to make it happen — in a way that is a lot more simple and fun than you may believe is possible.

Systems are Basically Matter, Basically Working to Matter

Everything that occupies space in the universe is a system. That is, everything that has mass, and so is matter, is a system. All matter is made up of atoms. And all atoms are made up of subatomic particles called neutrons, protons, and electrons. Sure, it would have been a lot more fun if they had named these subatomic particles pooties, dooties, and tooties, but you have to figure atomic physicists probably aren't looking for giggles when they name things.

Electrons are the smallest of these subatomic particles, and they were previously considered the smallest systems of matter known to exist. The atomic physicists have since determined that something called a 'quark' — the *new* elementary particle of the universe — is even smaller. Which means that if someone calls you 'quirky,' you can reply to that subjective assessment by pointing out that, objectively, you are 'quarky,' and that if you *weren't* quarky, you wouldn't exist. This will likely affirm the person's stated belief that you are quirky, even though you addressed the matter with a scientific fact, if not an actual adjective.

There are six types of quarks; they're referred to, a bit oddly, as flavors; and they're even more oddly named '*up, down, charm, strange, top,* and *bottom*.' While these quark flavors sound a bit like directional signs in Alice's Wonderland, or 'professional services' one can find, if you're looking, in Las Vegas, in fact they're the names of the subatomic particles that make up protons and neutrons, which in turn make up an atom's nucleus. We won't attempt to describe what they're all doing, but no doubt it's pretty wild and crazy, and quite possibly even a little freaky. (We're still talking about the quarks, not the stuff going on in Vegas.)

So, what's a system? When you break it down to the

basics, a system is matter, organized as a particular form of being, to conduct energy in particular ways, to do particular forms of work, to change itself and other systems in particular ways. That's basically what systems are, and it's all that they really do. You could say that everything is a system of matter, working systematically to matter to everything! Although if you were to say it in a public restroom at a hockey game while doing jazz hands and prancing around on your tippy toes, someone may punch you.

Systems do two things: They work. And they change. And there are countless unique and particular ways for the unique and particular systems of the universe to work, and to change. Yet there are only two universal ways, in particular, for a system to change. A system can either change positively, or it can change negatively. All change of all systems in our universe is some version of one or the other: Positive or negative. One of the two is happening with everything, all of the time, without exception. You can't always notice change in a system — for example, with a brick, or a sink, or Ryan Seacrest — but it's happening.

Changing the subject a bit, although it's really all connected: Physics tells us that all systems conduct energy. But because energy is the ability for everything to happen, and to be, physics also tells us that energy conducts all systems. Now there's a paradox for you! We may refer to this energy as 'Big E' Energy — or Life itself, or Being, or Spirit, or Essence, or Source, or Force, or God, or whatever other term you prefer. Call it 'Pops Powerhouse' or 'Babs Booster' if you like. Call it *anything*. Call it 'Everything!' Energy itself, doesn't care, because it *isn't* a 'self' — even if you care what it's called (that is, your own 'self' cares) on its behalf, because you project your own sense of self onto it, to help your ego relate to it.

So whatever you want to call it, the important thing to remember is that everything is, and everything happens, in our physical universe because of it — even though it has all the physical qualities of what we perceive to be nothing. This is a fact, and we'll keep on repeating it, to help you prevent your own brain from deleting it. Einstein referred to this fact not only in the highly literal terms of a mathematical equation, but in the more figurative terms of a metaphor as well — perhaps realizing that no one could intellectualize the squaring of light speed, beyond supposing it makes a big 'whoosh' sound.

'Everything is determined,' he said, 'the beginning as well as the end, by forces over which we have no control. It is determined for the insect as well as the star. Human beings, vegetables, or cosmic dust, *we all dance to a mysterious tune, intoned in the distance by an invisible piper*.' Such a musical musing about how everything works, coming from one of the great minds of physics!

Let's try a non-musical interpretation of what Einstein meant, one that is consistent with what we've been talking about (and perhaps something you can hum along with), and we'll see if it makes some sense (the explanation, not the humming): He said that everything is a *mysterious tune* (an incomprehensible system), in which *we all dance* (in which *everything that's happening is happening*), as a result of *intonations in the distance by an invisible piper*. Everything is *intoned* (created, animated, informed, organized, connected, sustained, and ultimately enabled) *in the distance* (beyond the field of time and space) by an *invisible piper* (the creative force and intelligence of the universe — or God, or Life, or Being; that is, *Energy*). Matter conducts energy. But Einstein is saying, here, that energy also conducts matter; his metaphorical 'Invisible Pied Piper' being the conductor.

In other words — specifically, words that are much less poetic in their content and arrangement than Einstein's, though are perhaps more comprehensible to so-called practical people who take all expressions of wisdom literally (and can get a little miffed if you don't, too): Work (all that is happening in the universe) is the result of force (energy) applied to matter (everything). Which means that matter conducting energy is *really* energy conducting matter. It's a mind-blowingly simple paradigm of our singular universe that is mind-blowingly complex in its infinite manifestations.

We mentioned earlier, and it's worth repeating, that the material aspects of all systems, at the subatomic level, are vibrating energy. This means that, notwithstanding what we perceive to be 'reality' with our senses, there's no such thing as solid matter, because matter is, in its most basic form, vibrating energy. This is not merely a theory. It's a *fact* of physics. It's what our reality really is. Every material system is, ultimately, nothing more than the 'nothing' that is energy — vibrating at various levels, within a form of uncountable and continuous variations, in a state of uncountable and continuous transformations.

Therefore, literally everything *is* energy.

Without energy, there is nothing. Not even time and space. And without time and space, there's nothing, never, and nowhere! Which makes downtown street parking even harder to find.

Whatever you think regarding the nature of existence, even if you think it's not worth thinking about, the fact is that the one 'Big E' Energy of and beyond our physical universe is what everything is, and how everything works, thereby rendering matter as 'nothing' that only appears to be 'something.' This is why Einstein described reality as a 'persistent illusion.' It's all nothing. Although you should still get your mom something on Mother's Day. At least give her a call! And on a related note, the reality of our reality is all the more reason to live life to the fullest by relating fully to Life. Meaning you should manifest as much as possible, in every moment, the mind-blowingly amazing Life that you are. I mean, a very big and important life question would be: Why *wouldn't* you?

The mind-blowing reality of our reality is that it's all one unified formless energy, appearing as form, vibrating in a seemingly infinite number of coordinated variations to become and be the form of our universe. All of which means that the next time you ask someone how they're doing, and they half-sarcastically reply as if they're being clever or original (which, invariably, they are not), 'I'm livin' the dream,' you can (and, really, should) respond, without any sarcasm: 'That's correct; you *are* living the dream — physics has proven it, and I can explain why.' You can then explain why, if your interlocutor appears interested, which is highly unusual in my own experience, especially if you say it to someone from supply chain while attempting small talk before an online meeting.

What we're trying to say, here, is that 'reality' is an illusion — but so what? It is what it is, so participate in it fully. The idea is to work with it, go with the flow of it, knowing that it *is*. It's in your knowing that the Life of your life *is* this flowing that you'll find your ability to change how it's going. Or put it this way: If you think it's difficult to fight 'The Man,' or city hall, or a fourteen-year-old about 'screen time,' it's nothing compared to fighting the creative force and intelligence of the universe. Which we unconsciously tend to do all the time.

Systems Work, and Systems Change

Every system is constantly working because it requires work simply being a system. Even when a system does not appear to be doing something, work is happening on an atomic level; it's the work of the system being a system. A system's atoms are always working to be organized as that system, whatever that system is organized to be. For example, a rock is working, just being a rock, because its atoms are working to remain organized as that rock. There's even change going on, with that rock being a rock. You can't see it, but it's happening, because atoms and their subatomic particles are involved and moving around. The same goes for that road construction crew you've seen at the exact same spot along the highway every day for the past few months. There's work going on because that road crew *exists*, although this is not likely established in the road crew's collective bargaining agreement, unless perhaps someone from Tinker, Dinky & Winky negotiated the contract for management.

A system works in everything it does, as well. And whether a system is working to 'be' what it is, or to 'do' what does, when a system works, it changes. And in changing, it changes the systems that are part of it, and the systems of which it's a part. Just as every system is, itself, changed by the work of the systems that are part of it and the systems of which it's a part — which are also always changing, in the work that they do, doing what they do, and being what they are. Inherent in this description of the universe, explaining all of what is, and is happening, is the fact that all systems are *connected*. Not 'spending a lot of time on Facebook' or 'knowing a guy at the landfill named Vito' kind of connected, but physically connected, on an atomic level — and, of course, through the creative force and intelligence of the universe that is Energy or Life itself. We will talk about how this applies to the system that is you when we get to the part about the system that is you.

Systems are Universal and Unique, and so is Their Work

Every system embodies the universal attributes we just described. But each one is also unique in the details of its attributes. Snowflakes get all the credit for being unique, but there's nothing unique about a snowflake's uniqueness, because everything in the universe is, in some way, unique. You might say 'uniqueness' is universal! And if you do say it, and someone says, 'I've said that,' you might say, 'You don't say!' And see what they say.

The fact is, every system in the universe is universal *and* unique in its form. The universality of uniqueness applies to every ant, sardine, and Hallmark Christmas movie script. If you're a hipster and think you're unique because you dress like you're in an Apple commercial, keep in mind that, while you *are*, indeed, unique, there's nothing unique about being unique. Oh, sure, we all perceive varying levels of uniqueness, particularly in how we perceive others, but that's all subjective — a reflection of our own, unique perspective.

A system's particular form of being — both its unique and universal attributes — determines the particular way it conducts energy, and thereby the particular form of work it does. The more diverse and complex a system, the more diverse and complex the work it does. When it comes to particular systems and the particular forms of work that they do, the stuff that stuff does depends on the stuff doing the stuff. For example, cats do cat stuff, cars do car stuff, and cans do can stuff — though a can can't do much except be stuffed with stuff, including but not limited to cat stuff and car stuff. Car stuff the inanimate system of a car does is a lot more diverse and complex than the can stuff the inanimate system of a can can do. Likewise the cat stuff the animate system of a cat does is a lot more diverse and complex than the car stuff an inanimate car can do. Cats and cans we can also compare, although you likely don't care so we won't take you there.

As diverse and complex as the system of a cat may be, the cat stuff the system of a cat does is a lot less diverse and complex than the human stuff the system that you can do, because the system of a human includes the system of a human brain, which is infinitely diverse and, as theoretical physicist Michio Kaku points out, 'the most complex object in the known universe.' Besides that, we know that we're more complex systems than cats, because of our experience with cats. Cats swat at fuzzy things that move. Humans design and build spacecraft that move. We also perform surgery on cats, so they can resume their swatting at fuzzy things. And although they move around *a lot* better than we do (our own inert cat, notwithstanding), cats cannot build spacecraft or perform surgery on other cats.

Hopefully, we have established, through our examples, that a system's particular form of being determines the particular forms of work it does. And the particular form of work a system does determines how it changes other systems. Therefore, forms of change are as diverse as the systems changing. Meaning the forms of change in the universe are limitless in their uniqueness. And yet — *and yet!* — for all the unique and diverse forms of change going on in the universe at any moment, among all of its unique and diverse systems, there's only two universal and basic forms of change happening to the universal form of every system. We mentioned them earlier, and that we'd get back to them later, and now is that 'later,' so we'll mention it again: There is positive change. And there is negative change. Also, there is loose change, a reality of our monetary system with seemingly more negatives than positives, likely due to rules that *prescribe what should be* administered by civil servants between their contractually established breaks during their exactly eight-hour workday.

The Basic Difference Between the Two Basic Forms of Change

Everything is relative. And everything is changing in a

positive or negative way. Which means positive and negative change are relative. But because change is relative, it's therefore subjective — subject, in particular, to how it's perceived. Meaning an objective differentiation between positive and negative change is necessarily subjective. But as we give it a try, let's try to be objective about it.

For our purposes, we will define positive change in a system — which we may also refer to as 'construction' of the system — to mean it has *more* ability to do its work. When a system changes positively, it has more ability to be what it is and to do what it does. Similarly, let's define negative change in a system — which we may refer to as 'destruction' of the system — to mean it has *less* ability to do its work. When a system changes negatively, it has less ability to be what it is and to do what it does. Since we know that a system doing nothing and simply 'being' is, itself, a form of work, we can add here that positive change means a system has more well-being in its state of being (it being, after all, more 'well' because it manifests and conducts more energy, or Being), while negative change means a system has less well-being in its state of being (being less well, manifesting and conducting less energy, or Being).

This is a good time to talk about Ohm's Law. There are, of course, times when it is *not* a good time to talk about Ohm's Law; for example, when you finally get the attention of a busy bartender; or you're at the airport with the family and just realized your flight was yesterday. But now happens to be the perfect time to talk about it. So let's talk about it!

Ohm's Law is a law of physics that relates to electricity, the well-known and otherwise popular form of energy enabling just about everything that's happening with you and the world around you. This *rule describing what is* basically says that, in an electrical circuit (a system), the amount of electrical current (energy) passing through the circuit (system) and manifesting as output (work) is invariably related to two simple variables: The first is the amount of energy, the voltage, going into the system. The second is the amount of *resistance* to the energy — the obstacle, or constriction, or 'stress point' — in the system itself that inhibits energy's flow through it, and thereby inhibits the system's ability to do work.

Very simple, don't you think? If you have 100 volts of electricity going into a system, but there's a breaker (resistance) in the system to allow only 50 volts through it, that system will only produce as an output — as its work — 50 volts of electricity. Its output, its 'work,' will be limited or diminished by the resistance to energy flow in the system. If, on the other hand, only 25 volts of electricity goes into that very same system, all of the energy will pass through the point of resistance, but that system will only work on the 25 volts of electricity that went into it in the first place. Its output or 'work' will be limited or diminished by the amount of energy that went into the system.

Applying Ohm's Law to our basic concept of systems conducting energy, *enabling the flow of energy through* (construction of) a system, and *disabling resistance to the flow of energy through* (destruction of resistance in) a system, both mean the same thing: Positive change. Likewise, destruction to a system, and construction of resistance in the system, would also mean the same thing: Negative change.

Pretty simple, right?

If you're not following along, we'll get you there, so don't get stressed. Because when a system is 'stressed,' it is negatively changed. It's changed, let's say, 'beyond' its optimal state of being, and therefore beyond its optimal ability to do work, so the system is less able to conduct energy. This is why *you* never want to *be* stressed — or, for that matter, cross a bridge or person that is stressed, because, being stressed, they're not working well, and so things won't go well if you cross one of them.

We now understand the **two basic forms of change** that happen in a system, and between systems:

There is ***positive change***, and there is ***negative change***.

- **Positive change** is *construction* to a system, or destruction of resistance to the flow of energy in that system — either way, the system is **less stressed**.

- **Negative change** is *destruction* to a system, or construction of resistance to energy flow in that system — either way, the system is **more stressed**.

We know that one or the other form of change is happening, all the time, with all systems. And, in case you didn't know, change in one system impacts the change of another system to which it's connected.

It may be true that a butterfly fluttering its wings can cause a typhoon on the other side of the world — this being the example often used to describe Chaos Theory, and how it works. And we know it *is* true that quantum physics establishes physical phenomena occurring that transcends observable connections to the point of being inexplicable by the laws of plain old physics. But we're not talking about the presently unexplainable potential realities of quantum physics here. That would be ridiculous![5]

Here, we are talking about the altogether 'explainable' — that is, we're talking about one of the most basic concepts of basic physics, that being: Work is the result of force (energy)

---

[5] Talking about quantum physics isn't ridiculous, when the people talking know what they're talking about. But *me* talking about quantum physics is ridiculous, unless I'm just mentioning how me talking about it is ridiculous, which isn't, itself, ridiculous. Unless of course I've made it ridiculous with all this talk about when talking about quantum physics is and isn't ridiculous. To continue with this ridiculous line of thinking would be silly, so let's move on.

applied to an object (a system of matter). We're talking about how work impacts the connections of and between systems — creating or strengthening those connections through construction (positive change); or weakening or eliminating them through destruction (negative change). Depending on the work that is happening. Which is dependent on the particular system doing the work (its particular form of being) — and the *state* of being in that particular form of being.

So, there you have it! That's all we're going to explain regarding the basics of systems, how they work and change, and how it all relates to energy. Congratulations! You pretty much now understand how everything in the universe works — in a childishly simple scientific way. Hopefully, you had a little fun along the way! Either way, for our purpose — which is to help you to save the world, by helping you define the problem of saving the world, by helping define you, the world around you, and your relation to the world around you — it's all we need to cover. You now know everything you need to know about 'everything' in terms of the universal aspects of it all — that is, as it applies to all unique systems, and relates to energy.

To be clear, and otherwise manage your expectation of the outcome of our explanation, none of what we have shared will necessarily help you understand how every unique system works, and so the workings of things like the stock market, your health insurance coverage, and the ShamWow will remain, for most of us, an eternal mystery. But that's okay! Just because it's impossible to explain and understand everything, specifically, doesn't mean we can't explain and understand everything, generally.

This brings us to our explanation of the unique and universal system that is you. This is where everything gets a bit more complicated, because *you* are a bit more complicated — or rather, your brain is. It's the most complicated system in the known universe — remember? Of course, there's a lot we don't know about regarding all the systems in the universe, so again, we're just talking about what's known. But then you knew that already.

The Unique and Universal System that is You

Like every other system in the universe, you are a material or physical form of being. But as a human being, you are also — because *you experience life as* — two other forms of being. You are a mental form of being. And you are an emotional form of being. If anyone ever tells you, 'Calm down, there's no need to get physical' (or 'mental,' or 'emotional'), you can reply that you already *are* whatever you were told you don't need to 'get,' because you're the system of a human being. Also, you probably want to pause and objectively observe your states of being because people usually say there's no need for you to be one of your three forms of being whenever you're doing something you probably shouldn't be doing.

Among your three forms of being, your physical form of being is especially important because your mental and emotional forms of being manifest and exist *through* your physical form of being. That said, however, you *experience* your physical form of being, including your emotional form of being — not to mention all of your doing, and the doings of other systems in the world around you — *through* your mental form of being. You also experience Being itself, through your mental form of being, as 'awareness.' This includes when you experience Being through your emotional and physical forms of being — specifically, as 'love' in your emotional form of being, and 'ability' in your physical form of being. The point being that you are *experiencing* Being *through* your forms of being, *as* your states of being.

Your three forms of being, in being a human being, are

interdependent systems, and together they comprise the system that is you. Like all systems within a single system, your three systems change one another. When one system becomes more positive or negative, the other two do the same thing. It's inevitable because it's physics. And the laws of physics apply to the systems that you are — and the one that is you.

All three forms of being that comprise '***unique you***' impact your every experience of life, both within and around you. As the state of your forms of being change, *you* change. As you change, the work of the system that is you — that is, *what you do* — changes. And as what you do changes — including the doing of you simply being, in whatever is your state of being — the world around you changes with it. This, again, is a fact. Not a theory. Not an opinion. It's a fact. Because, again, it's simple physics. It's how every system works.

Let's, then, discuss in more detail the system that is you. That is, ***unique you*** — the unique system or form that is you. It's universal in nature because all human beings are the same basic system. But because our universal forms of being all manifest uniquely in every human being, with the states of these forms of being uniquely changing all the time (albeit for the same universal reasons), we will refer to the system that is you as ***unique you***. In talking about — that is, in defining — the universal attributes of ***unique you***, we will also necessarily talk about ***Universal You*** — the universal formless Energy or Being that is also you.

We will consider both of you because you are, paradoxically, both:

You are ***unique you***.

And you are ***Universal You***.

pt. ends p. 127

But our starting point in defining you is the 'you' that you have come to 'know' as you — ***unique you***. And our starting point in defining ***unique you*** will be your physical form of being, because without your physical form of being, you don't have a mental or emotional form of being, not to mention it's difficult to find a hat that fits or get seated at a restaurant.

Your Physical Form of Being

We mentioned the Big Bang earlier, because that's how everything began, according to the facts of physics. And it's worth mentioning again because, as theoretical physicist Lawrence Krauss put it, 'If we really want to understand ourselves on a fundamental level, we need to understand the Big Bang.' More important to your existence than the much smaller albeit equally necessary 'bang' involving your biological parents (no offense to either, all due respect to both, and apologies to you, because who wants to think about *that*), the Big Bang is how your physical form of being came to be, and it therefore quite literally puts 'everything' about the system that is you into context — specifically, the context of everything.

In the beginning, there was nothing — not even the three-dimensional fabric of time and space. (If you can't imagine what that means, join the club. And if you join the club, be sure to check your monthly dues statement because they sometimes charge for 'incidentals' that shouldn't be there.) Then, about 13.4 billion years ago, out of literally 'nowhere' and 'nothing,' energy appeared. Pure and perfect 'Big E' Energy. Unfathomably dense, unfathomably hot, unfathomably violent, and unfathomably miniscule — a million billion trillion times smaller than an atom (give or take a few zeroes — at which point, what's it matter, given this point wasn't yet matter?). Meaning 'Big E' Energy really started out small.

And then everything changed.

Because that point of energy was everything. And *it* changed. Continuously. At an unfathomably rapid speed. Faster, even, than the speed of light. Astrophysicists say that, based on their observations of the universe — in particular, how the galaxies continue to move away from each other at increasing speed — the instant this unfathomably small 'Big E' Energy somehow appeared, it expanded and transformed so quickly that it was necessary to create a new measurement of time to track the sequence of change. Physicists named these infinitesimally small units of time 'Planck time,' of which there are approximately 100,000,000, 000,000,000,000,000,000,000,000,000,000,000,000 units in a single second. Amazingly, if not miraculously — and it seems to me, the latter — more change happened within that first second of the universe's existence than in all the time the universe has since existed. If that doesn't blow your mind, nothing will — or at least nothing should. And if you can't have your mind blown — not by science, or art, or nature itself — it's a sure sign that you need to be open to being more open.

Within the first second of the Big Bang, while expanding faster than the speed of light, this Energy split into what continues to be the four fundamental forces of the universe: The gravitational force; the weak nuclear force; the electromagnetic force; and the strong nuclear force. Four forces of the same Force, forced apart by — what else? — the force of that Force. As the universe expanded — which happened at the *exact* speed and gravitational force necessary to enable its existence (matter could not have formed if the universe had expanded just the slightest bit slower or faster, or if the gravitational force had been just the slightest bit stronger or weaker; and by 'slightest bit' we mean an incomprehensibly infinitesimal difference that would, or should, blow your mind to contemplate) — energy then cooled enough to be formed into subatomic particles, which eventually combined to become the atoms that are the building blocks of all life in the universe still today. Including yours and mine.

Again, this all happened in the very first second of the existence of the universe. And it happened only because the creative energy of the universe suddenly appeared, out of nothing, into nothing, and made it happen. The odds of it happening without the intention and intelligence to make it happen have apparently, somehow, been calculated, and those odds include — now get this! — *thousands* of zeros. Thousands! Cambridge University astrophysicist and mathematician Fred Hoyle said the odds of the universe being created were smaller — *a lot* smaller! — than the odds of you winning Powerball *and* Mega Millions every week for the next fifty years. Theoretically, it could happen, but if it did, we'd know the system was rigged.

And that's the point. The system of our universe didn't 'just happen.' It was 'rigged' so that it did happen, by an intelligence that none of us have the intelligence to comprehend. 'A commonsense interpretation of the facts,' Hoyle said, 'suggests that a super-intellect has monkeyed with physics, as well as with chemistry and biology, and that there are no blind forces worth speaking about in nature. The numbers one calculates from the facts seem to me so overwhelming as to put this conclusion almost beyond question.'

Numerous astrophysicists you probably never heard of from world-class academic institutions you probably have heard of say the same basic thing. This is something to keep in mind the next time you think that 'you' and your thinking — especially your worrying — can create a better solution to a problem you're dealing with than can the creative energy of the universe, to which you need only open yourself for it to help.

So! Matter was created out of the four fundamental forces of energy, but only after prevailing in an epic battle with something called anti-matter. 'Epic' is an overused word these days, especially by kids describing their experience playing a competitive video game to people like me, who tell them they should read a book or do push-ups instead. But because the battle between matter and anti-matter impacted the nature of the entire universe, we can refer to *that* battle as 'epic' and it's not hyperbole. Since (let's refer to it as) 'our' mind-blowingly amazing first second of existence, the universe has continued to expand, as energy and matter have continued to change forms, with human life, on planet earth, being one of those forms — including human life forms that you have to check on to make sure they left a decent tip. This leaves the inevitable philosophical question: *Why?* (We are talking about the broader existential question, here, and not the narrower one about being a cheapo.)

Why was an infinitely complex yet interconnected material universe created by Energy? And then why was the unique form of life that is humanity created — with its unique capacity for self-destruction *and* self-awareness? And finally, why, among all the incomprehensible number of possible forms of a human being that *could* exist, was the system that is ***unique you*** created? Who knows the answers to these deep and profound questions? Certainly not me! *No one* knows why. All we *know* is that it is clearly the intention of Energy for everything to *be*. Could it *be* that 'everything' *is* because it gives Energy something to *do*? Again — who knows? Only Energy does. And Energy is not a 'who.' Even though many people — all of whom are, in their ***unique you***-ness, a 'who' — hold beliefs that project their own 'who-ness' upon it.

We can't know *why* Energy would 'intend' for everything

to be. Why does matter exist? Why do black holes exist? Why did the reality TV show *Vanilla Ice Goes Amish* exist? It's all a profound mystery, impossible to understand. The 'why' of existence is indeterminable. But we know *what* everything is, including you, and that's a system. You're a material system, comprising organized matter, which we're referring to as your physical form of being. You're a system of smaller systems, some of them mind-blowingly smaller than your physical form of being. And you're a system of larger systems, some of them mind-blowingly larger than your physical form of being.

To best understand the system that is your physical form of being, we'll need to consider the systems that are part of you, and those of which you're a part — as this will help explain everything, generally, and in particular how you relate to it all. Also, it will highlight your mind-blowing amazingness, even if it's true that sometimes you do things you wouldn't want the authorities or even certain judgmental friends to know about.

The Smaller Systems that are Part of You

Let's first talk about the systems that are part of you, and let's start small, with the mind-blowingly small systems that are your cells. There are about a hundred trillion of these self-contained biological systems comprising the system that is you, each one capable of conducting and generating electricity. Mind-blowing, right? Especially when you consider that about 50,000 of your cells died, and about 50,000 new ones were created, in the time it took you to read this sentence. Now *that's* change happening in the system that is you.

And that's nothing — although cells are really something! — compared to how mind-blowingly small are your molecules — the systems comprising the systems that are your cells. Especially mind-blowing are those molecules called DNA, which more or less *tell* your cells what to be, and do. DNA is what makes ***unique you*** so unique. And yet it's 99.9 percent the same as everyone else's — and therefore it's a thousand times more universal than it is unique. This means that all the hosts from Fox News and MS NOW (formerly MSNBC, if you missed the rebrand) are pretty much the exact same system![6]

And then there's your atoms — or at least they're 'yours' for a while. Atoms are the systems comprising the systems that are your molecules. Atoms not only *comprise* the system that is you, but eventually they also do *not* comprise the system that is you, because while 'your' atoms organize together as the system that is you, they are also passing in and out of the system that is you, zipping and zapping and zinging around like nobody's business, literally connecting you to the entire universe, even as their subatomic particles zip in and out of the known field of time and space. This is why you *are* everything in life, even from a material standpoint. Which is the point of all the material we're sharing about everything.

Here's what we mean, here, if we happened to lose you there: It's estimated that 98 percent of the atoms in a human body change every five to seven years. Meaning atoms are zipping around between you and the world around you. 'Zipping' being my own unscientific term for

[6] This reminds me of an idea for a TV show: A weekly debate between the evening hosts of Fox News and MS NOW. It would get aired on both networks and match up the hosts based on their time slots. You'd need strict rules of engagement and include a mute button for violations. To ensure fairness, you get a charismatic nonpartisan robot to moderate, and ensure real-time fact-checks and evidentiary video clips are available upon request. The point would be for each audience to hear the other side's point of view, and to perhaps even get more agreement on what's the *real* 'fake news.' Not to brag, but this would be the best thing that could happen to America short of moving the Super Bowl to a Saturday, or temporarily banning all forms of social media until we colonize another planet.

what atoms do. Maybe they *zap*. Maybe they *zing*. Whatever they're doing, they're doing *some*thing. And that 'something' is participating in a cosmic atomic-exchange program that is the basic work of the universe. This is an important fact about the system of our universe, and the system that is you: Atoms pass between systems everywhere, all the time, with everything. The four fundamental forces of the universe play their own unique role in all of it, organizing how particles interact and change. And oh, by the way, we should, here, say that ***unique you*** controls absolutely none of what we just described, while ***Universal You*** controls the entirety of it.

Bringing this all back to you, which we need to do, or probably just did: The fact of your participation in this cosmic atomic exchange program defines a rather important aspect of your factual and physical connection to the universe, and your related mind-blowing amazingness. It's why not only is your physical form of being a *part* of the universe, but it's why *the universe is a part of you*. This is not merely a hopeful theory, or a poetic sentiment, or the posturing speculation of some stoner kid at a Phish concert who takes about three showers a semester and refers to his girlfriend as 'dude.' What it is, good reader, is a scientific fact: You're not only created, animated, informed, organized, connected, sustained, and ultimately enabled by the same Energy, but you're also comprised of the same basic matter, designed and functioning the same basic way as the rest of humanity has for hundreds of thousands of years — as well as every basic system has, for billions of years. As the (very often) antagonist (very often) says to the protagonist, in the (very often) climatic scene of (very often) unoriginal movies: 'We're not so different, you and me.'

And as is the case with your individual physical form of being, your individual cells, and your individual molecules, each one of the atoms that is temporarily part of your physical form of being is its own, self-contained system. It's a system of protons, electrons, and neutrons acquiring mass through something called a Higgs boson particle, which evidently comes from an energy field beyond — and yet is referred to within — the three-dimensional field of existence we perceive as time and space. Physicists have done the math, and estimate you have around 7,000,000,000,000, 000,000,000,000,000 of these self-contained systems that we call atoms — give or take a few, depending on how big you are and what you had for dinner. And they are organized together to form the system that is you.

Pretty mind-blowing! Especially when you consider that, even though all of 'your' atoms are constantly changing in and out of your physical form of being, your physical form of being remains organized by these other, new, completely different atoms in a way that, while continuously changing, is basically unchanged. This is why you look the way you look all the time, and it's hard to notice any change unless you spent the last day or so in an airport. It's likely pretty hard for you to imagine your physical form of being as being mind-blowingly well-organized individual self-contained atomic systems, because you only perceive yourself as one solid system. It's why you can't walk through walls, or do the crazy stuff they do in *The Matrix*, or even bump your head without wishing you hadn't.

But the fact is, the *reality* is, you are mostly empty space. That is, your atoms are mostly empty space, with mostly empty space between one another. If you happen to ask one, an atomic physicist will tell you that well over 99.9999 percent of your physical form of being is *nothing*. When you consider all the empty space comprising 'your' atoms and separating 'your' atoms from one another, the physical form of being — the so-called self-contained system — that is ***unique you*** amounts to almost nothing. As a matter of fact, regarding the facts of your matter, if you were to take all of the 'nothing' out of you — that is, if you were to remove all the empty space comprising your physical form of being — the solid atomic matter that would remain of you could fit into a sphere the size of the period at the end of this sentence. Easily! And if all of *that* doesn't blow your mind, consider that if all your matter were somehow converted to energy, you would comprise about 80,000 times more energy than was released by the atomic bomb that destroyed Nagasaki. If you find it hard to believe that a human being embodies so much energy, while at the same time comprising so little matter, you can do the math yourself, using Einstein's equation. A considerably less scientific method would be to observe a toddler five minutes after getting into someone's hidden stash of candy bars.

This stuff about your atomic composition is mind-blowing *and* something to 'keep in mind' when choosing how to look at, and see, the *real* you. You're mostly nothing, atomically speaking. Not that 'atomically' is a particular way to speak. Although, come to think of it, 'atomically' is the particular way that *everything* happens. Nothing's happening if it's not happening atomically. All of which means that, atomically speaking, you're mostly nothing. But because you're Energy, you're really everything.

Hopefully you can see why you are, truly, mind-blowingly amazing. And if you're still not convinced, how about looking at it this way: Let's say you're a schoolteacher with twenty first-grade students in your class, or you're a town manager and supervise twenty public employees. Now imagine how complex and difficult it would be to organize all of them (the kids, and the public employees) into a singular and cohesive purpose. Sound challenging? Sure, it is! Now imagine if you had to organize several *trillion quadrillion* or so first-graders or public employees into a single and cohesive purpose. Have fun with that! And, oh, by the way, if you think an atom is easier to organize than a first-grader or public employee — well, it isn't. Because for one thing, first-graders and public employees don't pop in and out of the field of time and space or appear in two different places at the same time, like the electrons of your atoms do. It may seem that way sometimes with certain first-graders and public employees, but it really *is* that way with the electrons of your atoms. Which means not only are your atoms going in and out of your physical form of being, but your subatomic particles are going in and out of the field of time and space. This, good reader, is our reality — believe it or not. As Neils Bohr put it: 'If quantum physics hasn't profoundly shocked you, you haven't understood it yet.' This, from a guy who won the Nobel Prize for his work on the atom. Which means that he had a pretty good handle on what's happening with everything.

You're also comprised of systems which aren't so mind-blowingly small. But they're nevertheless mind-blowingly amazing in how they work, and in the very fact that they do work, because if they didn't work, neither would you. Consider your seventy-eight individual organs. Or your eleven individual organ systems. Or your five vital organs. Or just *one* of your vital organs — like your brain, which is the system of your physical form of being that primarily informs your mental form of being — that is, your mind. It's for this reason we need to keep in mind what's happening with your brain, because if it's true that you change the world by changing how you look at it (which it is), it's also true that you change how you look at the world by changing your brain. Not just changing what it *does* in its work, or for that matter how it works when it's working, but physically changing its form of being — that is, what it *is*. And it so happens that your brain changes its form of being when you change your mind — in particular, when you change what you think about.

Depending on how much work your brain is doing right

pt. ends p. 127

now, you may be wondering: How do 'you' change your mind, by changing the physical form of your brain — by changing your mind? To explain the brain, we have to mention your mind, your mental form of being, because even though it's formless, as is everything 'within' your mind, your mind changes your brain as much as your brain changes your mind. And this, again, is something we need to keep in mind. Which we can do, now, by informing your brain about your brain. Which we can do by sharing a few thoughts about your thoughts.

What exactly *is* a thought, and — since we're still talking about your physical form of being — can it be described in physical terms? Before there was such a thing as neuroscience, it was the philosophers who considered this question, at least among the people who made a living doing it. But since they lacked knowledge of the brain's physiology, thoughts were all philosophers had to offer on thoughts, and so it all more or less amounted to nothing. Which is more or less where we are today, with our thinking on thoughts. According to Charles Jennings, director of neurotechnology at the MIT McGovern Institute for Brain Research, and therefore someone who is thought of as a thought leader on thoughts, a thought is the product of billions and trillions of systems working together — more specifically, about 100 billion nerve cells, called neurons, that work together through trillions of connections, called synapses, each of which transmits its own 'signal' of electrical energy, with some specialized synapses sending several hundred simultaneous signals in a single second. Try saying *that* five times fast! (It probably requires *a lot* of synapses simultaneously sending signals.)

And 'somehow,' says Jennings — in a notably less-than-expansive explanation, because it's all that science now understands — all of this mind-blowingly amazing coordination of work, involving billions and trillions of systems, produces a single thought. *Somehow*, the man says! Meaning somehow science has brought us to a point in our knowledge of the physical nature of a thought, but other than generally knowing how electrical energy is organized to form one, we don't know much if anything about a thought's so-called 'form of being.'

This all means that, as far as we can tell — meaning as far as the neurologists with the scientific expertise can tell — a thought is an energy form, formed through an absurdly complex process, in the absurdly complex form of your brain, which also somehow includes chemical reactions, which we won't get into, likely because of my own brain's chemical reactions, which are presently reacting in a way to help form the thought, 'There's no way I'm even going to attempt to get into how chemical reactions impact thought.'

The main takeaway, here, being that there is a mind-blowingly amazing confluence of work required for every one of the 60,000 or so thoughts people have every day. Even the stupid ones! And although it's mind-blowingly complex, the brain also functions, in a way, like a simple machine. The 'work' the system of a brain produces in the form of a thought is informed by its original design, and modified by its various experiences, perceptions, beliefs, and thoughts. In other words, the brain's output reflects its input, based on, you might say, a 'basic' design. This explains why people typically think about ninety-five percent of the same thoughts every day. Not the same as one another — no, certainly not! But we each *passively* think pretty much the exact same thoughts we each thought the day before. Which is why, in turn, our lives go around in circles. And it's why they'll continue going around in those more or less exact same circles. Unless, that is, we actively change our thoughts.

This brings us to the all-important matter of how our habits work, which all relates to how the physical human system works. We think of our habits as being circular behaviors, and they most certainly do manifest in the things that we do. But causing those circular behaviors is a circular process of our brain's work. The human brain — yours included! — is 'wired' (that is, its neurons and synapses are formed and organized) in a way to 'process input' (that is, interpret experience) in a particular way. Here's how it works — or rather, how *you* work:

First, you experience what we'll call a 'stimulus.' This is something that happens *to* you; it's something that you don't control, or at least it's not something you choose to happen. This stimulus may happen within you (a thought or feeling, such as 'I'm bored' or 'I'm uneasy') or around you (it's a certain time of day, such as lunchtime). You don't 'choose' to feel bored or uneasy (at least not in the context of what we're talking about here, unless you're a teenager visiting an amazingly interesting place while on an expensive vacation with your parents), just as you don't choose for noon to arrive on a weekday — and you may not even notice any of it happening. But it happens.

And then what happens? Your automatic habitual response happens. What really happens is that your brain, which is organized or 'wired' to automatically respond to that particular stimulus (boredom, uneasiness, lunchtime) with a particular response (let's pick an obviously destructive former habit of my own, like smoking a nicotine cigarette) that you associate with a particular reward (I'm more relaxed; I feel better) — and so that is what you do. Like a robot on autopilot. You do something that is objectively self-destructive — destroying, in this particular example, your physical form of being. And when you experience that self-destructive 'reward' to your response (natural enjoyment of the state of relaxation), it reinforces and strengthens your self-destructive response the next time that stimulus manifests. This is why, in the most basic and simple terms, so many people do so much obviously self-destructive stuff all the time. This 'habit loop,' as it's described by writer Charles Duhigg in his book, *The Power of Habit*, simply describes the basic work of the human neurological system that is responsible for the fact that we do, indeed, live our lives in literal circles. And this means you do, too.

Sometimes your habits are constructive to the system that is you. But far too often, as in the case of cigarette smoking, your habits are destructive. Constructive or destructive, positive or negative, no matter how a habit changes your physical state of being, your brain continually changes to accommodate the process of you thinking the thoughts you think. Meaning your brain doesn't just work differently when you think different thoughts. Its form of being changes to work differently. Through a remarkable process called neuroplasticity, your brain morphs — it physically changes its form of being — to accommodate your habitual thinking, to repeat it. Now, of course your brain doesn't morph into a hairdryer, or a bowling pin. It's morphing into a new form of the same human brain, with the same basic form. But it *is* physically changing, changing *what it is*; and by so doing, it changes *how it works*. And so, it changes *what it does*, working.

Herein lies the power of a habit: By thinking over and over a particular constructive thought ('time to exercise' or 'the universe supports me') or a particular destructive thought ('time for a cigarette' or 'the universe is against me'), your brain physically changes to accommodate that thought, so it is naturally, automatically repeated in response to the next relevant stimulus you experience. This habit *becomes* a part of your physical form of being. So it becomes your belief. And so it becomes your life. In this way, neuroplasticity proves that mind over matter is real, and that it applies to the matter that matters most — brain matter. And brain matter matters most because the work it does changes — for better, or worse — the system that is you, the work that you do, and therefore what happens in the world around you. 'The world is a product of our thinking,' Einstein said, 'so in order to change it, we must change how we think about it.' We can see, now, what he was thinking when he said this.

To change how you passively think the mostly-same thoughts you think every day, you must actively change the most complicated system in the known universe — your own brain. Fortunately, this work 'you' must do on your own brain *isn't* complicated. It's actually incredibly simple. Maybe *not* easy. Well, *definitely* not easy. But it *is* simple. And affordable. And convenient! It doesn't require any special knowledge, skills, or equipment — not even an app. Everyone can do it. Anywhere, at any time, in any circumstance. You only need to be ***aware*** you can do it, ***believe*** you can do it, and ***choose*** to do it. In this way, you could say that changing the most complicated object in the known universe is as simple as **ABC**.

We often make the mistake of trying to change our habits by choosing different things to do — that is, different actions or behaviors. What we need to do, instead, is to *first* choose different thoughts to think, regarding what we do, and for that matter, what we are. Then, we need to choose to think those same new thoughts. Over, and over, and over again, until we think those thoughts naturally, and they become a natural part of who we are. This is, by the way, the reason we keep repeating certain facts and thoughts about what you really are — which is 'everything,' mind-blowingly amazing, and able to save the world. As annoying as it may well be, this is purposeful, and likely necessary, to counteract your false belief that you are otherwise: Separate, limited, and confined by your own worldview. We are equipped with a remarkable world-changing power, to change our thoughts. But the problem is we don't use it because we aren't aware that we have it. Although *you* are, now, aware that we do.

We have another problem, which is that the human system accommodates negative thoughts more easily than positive ones. As we pointed out earlier, most people think mostly negative thoughts, even though we much prefer to focus on the more positive ones. Studies of human thought patterns indicate that over eighty percent of our thoughts are negative. Which is a statistic that's hard to be positive about. *Why* are we inclined to think negative thoughts, even though we don't enjoy thinking them? It gets back to brain design. We think negative thoughts because the basic system of the human brain is designed to create and sustain the egoic sense of a separate self on which all negative (self-oriented, separating) thoughts are based. It's a problem we've inherited — one that, at one point in our human evolution, wasn't a problem — and, in fact, it was a solution. It was *the* solution — to keep us alive.

Before our brain, and our ability to use it, evolved to the point that the only real threat to our survival was ourselves (if we want to call that 'evolving'), our ability to survive the natural world was enhanced by this built-in impulse to fear, desire, and judge what we observed in the world around us — to project onto it our own ego-based perspective. These impulses kept us safe, nourished, and procreating, among other things. They say there's a time and a place for everything — and that includes, even, the ego in our human evolution. That said, if there's a time and place to do interpretative dance during an executive job performance review at an auditing firm, I'd like to understand the details of that situation.

Anyway, at this point in our evolution — here and now, in our modern world, with all its different needs and challenges compared to, say, the beginning of the Pleistocene epoch, which took place more than two and a half million years before we invented the doily — our self-oriented impulses, and the beliefs reinforcing and sustaining them, are not only destroying our ability to thrive, but they're compromising our ability to survive. And our path to self-destruction will continue, absent a wide application of force to the human brain, one brain at a time. The 'application of a force' we're talking about is not of the 'frying pan to the head' variety; rather, it's about focusing our minds to manifest what we already are — which, while a process that invariably involves some form of suffering, won't leave a dent in your skull.

This is where awareness comes into the picture and makes everything possible, even though awareness is, of course, impossible to picture. And 'where' awareness comes into the picture is in your mental form of being, that being your picture — of everything. So, let's engage your mental form of being to consider your mental form of being — which, although formless, and like 'nothing,' in terms of matter, matters more than anything because it informs and forms every experience of your life, including and especially your experience of Life itself. As the creator of everything in your life, it is everything to your life. And it really comes in handy when you're reading a book about everything — or, for that matter, doing anything at all.

Your Mental Form of Being

If you thought that stuff about your physical form of being was mind-blowingly amazing, that's nothing, compared to your mind, your mental form of being — which, as we have mentioned, is essentially nothing. Yet it's the essence of everything! And without it, you don't experience anything. Not even the aforementioned frying pan to the head.

We can't say for sure, since not even you can perceive it with your five senses, but we're going to posit, or at least speculate, that your mental form of being exists as its own system, existing and working and experienced *through* the physical system of your body, with the system of your brain being especially important, doing especially important work. While your brain is a physical system that creates thoughts, a thought itself is formless energy, as is the mind 'within' which it exists, which is why we have to posit or speculate about it. It should blow your mind, to think about your mind, because while it manifests through a physical system, it is not, itself, material. This gets to the essence of the paradox that you are.

You are a physical system, conducting energy. But you are also energy, conducting a physical system. You are both the system of an individual human being, a 'self,' conducting the Energy that is Being; and you are also Being, the 'transcendent selfless,' conducting the system of a human being. This raises the ultimate question of what is your true nature: Which is real — which is true? Of these metaphysically and diametrically opposite two, which, in reality, is the real you? The answer to this question depends on how you define reality.

As a human physical form of being, as ***unique you***, you are a constantly changing form that is temporary. As 'Being' itself, as ***Universal You***, you are constant *and* eternal, formless and yet informing all forms. ***Universal You*** is the energy that enables your awareness, your experience, of it all. ***Universal You*** *is* that awareness. It's the awareness, the consciousness, of the entire universe. And it's you!

Which, then, better describes what's real and true? Millennia of human wisdom says that you are a spiritual being, having a human experience, more than a human being, having a spiritual experience. You are Being, informing your being; Life, informing your life; ***Universal You***, informing ***unique you***. Physics, now, tells us the same thing, with scientific evidence to back it up. But, again, which of the two is true for you is ultimately a matter of your own point of view. Because you live your life out of the self-created reality of your own thoughts. Your thoughts are your 'answers' to what is reality.

In reality, reality is one unified reality. In reality, our unique answers are pretty much always getting in the way of what's really going on with everything. Toltec wisdom describes these answers as a fog obscuring the world and life to which we're all connected. It's the madness with which Mark Twain said we're all afflicted. It is the source of all the pain and suffering humans inflict on our individual selves, other people, and the world that sustains us. It's the source of thinking that is so incredibly stupid and self-destructive that you have to wonder if maybe we *do* need the aliens to come and fix things for us.

All of this may well make the case that you are, in fact, your formless mind — since your life and reality, including and especially your own identity as either 'an individual self' or 'the transcendent selfless,' exist within and are created out of your mind. And yet — ironically, paradoxically, and perhaps even humorously, if you happen to see the comical aspect — it's your mind that convinces itself otherwise, that you are a physical system conducting energy, rather than energy conducting a physical system. This self-delusional and self-defeating let's say 'phenomena' of human perception occurs because your ego (the innate sense of 'self' existing in your mind because of how your physical brain is designed) naturally aligns its own survival with the survival of your physical form of being. Without which 'your' mind, again, does not exist. Which brings us back, again, to the question: Are you a human being, conducting Being; or are you Being, conducting a human being?

To help you answer this question for yourself, about yourself, and whether you're a 'self' or 'selfless,' let's bring awareness, attention, and some answers to your mental form of being, your mind. Which seems not only sensible, but also fair, because your mental form of being manifests as your awareness, attention, and answers — your 'answers,' again, and to be clear, being the thoughts and, especially, the foundational thoughts about reality that we refer to as 'beliefs' that 'form in' and 'inform' your mental form of being. We'll also bring some perspective to your perspective — which we'll refer to as the 'Big A' *Answer*, the one answer comprising and reflecting all of your answers to form and inform your worldview, ultimately determining what *is* your big answer — 'yes' or 'no' — to your acceptance and, therefore, full experience, of 'what is.' Your big answer — that is, your 'Big A' Answer — being your attitude.

This 'Answer,' *your* Answer, which is *the* Answer of your life, framing and defining and ultimately limiting it all, tells you if you're open to being more open, able to acknowledge and accept 'what is' in pure awareness. Your Answer tells you, yes or no, if you *are* the positive change you seek. It points to the very point of your life. It tells you if you're here to save the world or destroy it. It defines, in the most literal sense, your experience of life. So in technical terms, it's a colossally big whoop-dee-doo.

We'll talk more about your Answer. But let's begin expanding awareness of your mental form of being by talking about your awareness, because everything begins with awareness, not to mention, but we will, that it all ends there as well. We've said it before, but it certainly bears repeating, that every experience of your life — and so everything in your life — only happens within your awareness. And so, your life, and Life itself, are both one and the same as your awareness, which we may also refer to as consciousness, or presence, or Being. We could also, though, call it, say, 'Henry' or 'Hazel,' to help us remember it's only a label.

Herein lies the importance of simply and impersonally being aware, or present, or conscious, without your thoughts — your personal 'answers' — getting in the way: To be aware is to 'be' Being itself. Which is, again, the creative force and intelligence of the universe — the significance of which cannot be overstated, can only be understated, and should continuously be restated to help manifest your mind-blowing amazingness. Somewhat related, and also entirely related: It is likely that you think your thoughts are all-important and even necessary to you being a human being. They are, after all, the source of your identity and life as you know it. Indeed, your thoughts can be helpful in the way you work when they help you 'be' and 'do' more positive. But ultimately, your thoughts or 'answers' are obstructions, points of resistance, to you being Being itself. Which seems a good reason to be open to being more open than you are right now. Whenever 'now' may be. Which is always.

It should be noted that, in defining your mental form of being, it's plausible, sensible, and perhaps probable that there is an 'unconscious' aspect to your mental form of being, even a 'personal' and 'collective' unconscious — this being the Jungian paradigm of the unconscious mind. (The phrase, 'the Jungian paradigm of the unconscious mind' being one to never use while exchanging personalized wedding vows, or as you're trying to sell insulation at a homebuilders convention.) Of course, there's no way of *knowing*, through experience, that the unconscious mind exists, or doesn't exist, because by definition, that which is unconscious must exist — if, indeed, it does exist — outside of or beyond consciousness, and therefore beyond our human experience. Not to be 'Captain Obvious,' here, but we're trying to clarify things.

The scientific and perhaps philosophical question has many times been asked, although it's not likely a big topic of discussion on your homeowner's association chat group, what with all the inadequate lawncare and unapproved façade changes to complain about: Does the sound of a tree falling in the forest *exist* if no one hears it — that is, if the sound is never experienced? The same basic question applies to the unconscious mind: Does the human unconscious mind exist if it is not, and cannot be, consciously experienced? The answer must be a definite maybe! But there's nothing more than logic and perhaps circumstantial evidence to back it up. We don't know it to be true because we *can't* know it to be true. To know otherwise would be like seeing into the fourth dimension — which, if you ever have occasion to do, please let me know if you find any cheap sunglasses or unpaired socks, because they may be mine.

The unconscious mind is, then, and can only be, an idea; it's merely a product of our thinking. At least it is for those of us who think about it. Not that I think about it much. Although when I have, and now that I do, it seems to me a good and reasonable idea that makes sense and may well be true, even if it can never be anything more than an idea. All of which is to say that, as we define our human mental form of being, let's think of the unconscious mind as an idea to represent some kind of potential of the conscious mind. From the standpoint of it being a physical phenomenon, the unconscious mind could represent all of what the brain has been formed or 'wired' to consciously experience through thought, including an innate understanding of what we truly are, and how we relate to energy, and thus is the source of the archetypes and other basic 'structures' of our self-awareness that manifest in our consciousness. It may also be why creepy-crawly things give so many of us 'the willies.'

Our conclusion, then, for our note-takers, page-benders, and highlighters out there: The unconscious mind is an *idea* to represent the brain's *potential* to work; an idea to represent every possible thought, and every possible organization of thoughts, that could manifest in the conscious mind, but doesn't. Until it does. At which point, it's not unconscious anymore. Though it may well have been. But really, who cares? In the end, there's no way of knowing if the unconscious exists. Although something tells me, possibly my unconscious, that something in the unconscious may intend to be known.

But this we know, or at least you do: Your conscious mind — your awareness — *does* exist. And you know it exists because you experience it. Every observation, perception, thought, emotion, and physical sensation you have ever experienced in your entire life has happened *within* your awareness. You, reading this book right now — the work of you reading, and the content of what you are reading — is happening, and only happening, within your awareness. Just as every circumstance you have ever experienced or ever will experience, in your entire life, has happened and will happen within your awareness.

The *content* of your awareness — that is, that of which you are aware — depends on let's call it the directional system of your awareness — that is, your attention — and how, and toward what, you direct it. Sometimes, really most times, your awareness and attention are absorbed by your own answers. And as we've already mentioned, and will discuss more in a moment, they're often negative because your Answer, your worldview, is rooted in the ego's sense of self, the ultimate source and cause of all forms of negativity in your attitude. When you look at the world around you objectively, selflessly, without judgment and in full acceptance of what is, your 'Answer' is aligned to your awareness. As Eckhart Tolle would say, your Answer is 'yes' to what *is* in the present moment. Don Miguel Ruiz points out that this Answer, to say 'yes' to life, is the way of the warrior — the warrior ultimately being the one who fights to break free of the ego. This concept is not to be confused with the Ultimate Warrior, the noted wrestler who wore face paint and tight underpants, defeated the Honky Tonk Man in nine seconds, and body-slammed Andre the Giant without getting a hernia. Although who knows? Maybe the Ultimate Warrior was a seeker of full consciousness. You can't judge a book by its cover — or, for that matter, a person by their underwear and how they wear it.

It is important to know the answer: What is *your* Answer to 'what is?' Because if your Answer is not 'yes' to what is, it must therefore be 'no.' 'Maybe' is not really an option. And 'no' is negative. 'No' is closed. You say 'no' to 'what is' because you want something different (judgment), or don't want to lose something (fear), or want something more (desire). In this way, we all say 'no' to what is with stultifying regularity. It's the reason why Mark Twain said we need to *remember* we're all mad, in order to see life for what it really is.

You may be wondering how you positively change the world if you accept what is. Seems counterintuitive, but it's how things work according to the laws of physics — specifically, Ohm's Law. This rule *describing what is* helps explain why saying 'no' to 'what is' — why your 'nots' to what is — are like 'knots' constricting the flow of Energy, the creative force and intelligence of the universe, that is your ability to make happen what you want to be, and will provide the answers to guide you to what you need to do, to take you where you want to go. By way of brief reminder, Ohm's Law says the amount of energy that manifests in the work of a system is determined by the amount of energy that goes into the system, minus the amount of energy that is inhibited by the resistance of energy flow in that system.

Consistent with this rule of nature, your negative answers (let's call them your 'nots'), are ultimately points of resistance to the flow of energy that is the system of your mental form of being — your awareness, or consciousness, or presence.[7] This is why your answers are also like your 'knots' — a 'knot' meaning, among its various related meanings, in the context of what we mean here: *a tight constriction*.

If we think of the system of your mental form of being, your awareness, as *being* the Being or the Energy that you are, then we can think of your answers (in particular, your negative ones; your 'nots' to what is) as the knots constricting your experience of not only what is, but also what you are, and therefore what you and the world within and around you could be. By simply being, without the 'nots' constricting Being, which is everything, you are empowered to change anything. The answers you need to make positive change happen will come to you naturally and without effort. Free your mind of its compulsive circular thinking patterns, by being Being, and thoughts to inform positive change will naturally form in your mind. It *has* to happen. We're talking ancient wisdom, here, sure. But, again, it's also a fact of physics.

When your mind is open, creativity *must* happen, because you have allowed it to manifest. This is why many spiritual teachers have encouraged us to 'Let go and let God.' Let 'Big E' Energy do all the work — because, after all, it *is* the ability to do all the work! Give it a try. Let go of those troublesome thoughts. If it feels like you can't, because you shouldn't for some reason (some untrue reason, generated by your ego) redirect your attention and observe 'what is.' You will notice new and different things within and around

[7] These terms are interchangeable, for our purposes — although I do like the term 'presence' in particular, because it implies that *you are present* when in a state of presence, as opposed to *you* being *absent*; and also because the word 'presence' closely resembles the word 'presents' — and presence is the ultimate gift, because presence is the literal gift of Life. Presence *is* Life — which can only be experienced in the present. It is also helpful around the holidays, when presents are presented, because people stress about what presents to present when they should, instead, be present.

you immediately. That noticing is a new way of knowing. The result of — what else? Your awareness growing.

Circumstance — The Outer Stuff Going On That's Really Inner Stuff Going On

Let's talk about your circumstances. Not your specific ones, now, but all of them, ever. While you may think your circumstance has nothing to do with your mental form of being, your mind, if we break down the word, we see that it does. Circumstance means *around* (circum) *your position* (stance). You very naturally think of *your* circumstance as all that is, and is happening, *around* you. But this idea of what the word means, which you have been conditioned to understand it to mean, disregards the meaning of the root of the word, which is 'stance.' Your stance on what's going on around you is where you stand on it — it's *your position* on it. It's how you look at it. Your stance is your *attitude* about it. It so happens that the word 'stance' is a synonym for 'attitude.' And when we look at the word 'circumstance' in this way — as your *attitude* toward what's going on around you, your view of it, your position in relation to it — it more accurately reflects what's really going on when you describe what is your circumstance. It's *not*, objectively, what is. Rather, it's your 'Big A' Answer to 'what is,' manifesting as your various answers about it. Another way of putting it is that what you perceive to be going on around you is, in fact, what is going on within you.

Think about it: All that is and is happening around you is, literally, everything that's going on in the world — which your mind cannot and does not process. Your mind naturally and necessarily picks and chooses — consciously or (by far, mostly) unconsciously — what to focus on, among all that is happening in the world around you — that is, *that you are aware of*. Your awareness and attention therefore limit and determine what is your circumstance. This is not bad, or wrong — it's simply what is. When perceiving your circumstance, it's often the case that you don't direct your attention to what is happening; you focus, instead, on what you *think* is happening, or happened, or may happen. Sometimes, perhaps often, you're thinking about stuff that has nothing to do with what's happening — or you! Therefore your circumstance is not what is, objectively, happening around you; it's your attitude toward what you are aware of and directing your attention toward. All of which means your circumstance reflects your attitude. And you get to choose whatever attitude you want, whenever you want, every moment of your life. This is a mind-blowingly amazing, life-changing power, but you only have it if you are ***aware*** you have it, ***believe*** you should use it, and then ***choose*** to use it.

Attitude is important. And awareness is important. And their importance is related. The more awareness you have, the greater your ability, the greater your power, to notice when your attitude isn't what you want it to be, and choose to change it. It's hard to say when there's a good time to say it, but now seems as good a time as any to say that all of this is not to say you should be happy in unhappy situations. Life presents us with tragedy. The loss of loved ones, or their imperiled health or safety, are especially traumatic and understandably painful. Whatever the magnitude of the pain may be, it hurts inside, which no one wants to experience. And attitude — properly brought to bear and utilized — presents a way to deal with it, by bringing awareness to it, opening the way to, at some point, somehow, some way, transcend it. We can only hope that, if you are dealing with the potential or stark reality of some form of tragedy, what we are sharing here is in some way, however big or small, helpful. And most of all, we hope it helps you open enough to let go of your pain in whatever ways you can that are not more destructive than the experience of the pain itself.

In reflecting your awareness, we can think of your attitude as a *measure* of the amount of Life, or Being, or Energy manifested by the system that is you, manifesting in all the work that you do. And because we know that energy is the ability to do work (and because we know that work is everything that is happening in the universe), it is a rule of nature — a rule *describing what is* — that with a more positive attitude, you have more ability to do everything, and with a less positive attitude (that is, a more negative attitude), you have less ability to do anything. To paraphrase the self-help pioneer Zig Ziglar, your attitude toward life reflects your altitude in life. Think of it as determining how high or low you go on the metaphorical mountain climb that is your life's journey, if the Dante-esque metaphor resonates.

And remember, everything in life changes all the time, so while you're on life's mountain, at any and every given point along your journey, you're either making the challenging climb up, actively improving your view and experience of life, or you're taking the easy way down, passively rolling toward rock bottom. The amount of energy — the amount of *Life* — that you manifest while on the journey of life determines the way you are going. The more positive work that you do in life, effectively saying 'yes' to it, the more Life comes into your life — because you are open to it. This is how you make life better and save the world. And it *really* helps your view from the mountain. When you're saying 'no' to life, you're effectively closed to Life, you end up at the bottom, and that mountain casts a dark shadow over your view.

Another way of saying what we're saying, here, is beware of the knots that are your answers, which you can only do by being aware. It's why, if you look at the Garden of Eden as a metaphor for consciousness unobstructed by ego, it makes sense that the fruit from the tree of 'knowledge' is, then, a symbol for ego; it's humanity's false sense of God-like power that comes from a sense of self and our ability to create our own answers to 'what is.' It is what ultimately *separates* humanity from God: The God-like sense that Schopenhauer and others saw as our fatal flaw: Believing the world *is* our own, limited worldview. To eat of this fruit, to be self-conscious and self-oriented, is to be disconnected from the bliss that is our experience of God, of which we must be a part. The rest of nature doesn't have this problem, but we humans do. This form of so-called 'intelligence' is a gift, but it's a curse; it's a self-imposed expulsion from Eden that is the source of all human-created fear and suffering. People who insist they are objectively 'right' to view this story as literal history not only miss the point of it, but they are examples of its warning.

We make the problem worse, the more we focus our attention on our self-oriented answers. We create with our ego-based answers the bricks of a wall self-constructed around us, blocking our ability to 'see' the plain and obvious reality that Eden, the Kingdom of Heaven, is still right here, now, before us. Children have the greater ability to see it, and experience it, because they are not burdened with our deep-seeded answers, the burden of 'knowing' a false reality, projected by ego. They are, in a word (actually, two), more open. As grownups, we have been conditioned to live in a closed circle, disconnected from Eden. It is why so many of us destroy ourselves and the world around us, and otherwise get ourselves tied up in a knot over nothing. The German philosopher Meister Eckhart said: 'To be full of things is to be empty of God. To be empty of things is to be full of God.' And the magically wise Mary Poppins put it plainly: 'This I know for sure: People think too much.' This mental game of life we're playing is of the 'zero sum' variety: We can't pay attention to 'what is' while we're paying attention to what *isn't* — that is, our thoughts about what was or may be. We can't do both. We do one, or the other. We are open, or we are not.

Definition, by definition, is ultimately a limitation. And there is no limitation to Energy, the creative force and intelligence of the universe. There are only perceived limitations to the forms informed by Energy. This idea was very famously related during the climactic scene of the original *Star Wars* movie, when the Jedi master Obi-Wan counseled his apprentice, Luke Skywalker, in the critical *moment of truth*, when the challenge of the deed to save his world was upon him: '*Let go*, Luke. *Use the Force*.' Let go. Just let go. Let go and let God. Luke did it, and prevailed. Most of us can't or won't let go. We lack faith. We lack belief in the reality of our mind-blowing amazingness. We identify with our self-oriented thoughts, deeply believe our self-oriented beliefs, and cling tightly to our own false sense of reality. And we don't let go of it all because we're afraid. The Buddhist philosopher Thich Nhat Hanh points out, 'People prefer their own familiar suffering to their fear of the unknown.' And it is *the* heroic deed in life to overcome this fear, and let go of and allow the sense of self to die, so as to enable the manifestation of one's full potentiality, and therefore be able to save the world.

Human sources of wisdom — from the time before Jesus, to George Lucas, and now beyond — have been teaching this same basic truth. It's all the same, universal idea, expressed in a unique and different way. Same story, same journey, same heroic task — only the heroes change, from time to time and place to place. If you don't believe the attempted logic of what we're saying here, go ahead and try it for yourself. Simply be, without thought — observing thought rather than 'being' thought. Let go of your compulsive ego-based thinking. Experience being, without 'being' your answer; without your Answer in the way of the experience of being

pt. ends p. 127

Being. See what happens. At first, and for quite some time, you will notice how quickly your thoughts impose themselves on your awareness. 'Look at me, look at me!' your thoughts may as well be saying. Look, that's fine, but then let go.

Hopefully we have at least got you thinking about how thoughts are the ultimate obstacles to everyone's experience of everything. What is the opposite of awareness? It's ignorance. And we all experience it some way if we think of the word 'ignorance' to mean *ignoring 'what is'* when our own answers are in the way. It's why so-called 'smart' and 'successful' people can at the same time be very ignorant — which, if you don't accept what is, can be exasperating to deal with.

Selfishness versus Selflessness — The Singular Battle for Life in Your Life

When you think thoughts aligned to the reality of your connection to the world around you, in which you are not a separate self, bound by ego, but rather the whole of everything, free of ego, you are thinking 'self-less' thoughts. These thoughts are full of energy, and positive. When your thoughts are aligned to the illusion of your disconnection from the world around you, in which you are a separate self, a fragment of everything — when they are 'self-ish' thoughts, emphasizing the self, and therefore trapped by the destructive barrier of ego — they lack energy, and are negative. In this self-created circumstance, frankly, you're a wee-wee.

The difference between these diametrically opposite states of mind is analogous to how biological systems work. Open systems that are connected to the systems around them survive and grow, resulting in creation. This is why evolution and creation are the same thing, and not contradictory concepts. Closed systems that are disconnected to the systems around them, like a mind trapped by circular logic, wither and die, resulting in destruction. This is why it's important for you, the real you — that is, the awareness that you are — to be more of an open system. Which is why it's important to be open to being more open.

How do you know the difference between the different states of your mind? You experience it. You can *feel* it. You know the difference between positive and negative thinking not through more thinking, in your mental form of being, but rather through your emotional states of being, in your emotional form of being. You *feel* your emotional state of being — especially if you're paying attention to it! And even if you don't notice your emotions at all, your negative feelings are nevertheless damaging your body through stress just the same, negatively changing the state of your physical form of being. And those feelings are negatively changing your actions, what you do.

We have overlapped into the subject of your emotional form of being, but that's because your mental and emotional forms of being overlap. They are interdependent, connected systems; they are 'designed' by Energy to inform, and be informed by, one another — creating positive or negative changes in and through your physical form of being. Your emotional state of being tells you if your thoughts are creating a negative or positive mental state of being. Positive thinking makes you feel more positively — it makes you feel better, lighter, warmer, and freer; it makes you feel more connected to Life and the life around you. Negative thinking makes you feel more negatively, tense, and constricted — it makes you feel worse, burdened, colder, and trapped; it makes you feel more separate from Life and the life around you.

Again, 'positive thinking' is here defined as thinking founded in selflessness — reflecting the at-one-ness of, and 'atonement' with, all things, *being* wholeness; one could call this sense of wholeness a state of holiness. And 'negative thinking' is here defined as thinking founded in selfishness — thoughts of judgment, desire, or fear reflecting a sense of separation, *seeking* wholeness because you sense you are not, yet, whole; this, then, we could refer to as a state of unholiness. The former reflects awareness of what is, the Answer that is 'yes' to what is; the latter reflects ignorance of what is, the Answer that is 'no' — because 'what is' is obscured by your illusional, delusional, selfish thoughts; the 'nots' or 'knots' that are your answers.

Here's the point, here: You have a choice. You can choose your perspective. This is Einstein's choice about whether you live in a hostile or friendly universe. Both versions of the universe exist, both are true — the question is, which one do you choose to see? And the other question is, *do* you choose to see — or do you just see what you see the way you see it, and remain stuck in however you see it? What's your Answer — is it no, or yes? Is it negative or positive? Do you see your circumstance as 'hostile' or 'friendly'? Do you see yourself as a separate being, self-ish, disconnected from a universe that's against or withholding things from you; or do you see yourself as *Being*, self-less, connected to a universe that supports you and that you are? Are you absorbed in ego-based thoughts of past and future, disconnected from the timeless 'now' — the singular point in eternal time in which Being exists? Or are you able to free yourself of these answers, and connect to now, and experience Being? And would you like me to stop asking you these heavy, deep, life-defining questions now, so you have a minute to answer them? Or would you like me to . . . never mind.

Did you take a minute and answer those questions? It's fine if you didn't. You just want to keep reading! But you should know your own answers: What *are* your beliefs — your answers, your Answer! — about you and your relationship to the world around you? How did you adopt your beliefs? Did you passively and unconsciously acquire them without realizing it, or did you actively and consciously choose them? For most people, the answer is the former. For all of us, the answer should be the latter. Because your ability to choose beliefs that are aligned to the positive outcomes you desire is a veritable superpower, enabling you to attract the support of the universe in the work you do to make the world a better place. It's there, within you. To save yourself — and to therefore save the world — you simply need to use it. And also remember that if you *don't* use this ability, it will atrophy from disuse, just as every other human ability does.

The reason you don't actively and consciously choose your beliefs is that you don't — or at least you didn't, for much or maybe all of your life — believe that you can. Which is a paradox, or at least ironic, and you can definitely make the case that it's silly, because it's precisely *because* your beliefs are so powerful that you don't believe you can — or should — change them. Doing so, of course, requires awareness of your beliefs. And this requires that you pay attention to them. Which brings us to why we need to pay attention to your attention.

Attention to Your Attention

Even though we've been talking about and seeking your attention, we haven't really talked about what it is, and how it relates to you. Because it most certainly does 'relate' to you. In a way, you could say, you *are* the center of your attention. 'You' are not only the 'center' or space or point from which your attention manifests and is directed, which we've been calling 'awareness,' 'presence,' 'consciousness,' 'Being,' 'Energy,' and '***Universal You***.' But you are also that to which you point your attention. You become the center or point to which your attention is directed, and manifests. Buddha and Jesus taught us the same thing, and they even said it in pretty much the same way: As you think, so you shall be. Whatever is the object or content of your attention becomes absorbed in and as your mental form of being.

Therefore, as that *from* which your attention manifests and is directed (awareness, Energy, ***Universal You***), you are also, at the same time, that *to* which your attention is directed, and manifests as (what you are aware of, what Energy makes happen, ***unique you***). And so we're saying ***unique you*** embodies the collective stream of everything you observe, sense, perceive, think about, judge, desire, fear, and imagine; or, more simply put, your interpretations of your inner and outer reality; or, even more simply put, the 'answers' to which your attention is directed. These 'things' — these interconnected illusions; these answers, comprising your Answer, which all amount to 'nothing' — comprise ***unique you***. You become what is the center of your attention, including the thoughts you impose on what is.

So, to summarize: You are Being, the awareness through which your mental form of being manifests. And you are your observations, perceptions, and thoughts which manifest in your mental form of being. You are awareness, *and* the contents of your awareness as well; and the two are connected by and through your attention. You are ***Universal You***, and you are ***unique you***. Just as a ball of clay is a ball, and it is clay as well — it's a ball because it's a ball; and it's clay because that's what the ball is made of. And this makes you, in a very literal sense, the center of attention. The center of your own attention, to be precise. And it is your own attention, and no one else's, including all the people in your life who irritate you. Which is why, when you let other people irritate you, you're letting them own you in a very real way. These people are, as the saying goes, living in your head, rent-free. Unless you can get them to sign a lease. And as someone who gets irritated by *a lot* of people, *a lot* more often than I should (especially by people who, usually unknowingly, are contributing to my experience of *waiting*), I can tell you from a perspective of extraordinary knowledge and experience: It makes you feel bad, and is self-destructive. As the Buddha said, 'Holding on to anger is like grasping a hot coal with the intent of throwing it at someone else, you are the one who gets burned.' Which is, of course, stupid. And as my dad once said, for some reason forgetting to use a verb, which my brothers and I never let him forget, and which to this day I have never forgotten: 'Don't stupid.'

We mentioned how irritation makes you feel bad. All negative, self-oriented thoughts do. Fear, desire, judgment — none of it makes you feel good. It may give you a rush, or a false sense of power, but it doesn't make you feel *good*. Do you *notice* how it all makes you feel, or do you merely experience it 'in the background,' allowing it to cause stress to your physical form of being? As you reflect on your answer, hold on to that thought — or better yet, let it go, as we consider, at last, your emotional form of being. We're talking about your emotions last, but they are by no means the least important of your forms of being, even if you like to think of yourself as too tough, or practical, or whatever euphemism you have created in your mind, to pay attention to your emotions. It is invariably self-defeating and indisputably ignorant to ignore your emotional form of being. Because your emotional state of being reflects your mental state of being in your physical form of being — connecting all three forms of being through experience. Your emotional form of being also informs the work that you do. Because whether or not you do work, and how well you do the work that you do, is necessarily informed by how much you feel like doing it. And how much you feel like doing something is experienced through your emotional form of being. This is something to keep in mind the next time you feel like doing something you shouldn't, but do, and the next time you don't feel like doing something you should, but don't.

Your Emotional Form of Being

The system of your emotional form of being, like the system of your mental form of being, manifests through your physical form of being. As we have already mentioned, its work as a system is to tell 'you' — that is, your awareness — what is your mental state of being. But like all communication systems, it only works if your mental form of being pays attention to what's being communicated.

Wait a second, what the—! Hey, look, everyone, it's your emotional form of being — and it's trying to get your attention. It's jumping up and down and waving! But why is it wearing *that*, of all things? Hey, no judgment, here! (But, seriously . . . *that*?) Anyway, it looks like your emotional form of being is in a negative state, and it's got something to say about it:

'Hello, mental form of being! It's me, your emotional form of being, communicating to you through the sensations of your physical form of being. You're worrying right now, I can tell. You are worrying about something that happened already, or may happen someday, because there's nothing to worry about now. Nice work, oh-great-and-mighty creator of our universe! And thanks for nothing! That's right, you heard me: Thanks to *your* preoccupation with phantom projections — that is, thanks to your own beliefs, your own personal answers about your circumstances, which you're *sooo* certain reflect 'reality' — you're creating real stress in *our* body right now. You are *so* self-absorbed! And now your entire 'self' has to suffer for it.

'I mean, *look at yourself*, you infinitely big dummy! You're creating destructive change to *our* physical form of being.

And it's not pleasant. Vague unease, mild nausea, tightened face, shoulder, and back muscles, and a literal pain in the neck . . . *not* pleasant! And you're reacting in a way that's not helping the thing that you're stressed about. Did it cross your mind — I mean, ah, did it cross *you* — that you're creating problems with all our major physical systems that make us work? I mean, *you're* the one that manifests through the brain of our physical form of being. Don't you read about this stuff? This self-destruction of *our* body — that *you*, and you alone, are creating — manifests in all sorts of unique ways, which you know as well as I do through your experience of these physical sensations. Do you not realize that I'm stuck with our state of being, whether it's positive or negative? For that matter, do you realize that you're now in a negative state of being! Do you care?

'Hey, look, I'm here to help. You really ought to let me do *my* job, to reflect back to you in my state of being what is *your* state of being. I'm here to let you know how you're doing. I have one job, really, and that's it. Which you would *notice*, if you paid attention to how I'm doing, instead of directing all your attention to your own selfish negative thoughts. You're always so wrapped up in yourself! You ignore everything else. Including me. Which is to your detriment. Which is to *our* detriment.

'So, if you don't mind, mind, please keep this in mind: Whenever you're negatively changing *our* physical form of being — our body — it isn't going to help any one of the three of us. It's not going to help any of us now, or in the future. And it sure isn't going to change anything that's already happened. Not to be negative, but even though I'm the one manifesting as tension, you made me do it! So do us all a favor, won't you, all-powerful creator of our reality, and pay attention to *me* every now and then, instead of always being so self-absorbed. I mean, I am a creation 'of' you. Not that I'd want to bring you to school for career day, but let's

pt. ends p. 127

face it: *I am born of you*. I'm your only child, so to speak; and it would be nice if you acted like you cared. My other parent, our physical form of being, of Mother Earth, lives and dies over everything I do. So how about not acting like you're above it all, oh great-and-mighty creator of our existence, and acknowledge what's going on with me!'

Of course, your emotional form of being doesn't communicate verbally to your mental form of being, but it nevertheless very clearly tells your mental form of being exactly what's going on. In fact, your emotional form of being could not express itself more clearly, because there's no ambiguity about the experience of a feeling. There are no subjective interpretations of a feeling. It's either good or bad. Positive or negative. Comfortable or uncomfortable. When you're the one feeling a feeling, you either feel content and at ease, or discontent and anxious — call it 'dis-ease.' (Interestingly, when you're feeling 'dis-ease' in your emotional form of being, your physical form of being is more likely to manifest disease.)

Here's a few admittedly not-so-fun facts about what happens when your mental form of being ignores your emotional form of being and allows stress to manifest: Stress is a factor in five out of six of the leading causes of death — heart disease, cancer, stroke, lower respiratory disease, and accidents. It's also estimated that over 75 percent of doctor visits are for stress-related issues. This doesn't account for the many people who have these issues but don't go to the doctor. And it may or may not count what people do to their bodies as a response to stress in the form of addictive behaviors like overeating, drug and alcohol abuse, sexual obsession, physical and verbal abuse of others, and even self-mutilation. No other species self-destructs the way we have done, still do now, and will do, indefinitely — unless and until we change. So we better damn well pay attention.

It's especially important to pay attention to your tension

when you're feeling tense, rather than to just 'feel tense' and therefore to just 'be' tense. It's why it's *always* important — that is, it's always helpful to you; it's a necessary first step to a more positive experience of, and outcome from, what you're doing — to pay attention to your emotional form of being, and observe what state it is in. Doing so, you'll notice *exactly* what state your mental form of being is in — positive or negative, and to what degree. You'll bring into awareness your state of being; and within the space of 'what is' now, you now have the ability to choose what will be.

The ability to create this space of awareness within yourself, to choose how to think and feel, is now popularly referred to as 'emotional intelligence.' Not surprisingly, your emotional intelligence — according to Daniel Goleman, the world-renowned psychologist who literally wrote the book on it — is a greater predictor of your success in life than is your IQ or demographic background. Success, as defined by Goleman, being your ability to set and achieve goals, create sustainable relationships, lead other people, and experience peace and contentment. All abilities that enable you to enjoy life and make it better. You have a great power at your disposal. You simply have to choose it, to use it. Which makes choice, itself, an incredible power. But you only have this great power if you're aware that you do. And hopefully, now, you *are* aware. So what are you going to do about it?

You can actively choose your 'way' to experience circumstance, and experience contentment, happiness, joy — or even bliss! — in whatever is happening in the present moment, right now. Or you can continue to passively allow your ego to determine the way you experience whatever is happening, which usually involves ignoring what's happening, because you're preoccupied with what already happened or may, in the future, happen. In which case, you will experience some form of discontent, or unhappiness, fear — or one of its destructive manifestations like greed,

pt. ends p. 127

anger, or hate. Meanwhile your brief time in this world moves on, inexorably hurtling toward its inevitable conclusion. At which point, you'll be gone, having left behind what you've done — and having failed to leave behind what you could have done.

So, what have we learned here, good reader? Your emotional form of being, through its state of being, communicates the most important information in your life — that is, it does, when you're paying attention to it. It's even more important than — you may want to sit down for this, because you may find it shocking to the point of requiring medical attention! — whatever information you get the next time you stare at your cellphone.

Your emotional state of being tells you if you are experiencing a connection to Being (in the form of peace, love, compassion, or joy) — or a disconnection to Being (in the form of anxiety, fear, callousness, or despair). Your emotional state of being tells you if your ego is informing your thoughts, creating 'selfish' thoughts, or not. It tells you if your thoughts are founded in a moment in time other than now — the past or future — or not. It tells you if you are living in a metaphorical hell, or in 'the Kingdom of Heaven here on earth.' It tells you, through its physical sensations, *exactly* what's going on in the state of your mental form of being. It tells you *how* you are experiencing life. And so it tells you the state of your life — infinitely more than does your bank statement, or business card, or the pictures you post on social media.[8]

We have mentioned, more than once, that when there are fewer obstacles (less ego-driven 'selfish' thoughts), there is more Energy manifesting in the system of your emotional

---

[8] People who spend a lot of time trying to show other people how interesting or fun their life is by posting pictures on social media . . . spend a lot of time trying to show other people how interesting or fun their life is by posting pictures on social media. I mean, what else is there to say? We live our lives on the inside. Social media posts don't change that.

form of being. Experiencing this Energy *feels* positive because it's a sense of connection. It feels warm and full. You *feel* the 'fullness' of peace, contentment, compassion, and joy. We can think of this as the selfless form of 'love' Jesus talked about when he said, 'God is love.'

To experience Energy through one's mental form of being, is to experience awareness or presence. And to experience that same Energy through one's emotional form of being, is to experience love or compassion. Compassion is a special form of pure love that is the experience of our connection to others, even allowing us — yes, *allowing* us, for it is a gift that enables us to open more, for more love — to share in the suffering of others. To experience love is to bring forth what is within you, which the New Testament teaches is needed to 'save' you — because it *is* you. Love, you see — which you will, if you see — is what you really, truly are. It's why you feel good when you feel it, and you feel bad when you don't. Abraham Lincoln said, 'When I do good, I feel good. And when I do bad, I feel bad. That is my religion.' If the purpose of a religion is to help a person connect to God through the experience of connecting to life, and Life itself — which, seems to me, it ought to be — Abe had a good one.[9]

On the other hand, when there are more obstacles (ego-driven 'selfish' thoughts), there is less Energy manifesting in your emotional form of being. This is Ohm's Law at work in the system that is you. Experiencing these obstacles — these 'nots' to what is; these constrictive 'knots' — blocking 'you' from your experience of this Energy, of the Being that is your true being, feels negative; it is a sense of disconnection;

[9] Religion, and religious people, are themselves neither objectively 'good' nor 'bad.' But the actions and outcome of one's religiousness can be objectively assessed as 'positive' or 'negative,' depending on how it impacts the well-being (as we have defined it) of oneself and others. It really all comes down to how much of a wee-wee you are, as opposed to, say, how often you go to church or announce to others your devotion to your professed beliefs.

pt. ends p. 127

it feels cold and empty. It feels like there's a hole inside, as opposed to feeling 'whole' inside. You feel the hollow feeling that is the absence of peace, contentment, compassion, and joy. It's the terrible and fearful feeling of disconnection from everything, of 'being' cut off and separate from what you really, truly are. In this state of being, you always want something different than what is. You fear loss. You want more. You negatively judge what is. Your answer to life is 'no.' And so you feel disconnected from everything, alone in the universe, which is a scary and otherwise unpleasant way to live.

There's More to Emotion than 'Meets the Eye' — That is, 'Observable by Your Attention'

It should be noted that your emotional form of being not only manifests as your feelings, but also as your instincts and impulses. It is in the experience of an instinct or impulse that we have further circumstantial evidence that the unconscious mind exists. Because if it makes sense, and is aligned to your experience, that your conscious thoughts create your feelings, it should also stand to reason that your instincts and impulses — which are, by definition, emotional responses that have little if anything to do with conscious thoughts, but are, rather, visceral responses to brain activity that does not manifest as thought — are created by what's going on in your unconscious mind. This is why, for example, a properly timed 'Boo!' can have the gravity-defying impact of a rocket engine.

When we're talking about instinct, we're talking about the basic work of our shared human nature, guiding and driving our lives in unseen ways. 'Moving us around like pawns,' as the noted writer on the human condition Robert Greene puts it. 'Refusing to come to terms with human nature,' he writes, 'simply means you are dooming yourself to patterns beyond your control.' No doubt, if Robert Greene were a super villain and not a noted writer, it is likely he would have added: '*Doomed*, I tell you . . . doomed! Bah-*ha*-ha-ha-ha-*haaaah*!' This is why it's equally important, perhaps sometimes even more important, to bring awareness to your instincts and impulses, because you don't have the opportunity to observe the unconscious activity that creates them. This can get you in big trouble, because driving a lot of your instincts and impulses is your powerful sense of self. Unfettered by the cerebral cortex, the part of your brain that has evolved to modulate this drive by rational thought, you can end up doing all sorts of stuff that is destructive to you and the world around you.

If you're lucky, it only manifests when you're home alone on your couch and yelling at someone on television who can't hear you, in which case you have the literal space around you to summon the deeper space within you to realize you're acting like a wee-wee, and you can stop if you so choose. However, if there are other people around you when your emotions take you over, you can end up embarrassing yourself, your family, and possibly several generations of ancestors by some extraordinary behavior usually associated with a deranged criminal or a toddler who missed naptime. You can end up hurting people you don't know, or people you do know, and even and especially people you love. And you inevitably will end up hurting a person you need to know better — yourself. Our prisons today are full of people who failed to observe and overcome the prison within. Look at all the so-called powerful people presumed to 'have it all,' but who evidently never had enough, because the ego never has enough. The ego *is* never having enough.

People not only go to prison because of their self-oriented suffering, but sometimes it becomes so unbearable that they choose to take their own lives. The Center for Disease Control reports that suicide is the tenth leading cause of death in the United States, and it increased an astonishing 33% in a decade. If you have any doubt that we need to save ourselves from ourselves, this tragic fact should change your mind. It is almost impossible not to know, or at least know of, someone who has been impacted by this terrible tragedy. Even when the suffering that prompts the act of taking one's own life is related to a physical dysfunction of the brain — chemical imbalance, dementia, or otherwise — the ego's self-orientation is somehow involved as the ultimate source of fear and suffering. All of which is to say, puh-*leez* pay attention to your emotional form of being, and the state it is in! If you don't do it at all, start doing it now. And if you already do it now, do it more.

As you proceed to open up the door to yourself — that is, your true self-less 'self' — don't judge your emotional form of being, and whatever state it is in. It is important to accept what is, including your negative emotions. Observe them, acknowledge them, accept them, even embrace them. *Then* you can let them go. But don't judge — this is important! Just pay attention. On purpose, in the present moment, without judgment. This is how Jon Kabat-Zinn, the former MIT professor, defined mindfulness — upon which he based a successful stress-reduction therapy that has helped people all over the world. Your emotions will communicate the state of your mental form of being — positive or negative. They will tell you how your thoughts are impacting your physical and mental forms of being — positively or negatively. And they will impact, very directly, the work that you do (your actions, and your being) — positively or negatively.

This is especially important and helpful when you're choosing the work that you want to do. Pay attention to what you feel like doing. Become aware of what you love to do that somehow makes life better for others. There is a reason you love to do it. Your love for a particular form of work, which is Energy, is simply your ability to do that work, which is the same Energy, pulling you to do it. Do the positive work (again, work that is somehow, in some way, helping someone) you most love to do — the work that seems simple, and is fun, for you. The best way for you to save the world is whatever way that is simple and fun for you. And saving the world is the best way to enjoy simple fun. Both are, in religious terms, 'the work of God.' They have to be, because you have to have an open heart and mind to do both.

Point In to Point Out God

Speaking of religious terms and God, let's take a moment to mention how and why mythology, generally, and religious stories, particularly, offer helpful guidance to the nature of Life and how we humans relate to it — especially when considered in metaphorical terms. Take my childhood religion, Catholicism, for example, which is so full of icons and symbols and rituals that one tends to take in stride how bishops and cardinals dress like Bootsy Collins to administer those rituals. Critics will point to how the Catholic relation to God is so materialistic that its hypocrisy undermines if not contradicts the point of it all. But in defense of my childhood religion, there is one symbolic ritual that, if viewed metaphorically, very obviously points out that God — Life itself — exists within each of us, and thereby shows us how to save the world.

I bet you recognize this ritual, even if you're not a Catholic and never attended a mass, as it permeates staples of American culture — family meals, sports events, and mobster movie funerals, to mention a few examples. We are talking about the act of blessing oneself by making the sign of the cross. This simple act, which affirms the Catholic concept of God as a 'Holy Trinity,' also literally and figuratively points to how ***Universal You*** (aka the creative intelligence of the universe, Energy, Being, Life, Force, Source, Essence — *God*) manifests through and as ***unique you***. Though not explicitly intended, and quite possibly unintended, this most commonplace of all Catholic practices affirms that, in being a human being, Being manifests through our physical form of being in our mental and emotional forms of being. This being why it's worth taking a moment to explain why.

When you bless yourself, you make the sign of the cross on your upper body, your physical form of being. This is, remember, the foundation of who you are, as ***unique you***, a unique system — while at the same time being the vehicle through which you experience ***Universal You***. The first step of this ritual is to point to your head — and say, 'In the name of the Father.' You next point to your heart — 'in the name of the Son.' And then your hand sort of flows across the invisible line connecting the head and heart — 'in the name of the Holy Spirit.'

This brings us to our metaphor, and the point of pointing to what one points to when Catholics 'bless themselves.' God the Father of the Old Testament, first 'person' of the Holy Trinity, embodies all the attributes of the human mind, our mental form of being: Intangible, invisible, and existing beyond time and space. Creator of all reality. Embodying the omnipotence and omniscience of the Holy Spirit, God the Father is at the same time a personal 'He,' who manifests a disposition unique to the human ego. God the Father judges right and wrong, sometimes contradicting Himself in the process. For example, thou shalt not kill — *unless* I say so, in which case you should kill your own child, without question. (*Okay*, then!) God the Father plays favorites, too. And He especially likes those who recognize and praise Him — it's how and why he chooses his favorites! He's divisive, vindictive, and angry one moment; forgiving, benevolent, and all-loving the next. And, again, we are talking about a personal God, a self-contained God, an individual — first *person* of the Holy Trinity. We're talking about a perfect metaphor for the egoic human mind. It hit me: *This* is why Catholics point to their forehead, the brain, to recognize that God manifests through the mind 'In the name of the Father.'

And then Jesus comes along in the New Testament. The second 'person' of the Holy Trinity. The Son. A literal person who is begotten *of* the Father, just as one's emotional state of being is begotten of one's mental state of being. And Jesus likewise embodies all the attributes of the human heart, which we associate with the experience of our emotional form of being: Tangible, physical, and existing within the field of time and space. Jesus is God manifesting in the form of flesh and blood, born into suffering, just as we experience all suffering with our flesh and blood, in our bodies, through our emotional form of being. Existing in the field of time and space, Jesus teaches by the example of his life, through his actions, that one must sacrifice the physical 'self,' and our egoic attachment to it, to be reborn as the selfless Being. He teaches that love is the way, that God *is* love. And love is an emotional experience. That's why Jesus said, 'I am the way.' He was trying to tell us that selflessness, that *love*, is the way. It's a metaphor — *not* a literal call to dogma, as most versions of Christianity claim it to be — to teach us that we manifest and experience God through love.

Curiously, though not surprisingly, the third 'person' of the Holy Trinity, the Holy Spirit, gets the least attention of the three in the Catholic religion — and, really, all forms of Christianity. Perhaps this is because it's not in any way defined as a person, and so the human ego can't relate to it at all. The Holy Spirit is a real outlier in the Christian belief system. Not only does it not get its own book in the Bible, but it barely makes cameo appearances in the books about the other two. When you think about it, it's kind of hard to have the Holy Spirit make an appearance, when it

pt. ends p. 127

reflects the nature of God that has nothing to do with form, but rather informs all forms with all the qualities of nothing.

Viewed metaphorically, in the general terms of your relation to God, and in our specific terms of ***unique you*** relating to ***Universal You***, the Catholic ritual of blessing oneself literally 'points out' God to oneself by pointing inward. What a helpful ritual! Unless it's interpreted literally, in which case the concept of the Holy Trinity can be incredibly confusing — especially to children, who are open-minded enough to know it's confusing. Since this is meant to be simple and fun, we'll spare you the details and examples; but if you want to read more about the literal interpretation of the Holy Trinity from the 'experts,' you will see what I mean. The circular logic they use to justify their literal interpretation will make your head spin around. And if you're a Christian who feels offended by any of these thoughts, because they contradict *your* thoughts (which were likely taught to you by people who didn't put much thought into it, beyond thoughtlessly accepting what *they* were taught), please remember that 'feeling offended' is a function of ego, and cannot be experienced without it.

The Universal Problem of Changing Positively

We have established that change is always happening, with everything, all the time — including you. And we have established that you change everything by changing you. Mahatma Gandhi taught that each one of us must 'be' the change we seek in this world. Unfortunately, this simple, basic, and sensible idea — which, we now understand, reflects the reality of physics — has never been well-understood. The Russian writer Leo Tolstoy explained why: 'Everyone wants to change the world, but no one thinks of changing himself.' It's both our great human challenge, and opportunity, that the power to change what's around is our power to change what's within us; and our power to change what's within us is already there, ready to enable positive change, waiting for us to notice that it's there so we can get out of its way and let it out. But we just can't seem to get out of our own way.

Consider how seven out of ten organizations fail to implement their own strategic plans. This is a statistic that's been reported by some of the most prominent sources on business management in the world, and it's held steady across three continents (so it's not a cultural thing) and three decades (and it's not a generational thing, either). Seventy percent of organizations fail to change positively in the way they put time, energy, and various resources into changing positively — and this failure happens pretty much everywhere, and all the time. Meaning organizations want and try to change positively, but don't. This is an especially compelling statistic when you consider that it's easier to change people's behaviors in groups than it is individually, because there's a 'support system' inherent in the collective efforts of a group that helps enable positive change. The problem people have changing positively is even more difficult when we go it alone.

The evidence clearly demonstrates just how bad we are at positively changing. For example, nine out of ten people fail to follow through on New Year's resolutions by the end of January. We 'resolve' to follow through on these resolutions because we want to change for the purpose of enhancing our own well-being and quality of life. And yet, pretty quickly, we give up trying because it seems we just can't do it. We lack the ability to do it — to positively change. This all-too-common disability manifests even when there's a real life and death situation to motivate people to positively change. Consider how the National Institute of Health has reported that over 100,000 people die every year because they don't follow medical directions related to diet, exercise,

pt. ends next p.

and medication following a heart-related medical problem. People literally die, they allow the complete destruction of the system that they are, because they lack the ability to positively change. My own grandmother — my Gingee; one of my favorite people, ever — died this way. The doctor told her not to smoke cigarettes or drink alcohol or coffee because it was dangerous to her health. She was found dead in her bed with the plain evidence of her inability to change on her night table — coffee-stained cup, empty Scotch glass, and an ashtray full of cigarette butts. No doubt my dad's indulgence in hamburgers and processed foods, and his aversion to physical exercise more strenuous than walking to a cupboard or golf cart, contributed to his far-too-early demise.

People who destroy themselves through addiction are the unfortunate, sad, and more prominent examples to which far too many of us can personally relate. Drug addiction is especially destructive, killing people every day. It's the ultimate self-destruction. We have talked about the alarming rise in suicide rates. And the suffering and death we impose on each other through individual crime and wide-scale war is all too apparent in this age of overwhelming information, dispersed through the social media forums of the internet. We're destroying our planet to the point that it will no longer be able to sustain human life within in the next few generations. Rising ocean temperatures, melting icebergs, natural disasters, and record high *and* low temperatures on land are occurring with increasing frequency, all around the world, in recent years. Other than the fact that people who don't know or care anything about science characterize the extraordinary amount of scientific evidence we already have, collectively, as 'a hoax,' do we really need *more* evidence that we are self-destructing?

Clearly, the ability to positively change *is* an ability, and it must be the most important ability in the world, to the world. How could it not be? It's incredibly difficult, but even more simple:

Be more open. Be more *aware*.

The Part Where We Transition to the Next Part

We have, at last, defined the problem of you saving the world, by describing how everything basically works. We focused on the basics of you, and what you really and truly are; the basics of the world around you, and what's really and truly happening; and the basics of how you relate to the world around you — that is, the connections between everything. Most important of all, we explained how it all relates to 'Big E' Energy — Life itself — which *is* everything.

With that, let's now get to the path you must take to save the world. Like everything else in the universe, generally, and in human nature, specifically, your path to save the world is circular, and a paradox. It's universal, for everyone — but it must be unique, for you. And although saving the world is in many ways complex and difficult, we're going to make sure it's simple and fun. You're welcome! You deserve it. Although saving the world in your own unique way truly is its own reward; an unknowable reward — until you realize it.

PART THREE

The Path

The path to Life is through awareness
It's universal — and unique
Continue when the path is darkest
And you'll find the Light you seek

Follow your bliss and the universe will
open doors where there were only walls.
–Joseph Campbell

To this point, we made a point to point out the point of your life (to save the world), and this book (to help you do it), though it may have been the other way around. Either way, we got around (and around) to pointing out how it's all circular.

We then defined the problem of life, the cause of all our human strife; the source of our self-orientation and false sense of separation: The ego. This self-created wall exists by keeping one and all from, really, all that really is and our connection to it all. And *that's* a problem! One creating all the problems we all create. It's the 'tempting fruit' from Life's well-known forbidden tree; and when we eat from it, we get exactly what we're asking for: A world created by our thoughts, obscuring the Kingdom of Heaven here on earth.

Along the way of explaining the way ego gets in *your* way, as a way to open you to be more open, we openly supposed that those disposed to remain closed would probably have a problem with this book and have closed it. However! For the reader who's open to being more open, and therefore kept our book open to read it, we tried to break through your false ego-worldview with a simple fun moment, as needed. It was therefore a matter of plain practicality to keep you engaged in the book's factuality — *especially* what challenged your ego's reality — by keeping it simple and fun.

With that brief reminder of what we have covered to help your mind briefly recover it, it's time to round out our explanation of life by describing its path — that is to say, what is . . . *the way*. [HEAR: Rousing orchestral music that makes you want to do something heroic (or at least watch someone else do something heroic), while that one movie trailer voice guy says in his melodramatic movie-trailer-voice-guy way: '*First*, you read about the point of life. *Then*, you read about the problem with it. *Now*, it's time to read about life's path . . . the way for you . . . to save . . . *the world*.]

Let's begin explaining the path of life by saying 'the way' is an unusual journey, unlike any one anyone has ever undertaken. It's a journey wrought with the unfamiliar and unexpected, verily defined by the unknown — and unknowable. And so it's a journey that is *always* mysterious, surprising — revelatory, even — and unique. Though not in all ways — because it's also universal! And it's even mapped out, more or less, step by step.

Though, to be clear, you won't find 'the way' on any map, because as you no doubt now know, the way you change the world is by changing you. And the way you change you is by changing your worldview. Therefore the path we are talking about is a journey to overcome yourself. To *transform* yourself. By transcending your '*self*.' And so it is therefore a journey *of* and *through* your mind — which, of course, exists 'nowhere,' and so no map can guide you there.

That said, keep in mind that you *will* have to go places, and deal with stuff, and do stuff on your journey — even if it is all of and through the mind. But mind you, *everything* in life is experienced of and through the mind. So the only way to relate 'the way' is of and through the mind.

With that in mind, I'm reminded that even a map is

related . . . come to think of it, never mind. Just be mindful that 'the way' is a journey of and through the mind; and because all of life is experienced this way, it's the only way to relate 'the way.'

It should go without saying (but we'll say it anyway) that there is more than one way to relate 'the way' in this one way we all relate — that is to say, of and through the mind. Talking about 'the way' is one way to relate it. Writing about 'the way' is, of course, another way. Relating 'the way' by way of example is, in a way, the most relatable way of all. And there is one way to relate 'the way' in every way we relate to one another — by talking about it, writing about it, and showing it by doing it, including and especially by way of a show. It is, by the way, the way that 'the way' is most often related. In a way, you could say it's *the* way to relate 'the way.' And that way to relate 'the way' is by way of a story.

Why use a story to relate 'the way' when there are other, more direct ways to relate it? Because a story is universally, and uniquely, relatable. Or at least it is when it's written the right way. When we experience a story — by way of listening to it, or reading it, or observing it — an amazing thing happens. You could well say what happens is mind-blowing. Because we *open our minds* to it. When we hear, or read, or watch a good story, the same areas and functions of the brain are activated as if it were engaging in what we perceive as 'real-life.' The one big and helpful difference is that the brain takes in a story without ego so much in the way, distorting 'what is' through its self-oriented lens. There's not so much 'me' that gets in your way — except when someone else tells you that 'my way' of seeing a story is the *only* way, and you accept that way. This is, by the way, the way dogma is passed along, to define and therefore limit what you believe. We are instead talking about passing along life lessons, to open and increase belief in yourself.

A story engages the mind with what is happening to

pt. ends p. 149

'another,' while freeing us of the ego's judgment, desire, and fear imposed on what is happening to ourselves. And when the mind is clear of the ego's distortion, we can see 'what is' in truer proportion. Joseph Campbell saw storytelling in this way; that is to say, as a way to help us see: 'When the story is in your mind,' he said, 'you see its relevance to something happening in your own life, and it gives perspective on what's happening to you.' A story entices, encourages, and ultimately enables us to see ourselves in others, and our own lives in theirs, even though — or, perhaps, *because* — the unique details are different and detached from us.

Collectively, stories reflect all our common human experiences and help guide us through our lives. And because the ones we pay attention to are interesting, entertaining, and often a lot of fun, they support a function that is important and even necessary to our growth and survival — individually, and as a species — because the content enlightens us to, and enables us with, self-awareness. This is especially true of the story of the hero and 'the way' to save the world.

It's the oldest story, told most often, everywhere. It's also the story most relevant to every human life. It was told in *The Odyssey* and *Inferno* (which hardly anyone reads, but we all know about or at least heard of). It's told in classic novels, from *Don Quixote* to *The Hobbit* (and a lot of them before and after those were written). Shakespeare used it in *Macbeth* and *Hamlet*. It's acted out in action movies, such as *Star Wars*, *The Matrix*, and *Avatar*. Literally every Disney movie tells it (it's a requirement of the business). It informs the 'back story' of pretty much every comic book superhero. And it appears in the stories told in the world's main religions. In other words, unless you have lived your entire life under a rock, you are familiar with this story even if you didn't know it.

It is fair to say that every hero, in their own way, followed 'the way.' King Arthur, Luke Skywalker, Lightning

McQueen, and the Batman all followed the same basic path to self-awareness (that is to say, 'the way' to the self-realization of selflessness) — as Moses, Jesus, Mohammed, and the Buddha. Ancient gods from around the world have followed 'the way,' too — Greek, Egyptian, Polynesian, Roman, and Hindu. This fact — and it is, in fact, a fact; one revealed for all to see (that is, you will see it *if* you look beyond the surface, the specific details, to break down and examine these stories in terms of their basic storyline) — does not make any of your favorite heroes less special. Not by any means! It simply means that there is meaning in their stories meant to help you bring forth and become what is special in you. So no matter what you believe, in this way, all are true.

Joseph Campbell (a personal hero of mine) identified, named, and defined the meaning of this hero journey. Inspired by Carl Jung's concept of the 'archetype' and James Joyce's idea of the 'monomyth,' Campbell came to see — due in no small part to his broad perspective of the human condition, gained in no small part from his lifelong study of human expression through the world's folklore, mythology, religion, philosophy, literature, poetry, psychology, history, art, and, yes, even physical science — that the *same* sequential and circular pattern of human experiences manifested in hero stories from virtually every culture and era of human history. By studying the unique details of human expression over countless times and places, he discovered our universal experience. And he realized that, no matter the time or place in history, the story of 'the way' has, in some way, been told.

Campbell wrote a famous book (famous among a lot of artists, writers, and people interested in the human condition; though perhaps not so much among the 'child beauty pageant crowd') about 'the one story in many' called, *The Hero with a Thousand Faces*. Therein he helped us understand that saving the world is not a destiny limited only to a special few, but for all of us, potentially. The heroes of our stories — who found their true nature and calling in the crucible of life experience, and saved the world around them as a result — are all metaphors for *you*. Their stories are lights to help you see the path for your own journey, one we all must take in life, to overcome our sense of self, the ego, to find our true 'selfless' self, life's 'Holy Grail' — the energy of, and that is, the universe; the creative intelligence and force informing all life; the 'God of all creation' that is present in every myth and religion; Life itself — that exists within, and as, each one of us. In this way, the story of 'the way' lights the way to the Light itself: the Being of our being, experienced as our love and gratitude for life.

Campbell explained that, while there is one universal way for all to follow (because, after all, we are all one and the same), it is also true that we are all different, and so we all have to find our own unique way. And anyone *can* do it, and *will* do it — including and especially you! — when, as Campbell put it, you *follow your bliss*. Follow your bliss — that is, fearlessly pursue what you naturally enjoy doing that brings forth the presence, love, and ability within you — and you'll be saying 'yes' to the adventure of life. You'll find yourself on the heroic journey to save the world. And nothing will bring more Life into your life than that.

Again, this journey is necessarily as unique as you are — in the details. But generally speaking, it is universal (also just like you) in its essence, and general framework, in that it follows the same sequence of the same specific steps in which a circular pattern is followed — a going out, and a returning home. It is *the* proverbial 'coming full circle.' Always coming home, even as you're going out into the unknown. Such is the nature of this circle of life.

If you're intrigued by what we are talking about, or have a book report due and want to get this over with, let's lay out the sequential steps of our heroic journey. For it is, truly, *our* journey. If we choose to take it, as our own.

As we describe this mythological and sometimes, yes, magical path, you may well recognize some or all of its parts, perhaps from the experience of your own life, and likely from your knowledge of the stories of your own favorite heroes. Likewise, once you're familiar with this journey, you'll notice its elements in other stories that you think about, read, or watch in a movie. Eventually, when watching a movie, you can point out the elements of the hero's journey to the people watching with you. They may pretend otherwise, but your family, especially, will *love* it when you do that!

How to Become a Hero in (More or Less) A Dozen (Not-Always-So-Easy) Steps!

The hero story begins with the hero — who we will think of, here, as you — living a seemingly unheroic life. It may even seem like the diametric opposite of heroic. Life isn't going well on the inside, for sure, but maybe things are seemingly on the slide on the outside, too. And whatever's lacking, however you're unfulfilled, it's because your own worldview and related attitude are getting in the way. But you don't know this. You are not, yet, aware that your problem is your own awareness — specifically, that you are much more than the 'self' you perceive you to be.

So you're in this rut, let's call it. And then, there will be — and hopefully you notice it, when it happens — a call to adventure. An opportunity or challenge will present itself to you, to depart from your routine 'rut' of a life. This is a fairly self-explanatory step in the process, although the problem here is that you may not even *want* to notice the opportunity or challenge (they are both the same thing). You are, after all, comfortable with your own, familiar suffering, from not manifesting what is within you. We should note, here, that as the New Testament warns us, when you do not bring forth what is within you, it will destroy you. In other words, there's a downside to *not* following your bliss — that being, an uninteresting, unfulfilled, and ultimately unhappy life. And that's a description of the *ceiling* of your life experience. Things could be, and may be, worse. A lot worse.

Which leads us to the next step: An initial refusal of the call. Why, you might ask, would you refuse adventure — especially if your life is unsatisfying and maybe even boring? Well, because you are, after all, attached to your egoic worldview — attached to your own familiar suffering! It's a 'comfort zone' of sorts, uncomfortable as it may be. And your egoic nature, desiring what it deems 'secure,' is fearful of the perceived loss of letting go in order to move forward. When this happens, and you dwell on your fear of lack or loss (penny-pinching your way through life is a good sign you're dwelling on this), your life will manifest exactly what you are dwelling on: Lack, with little gain, missing out on the fun and adventure of life.

But if you are open enough — 'just enough' is all it takes (which is one reason why it's important to always be open to being more open) — a choice or a circumstance will propel you forward. Sometimes, it can seem like the opportunity of a lifetime. But more often it can seem like the worst thing that could have happened. Either way, you're on your way, into the field of the unknown, somewhere you've never been, or thought of going, or even knew existed. In this new world, you will have new 'eye-opening' experiences, and encounter new mentors, enemies, and allies along the way. You will experience tribulations, revelations, and discoveries of new powers. There is *a lot* going on in the field of the unknown! And you never know what to expect. So don't expect to know — unless you're expecting the unexpected.

This experience of being in the field of the unknown is,

usually, a proportionately big part of your story. It goes on for a while. Again, there's a lot happening; there's lots of trials and tribulations (as well as some 'next-level' experiences of enlightenment and fun!) — and it takes a while for all of it to happen. So this all happens, in the form of unique experiences (that are, at the same time, universal, of course). And then, when you are ready (even if you don't think that you are; and you very likely won't), you will venture into the darkness for a confrontation with your worst fear.

This is the aspect of your life that, in a large way and perhaps more than anything else, is holding you back. It is the confrontation with your own unique version of the egoic wall between the life you live, now, and your true selfless self that resonates with Life. If you have a self-destructive addiction, doubt yourself, struggle to break routine, can't commit to something new, or are just plain lazy, the attachment to your sense of self driving these habitual attitudes and behaviors is what you must overcome. In a mythological story of the hero ('mythological' really meaning 'metaphorical,' as Campbell helped us understand; meaning a myth doesn't mean 'untrue,' but rather it's the opposite — only just not what we consider literally, historically true) this encounter in your journey is represented as something like a cold dark cave, with a dragon living there, existing only to guard a treasure it cannot use . . . a treasure that will change your life forever and empower you to save the world. And that treasure is, of course, Life itself — to manifest within you more fully as your presence, love, and ability to do what you do best to save the world. You are open and saying 'Yes!' to life — and Life itself. You conquer what's holding you back by confronting and slaying the dragon. Which requires the fearful task of letting go of your egoic worldview, and accepting the difficult realization that it's self-destructive and not self-sustaining. It's the shit Toni Morrison said is holding you back from flying.

pt. ends p. 149

When you confront and conquer your dragon, you gain the treasure from your experience — that is, again, you gain *awareness*, including the ability to recognize and overcome your own fear. And, of course, you become more powerful as a result. You move on with a sense of what you need to accomplish, your purpose is now defined; and you're determined to see it through, whatever obstacles stand in the way. Most important of all, you *believe* — no matter the apparent odds against you — that you can conquer anything to achieve your purpose, and that you will prevail. That you are, now, prevailing! The transformation of your worldview is now well underway, and you are already seeing everything differently than you ever have before. And it's pretty great! How could it not be? You are living life more fully, bringing forth within you, Life itself!

At this point, you are ready, prepared as you can be, when the adventure requires a final act, one of supreme sacrifice. The sacrifice will be your very life — that is to say, it will be your life *as you know it*. We are talking about death, here. A death of the self. In a mythological story about 'the way,' the hero's death is sometimes literal; there is a destruction of the living body — the ultimate manifestation, and symbol, of the 'self.' But for *every* hero who undertakes this journey, overcomes fear, desire, and the God-like sense of 'knowing it all' (passing judgment on 'what is'), and moves forward to take this ultimate step — whether the hero and the story are real or fictional — there is *always* a death of the ego, the falsely empowering and truly imprisoning sense of being a separate self.

And to be clear, this death comes — again, whether literally or symbolically — preceded by the experiences of loss, and pain, and suffering. It is, after all, tremendously difficult and otherwise unpleasant to let go of your old worldview — particularly the way in which you happen to view *you* and what has *be*-come your *life* — your fundamental *beliefs* about life. It is why we deep-down fear 'letting go' so much and avoid it at all costs. Remember, an aspect of our shared human insanity is that we 'prefer our own familiar suffering to the fear of the unknown.' (We keep repeating this for a reason.) When your worldview is challenged, you fear for your life — because your life, as you 'know' it, *is* threatened. We cannot emphasize this enough, which hopefully explains all the emphasizing. It is not because we forgot that we said it already.

But the hero has the power, now, to overcome this fear; and with a belief in being more than the self, the hero *lets go*, with a deep realization and understanding it is for the greater good of which he or she is a manifestation. The previously 'known' life is, now, gone forever. A transition is made — into the depths of what is unknown, an abyss. And then, when it seems as if the journey has ended on a major 'downer,' so to speak (given how pain and suffering and death are, by widely accepted definition, a major downer), there is a resurrection and rebirth! In a myth, when there is some form of a physical death, this resurrection is of the body — with the body returning to life in a form that is more powerful and new, manifesting more Life. It's the story of the Phoenix, Jesus, Psyche, and Shang-Chi. It's the greatest story, ever. And it's about both you and me.

Again, though, whether the story is literal or figurative, the rebirth and transformation experienced by the hero is always *of the mind*. It is experienced as a transcending of the ego, enabling the experience of one's true nature — Life itself — manifesting as awareness, love, and your ability to do what you do best to make the world around you better. Your circular journey, 'the way' of your life, has brought forth the universal 'what' you really are through the unique 'who' you really are.

And finally, after gaining the treasure of Life as the reward for bravely undertaking this journey of sacrifice and bliss, there is a triumphant return home, to the place where the adventure began, so that the hero can share the gift of awareness — of Life itself — with others. Often this return home is culminated with a celebration of some kind. And depending on the cultural protocols, there may be some embracing, and dancing, and general rejoicing; and it is possible that refreshments or even cupcakes may be involved. But remember, don't get too wrapped up in the details, or you will risk missing the point of the story:

'The cupcakes at the celebration were chocolate.'

'*No*, they were *vanilla*.'

And the next thing you know, people are throwing perfectly good cupcakes at each other — in the name of God, no less.

Notwithstanding variations among the many different stories told of 'the one story' of the hero's journey, what is most important to understand is that these experiences can, and will, manifest in your own life — if, again, you *follow your bliss*. This requires belief — in yourself, and what you are doing to make positive change. It requires faith that the power of Life itself is supporting you in your journey, even (and especially) if it doesn't always seem that way (because it won't; and in fact, it will seem the opposite). It requires patience as part of this faith — when things don't go your way, or the way you think that they should go, or along the timeline you'd like it to go. And it requires that you use the power of belief and faith and patience to overcome your fear of the unknown and break free of the prison of your own ego.

You can see how this is very much a journey of the mind! You can also see why there will be people who think you are out of your mind for undertaking it. But keep in mind that these people likely gave in to their own fear during key inflection points of their own lives, failed to answer their own call to adventure, and respond to you negatively (with resentment, or belittlement, or even flat-out open hostility) because witnessing your courage is a painful reminder of their own failure to answer the call. When you observe this happening, you are witnessing the self-destruction of someone who didn't bring forth what is within them.

We all fear the unknown in some way. This is especially true when it comes to getting to really know yourself — your true, selfless self, manifesting through, and as, the 'self' you think you know. But know this: While the process of self-discovery requires a departure from the starting point, it also requires remaining in, relying on, and ultimately returning to, that starting point. And just as everything in the universe is a paradox, your path to save the world — to saying 'yes' to Life (and life) more (and more) than 'no' — is paradoxical as well: You must step out of your 'ordinary' world, which requires that you overcome an obstacle within. But this inner achievement only happens when you put yourself out into the world.

All of which is to say that you must go outward, which requires that you go inward; but to go inward you must go outward. It should be noted that if in the process of doing this you also 'shake it all about,' you may be doing the Hokey Pokey, which is something very different than what we're talking about, although I suppose it's not necessarily mutually exclusive.

We should also point out that the path of a circle's perpetual line perfectly portrays the paradoxical process we just presented. If you look at a circle — go ahead and try! — you will see that any particular point on it will appear to curve inward in one direction, and outward in the other direction. Which of the two it happens to do depends on you, and how you look at it. And when the circle rotates, or you rotate your perspective of it, every relation between the points along its infinitely interconnected line will appear to change. The formerly outward direction between two points may now appear to curve inward, and the formerly inward direction between two points may now appear to curve outward.

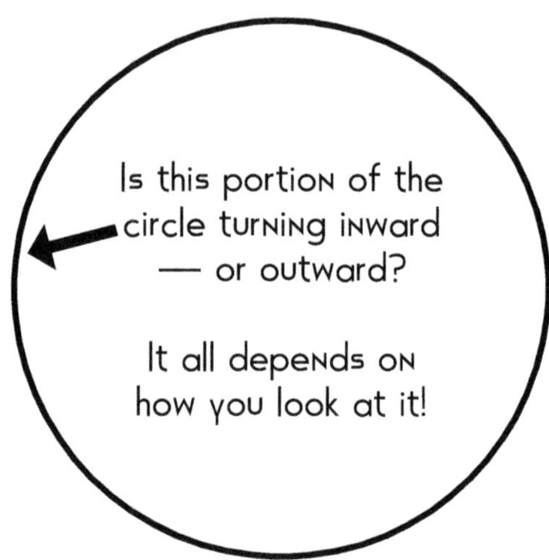

This is how perspective works: When you change how you look at something — including and especially your own perceived circumstance — it changes. Which, come to think of it, is a pretty good reason to every now and then 'shake it all about.' You know, shake things up a bit. Challenge your own perspective of . . . well, everything. Of course, this is a challenge, to challenge how we look at things. It is, in fact, our greatest of all challenges. It is *the* challenge we must overcome to save ourselves from self-destruction. The magnitude of which cannot be overstated. And so it's probably a good idea to restate it one more time.

We have continually talked about — harped on, even; perhaps to the point of being annoying about it — the well-known teaching from the New Testament: If you bring forth what is within you, it will save you. If you do not bring forth what is within you, it will destroy you. To 'bring forth' is to 'become aware of.' Because nothing happens in your experience of life outside or beyond your awareness. We established that you have the ability to bring forth what is within you. When you get right down to it, you *are* this ability. This is a fact of physics, remember, because *all* ability, no matter what it enables you to do, is Energy, Being, or Life itself. We also established that 'The Establishment' has not adequately established any of this well-established knowledge. And because of that, at least in part, it may be the case that you still don't believe you have this ability, even now, after we explained why you should.

And if it is what you believe, because you don't believe in yourself, you may well say, 'Well, yes, of course it's what I believe, and I believe it because it *is* my reality.' You have not found your ability to save the world (or so you believe), so you don't believe you have this ability. Makes sense! Sort of. But the problem is, if you don't believe you have the ability, you are not likely to find it. Your circular thinking *will* perpetuate your perceived circumstance. Because while it is normal, and sensible, and may be true that your beliefs reflect your perceived reality, it is also true — and *always* true — that your perceived reality reflects your beliefs.

Your reality is a product of your beliefs, not the cause of them — unless, of course, that is what you believe is reality. It's a circular problem. A vicious cycle. And it's especially problematic when you don't believe in *yourself* and so you're trapped within your disbelief — stuck there, going nowhere, with no awareness that belief is a choice. In this version of reality, belief is not a choice — because you don't believe that it is. But if you're aware that it is a choice, believe it is a choice, and choose to exercise that choice, you change your reality and free yourself from the self-made prison of self-defeating negative thinking.

Keep in mind that this negative thinking is always part of 'the way' of the hero's journey. It will plague you at the starting point and continue to challenge you throughout your journey. Self-belief is always a problem — unless and until you believe you are everything.

Either way, whether you don't believe in yourself, or you do believe in yourself, but would also welcome the help and encouragement of a simple, fun, sensible, fact-based, and otherwise satisfying explanation of why you should believe in yourself, this much we can say, to help you find your way (even though I have no way to know your unique ability to save the world):

Think of '**the way**' as the acronym **P—L—A—Y**.

And by this, what we are trying to say is that through the manifestation of Energy or Being or Life in the human system that you are — manifesting as:

PRESENCE in your mental form of being —

LOVE in your emotional form of being, and —

ABILITY in your physical form of being —

you are, in this way, saying —

YES to Life.

In a way, you could say that the acronym '**PLAY**' is a way to convey '**the way**' to save the world.

Does this idea sound childish? You bet your baby booties it does! Is it also based on the basic laws of physics, professed by millennia of spiritual leaders, aligned to the basic teachings of your favorite religion, and an easy way to remember how to positively change the world within and around you? On that, you can bet your life. And just to be clear, we're suggesting you take the chance, because — with the odds at one hundred percent certain that the more you open yourself to Life, the more Life will manifest, and work for you, in your life — it's the chance of a lifetime.

This playful idea is, by the way, a way to convey more than mere wordplay, because it also applies, literally, to the word 'play.' If you're going to save the world, the way *is* to play. And by 'play,' we mean 'do what you love doing that impacts your life and the world around you in a positive way.' Joseph Campbell put it this way: 'A good way to conceive of sacred space is a playground. If what you're doing seems like play, you are in it.' We are saying that, by playing, in this way, you are *following your bliss*. And so, you should do it, even if the people around you think you are out of your mind for doing so. (Which, in a way, you are — but in a positive way, because to expand your awareness, you have to go beyond and therefore 'be out of' your mind.)

Engage in work that is, to you, play, and you're saying 'yes' to life; you are bringing forth the Life within you because you are opening yourself to it. When your work is play, because you are following your bliss, giving of yourself fully, manifesting your ability in full, *nothing* can stop Life from changing the world in a positive way. All of which means that nothing in the world can stop *you*. Except, that is, your very own ego. That is to say, except, of course, you.

This brings us, now, to our play about play. To convey to you a story meant to help you find your way. As we pointed out earlier, you know the story we are going to share — because it's universal. But it is also true that you have never heard this one before — because it's unique. It involves two characters who are, by now, in many ways familiar to you — ***unique you***, and ***Universal You***. And while it's therefore a story that's all about you, it's also at the same time all about me. We should point out the point of it being about me: By opening up about my life story, with its veritable embarrassment of embarrassments in the form of mistakes, boringness, examples of ignorance, and other forms of self-deprecation, it's easier for you to see *my* egoic imperfections than your own; but through seeing mine, you may, then, see yours. And presto! Your self-awareness has grown. And that's the point of all of this, after all.

For the record, and to be clear, I *much* preferred to keep my personal life out of the book, and therefore left quite a bit out of it — for several reasons, actually; one of which relates to not knowing the statutes of limitations in certain jurisdictions in which I may or may not have entered at certain times on certain days for certain reasons, most of which I'm genuinely uncertain about. Directly related, revealing certain (many) details of my life would possibly (likely) undermine my efforts to set a good example for my sons, and would otherwise probably (definitely) be somewhat (very) embarrassing for some (all) of us. However! Being connected as we are as Being, and with all the circularity involved with everything, I just couldn't see any way around it. After all, the only way to convey the universal is in one's own unique way. Which is why this story about you is inevitably — though contradicting my egoic impulses of fear and desire — about me.

Our two-person play about play is set in ancient Greece. The erudite and thoughtful reader may well speculate that, by framing our story as an ancient Greek play, we are paying due homage to the major methodologies of metaphysical messaging — art, philosophy, mythology, and psychology; offering up to the gods of knowledge and wisdom, if you will, an *apropos* tribute to these infinitely unique forms of human expression conveying the universal human experience of the infinite; creating a symbolic bridge between the ancient and modern forms to relate, metaphorically, the timeless and formless. The 'not so' erudite and thoughtful reader may, on the other hand, not so much care and want to get on with the damn thing.

Turns out our erudite and thoughtful reader has it right, although our not-so-erudite and thoughtful reader has a good point. And so! With all of that as preamble, and without any further ado, I present to you my own unique story — a universal story, that is all about you . . .

PART FOUR

The Play (About Play)

A playful play about play
As a way to awareness —
As a way to show the way
On your way to awareness

The Second Greatest Story Ever Told
A Two-Person & Two-Act Play About Play

Dramatis Personae

Uniquio — The acclaimed writer, philosopher, and orator, who is here to pay a therapist a substantial hourly rate to listen to him talk about himself. He wears the standard tunic-like garment known as a chiton (pronounced chi-tn, with a 'chi,' not a 'shi'), a chaplet of garland around his head, and a pair of red Chuck Taylor high tops.

Universalus — The anthropomorphic manifestation of the creative intelligence of the universe, here manifesting as a psychiatrist who requires payment in full on the day of your appointment, making you have to deal with the insurance. He is dressed like Uniquio, but wears thick, black-frame glasses that are so large they resemble an actual pair of fishbowls (to symbolize infinite wisdom) and clunky white geriatric sneakers with Velcro straps (to symbolize being older than time and space).

Loquatio — The rapper who represents, and performs the function of, a Greek chorus. In addition to the chiton, he wears Air Jordans, a gold chain the thickness of an industrial rigging sling, and the Cat in the Hat's iconic striped hat. (Note to wardrobe: If copyright law prohibits use of the red and white striped hat, make it a white and red striped hat instead. Note to producer: The playwright should not incur legal fees related to the copyright situation with the hat, or for that matter anything herein described that may warrant legal action.)

ACT ONE: GOING 'OUT THERE'

The time and place are ancient Athens, Greece; the scene is a therapist's office in a contemporary style, with a large desk, bookcases, and, in the middle of the room, two large leather chairs. Floor-to-ceiling open windows overlook the city, and in the distance, we see the Parthenon, the Acropolis, and a billboard for divorce attorneys named Detritus & Screwuvius.

Scene One: Session One.

The curtain rises. Universalus is seated in the chair on the right, browsing through pages in a book. He places the book on the side table next to his chair and rises to greet Uniquio as he enters through a door, stage left.

Universalus: (*Greets Uniquio with a friendly handshake.*) Hello. And welcome!
Uniquio: Hi. Nice to meet you. I'm Uniquio. You look . . . familiar. Like an actor . . .
Universalus: I suppose you could say, 'I am that, I am.' I go by a lot of names. The important thing is to make your check out to 'Universalus' on the way out.
Uniquio: No 'Doctor' Universalus?
Universalus: Then I sound like a supervillain. Besides, titles are superfluous. At least they are to me. Please, have a seat.
Uniquio: (*Sits in chair.*) Well . . . it's nice to meet you.
Universalus: (*Sits in chair.*) It's good to see you. That is, it's good for *you* to see you. It's why we're here, after all. (*Smiles.*) A little 'therapist humor' there. By the way, congratulations on your incredibly successful book. I have a

first edition copy right here. Very nice publication — and so reasonably priced!

Uniquio: Well, thank you — and yes, it's *very* reasonably priced.

Universalus: I noticed the quotes on the back cover. The book got reviewed by some reputable publications. That must help with book sales.

Uniquio: The quotes? Oh, well . . . I wrote all of that myself. They're meant to be humorous.

Universalus: Oh! (*Seems surprised; looks over the back cover.*) This one says, 'An intellectual triumph that will transform world literature and awaken the reader's soul. If the reader's soul remains asleep, contact your metaphysician immediately.' (*Looks at Uniquio.*) So . . . you're saying, no one from *The New Yorker* wrote that?

Uniquio: No, that was me. There's some very small print there, explaining it.

Universalus: (*Squints and holds book close to read.*) I see. And so, no one from *The Washington Post* wrote, 'This towering achievement of and for humanity is a shining beacon of hope for our future — so long as humanity stops staring at their cellphones long enough to read it.'

Uniquio: Yeah, I can't imagine someone from *The Washington Post* writing . . . well, *any* of that.

Universalus: (*Looks at the book again, puzzled, as if it had turned into an oven mitt, and places it back on the table.*) Interesting. Well then! What brings you here, son?

Uniquio: To be honest, I needed a literary device to convey a unique example of the universal path to save the world. It's something to 'round out' the book.

Universalus: Are you talking about (*gestures to book on the table*) *that* book?

Uniquio: Yes, well (*gestures around the room*) *this* book. I figured the 'ancient Greek play' setting was a good way to end it, having a dialogue between my unique being and

Universal Being about my own unique life story in the context of the universal path to save the world.

Universalus: You're telling me we're in (*points to book on table*) *that* book, right now.

Uniquio: That's right. We're in (*gestures between himself and Universalus*) *this* book.

Universalus: To talk about *your* life story, trying to save the world in your own way.

Uniquio: Correct. To help frame the path for the reader's own heroic journey . . .

Universalus: To help every reader save the world . . . each in *their* own way.

Uniquio: That's right. And see how we just used our literary device to explain that?

Universalus: Hm. Don't you think that came across as a little . . . contrived?

Uniquio: I'd say that's highly likely.

Universalus: Well, saving the world requires 'enlightenment,' and according to social media data, it's exponentially less popular than celebrity beach pics. Not to mention it usually turns off people when you talk about it at parties.

Uniquio: I make no pretense about being enlightened. My life story is about gaining more awareness than I had, living constantly in my own head. It's about becoming a better person, to do better work for the world. That kind of thing. But I'm still my own worst enemy. I'm just, I guess, more aware of, and therefore better able to respond to, that enemy.

Universalus: If the 'enemy' is part of the growth process, is it really the enemy?

Uniquio: I never thought of that before.

Universalus: What can I say? It's how I put Pita on the table. And nice olive oil, or else what's the point. So . . . this story is about how you came to write this book. Which we're considering a 'heroic' achievement — saving the world. Do I have that right?

act one ends p. 207

Uniquio: Well, it's meant to help. And I mean, it *did* take me over ten years to write . . . not to mention all the reading and writing and experiences from earlier in life that went into it.
Universalus: It certainly sounds time-consuming. Did you ever figure out the genre?
Uniquio: It's intended . . . I'm not sure what you'd call that. I feel like it's a philosophy-comedy. (*Pauses, shakes head.*) If only there were a word for that. (*Shakes head again.*) Maybe the book transcends genres.
Universalus: Careful what you say. That'll be misunderstood by certain high-ranking public officials and your book will get banned — in at *least* five states.
Uniquio: (*Distracted, still thinking about a word for philosophy-comedy.*) I need to work on a good way to describe the book.
Universalus: Have you ever heard of a portmanteau? I'll give you a hint. It's not a Portuguese wine.
Uniquio: 'Portuguese wine' was my actual guess.
Universalus: Yes, I know. So that would be a 'no.'
Uniquio: Yes. It's a no.
Universalus: A portmanteau blends the sounds of words. You could make up one to describe your book. I could see highly creative publishers using them as one of their 'things.' (*Peers down at book again, cracks an enigmatic, 'Mona Lisa' smile.*) I see you had *Harper's Magazine* refer to you as the Bobby 'The Brain' Heenan of American Letters. (*Pauses, looks up at Uniquio, deadpan.*) Now that's just plain boastful.
Uniquio: (*Nods in agreement.*) Bobby 'The Brain' was the best. He really was. But, ah . . . I'm getting the feeling you haven't read the book.
Universalus: Look, son. When you're animating, sustaining, connecting, informing, organizing, and ultimately enabling all life in the universe, there isn't a lot of 'down

time' for reading. But I'm aware of the contents of your book, and comprehend that we're *in* the book, but we're not; and that you *know* I'm ***Universal You***, but you don't.

Uniquio: Correct. And you know everything about my life, but don't know anything.

Universalus: And the audience is sufficiently entertained to keep paying attention, or isn't.

Uniquio: That's right. It all depends on how each one of us looks at it all.

Universalus: Certainly. And to make sure we're on the same page: We're engaging in the present. But in the distant past. To discuss your recent past. To positively change the future of others. By engaging in the present.

Uniquio: I think that's obvious. (*Pauses.*) I have to say, it's a little unsettling, being in the presence of infinite awareness in human form. I mean, *you're* the creative force behind . . . everything. The inspiration of every scientist, artist, teacher, and leader; of every voice of wisdom in human history.

Universalus: But I'm also the creative force behind conspiracy theory chatrooms and those *Real Housewives* shows, so I need to be careful about taking credit for things. (*Looks at watch again.*) We need to start talking about your life story . . . I mean, your . . . *hero journey.*

Uniquio: There'll be some eye-rolling among my family, describing my life that way.

Universalus: The hero journey is available to everyone. It's the path of individual growth into self-awareness. Not to mention a good alternative to having your life spiral down the proverbial drain. There's nothing self-aggrandizing about recognizing your experience of this journey.

Uniquio: Yeah, well, tell that to my family.

Universalus: I believe we just did. And we really should get started. Let's begin with your childhood. A writer needs to read a lot, to learn how to write. Did you enjoy reading as a kid?

Uniquio: As a young kid, from elementary school through middle school — 'junior high,' as we called it — I read all the time. But probably my most memorable experience reading happened during my sophomore year in my high school library. I found a Woody Allen paperback that made me laugh out loud, reading it. For some reason I can remember how great it felt, laughing like that at the library. It surprised me, somehow. You could say it 'struck' me. Something resonated.

Universalus: Did you know you wanted to be a writer, that day in the library?

Uniquio: Oh no, that came much later. After I was well out of college. And then it took several years after that to realize I liked writing comedy the best.

Universalus: Oh! You write comedy?

Uniquio: Very funny.

Universalus: Do you mean you write 'very funny' comedy, or was 'very funny' your sarcastic response to my question?

Uniquio: Are you kidding me?

Universalus: I guess it depends on how you look at it.

Uniquio: I can't figure you out.

Universalus: Well, at least you figured *that* out. A lot of people think they have me figured out — and are *very* confident that they do! You said you enjoyed reading when you were younger.

Uniquio: I did. When I was in grade school, I loved reading the *Encyclopedia Brown* books, and *The Hardy Boys*, and *The Great Brain*. They were all books about smart kids who were able to figure things out that the adults couldn't. I liked that.

Universalus: An idea that clearly influenced your book.

Uniquio: I never thought of that. (*Pauses.*) Hm!

Universalus: (*Shrugs.*) With infinite wisdom, you have an insight now and then . . .

Uniquio: In junior high, I liked the classic short stories we read in English class. And the classic novels, too. *The Outsiders, The Catcher in the Rye, Animal Farm, Lord of the Flies* . . . I enjoyed those books. (*Pauses.*) But they were disturbing, come to think of it.

Universalus: How do you mean?

Uniquio: It made me uncomfortable when the main characters were dealing with trouble. I just wanted them to . . . to get *through* it, you know? To get back to normal — or at least to safety. It motivated me to keep reading, to see the main characters get out of danger.

Universalus: Of course, sometimes the hero never makes it to a safe place, in the literal sense. And nothing ever gets back to the old normal.

Uniquio: That's true. But even though they made me uncomfortable, I enjoyed reading those books. Time passed by like it was nothing when I was reading. It's like that now, when I'm writing.

Universalus: Time *is* nothing. It's an illusion. Still, if you're ever running late for one of our appointments, please call with a heads up. So it sounds like you've always been a reader.

Uniquio: I've always enjoyed fiction. Then I got into some philosophy and psychology when I was older. School textbooks were a different story. Likely because there was no story.

Universalus: Do you recall an interest or ability to write when you were a child?

Uniquio: Well, I mean, I'm not sure how good of a writer I am now . . . even though I walk around wearing *this* thing. (*Points to the garland chaplet around his head.*)

Universalus: Really? (*Picks up book and peruses the back cover.*) You said here that you wrote a book that's 'Biblically important, and then some.'

Uniquio: Well, again, it's all a joke — an attempt at humor . . .

act one ends p. 207

Universalus: You point out that comedy is the most effective way to convey the truth.

Uniquio: For some reason I keep forgetting you know what's in the book.

Universalus: Let's get back to your childhood. This was your big idea, telling your life story within the framework of the archetypal hero journey — the monomyth.

Uniquio: Hey, I'm just the system, here. *You're* the creative intelligence and force of the universe, informing everything . . . making it all happen.

Universalus: But as you point out, the system does the actual *work*. I'm just the *ability* to do the work. So, if this 'play' doesn't work, don't blame me, kid.

Uniquio: Fine, be that way. And by the way, I'm a little old to be called 'kid,' or 'son' — don't you think? I mean, people younger than me have grandchildren. I hardly even get carded at Applebee's anymore . . . and I pulled a muscle sneezing the other day.

Universalus: Everything's relative. To me, you're just a kid. Who likes to kid. And the important thing is to be a kid at heart. When I asked if you were good at writing as a kid, you responded by questioning your ability as a writer now. I couldn't tell if you were kidding.

Uniquio: In third grade, I wrote a report about Native American Indians. I got an 'F' because I didn't do the research for the assignment, and it was obvious. I remember being surprised to learn that American Indians didn't wrestle gorillas.

Universalus: Kind of ironic, with you being such a big Joseph Campbell fan. His lifelong work began with his interest in Native American culture and myths.

Uniquio: Yeah, I know. And no doubt Joseph Campbell would have been disappointed in my third-grade report. I even drew a picture for it, with an Indian chief holding a gorilla over his head, like a professional wrestler about to body-slam him.

Universalus: I have no idea how to respond to that. And I'm omniscient.

Uniquio: I spent a lot of time drawing as a kid. I guess I wasn't bad at it. And . . . well, this isn't exactly writing, but when I was in first grade, I had an alter-ego called 'the old man.' I assumed this other character, and Scotch-taped cotton balls to my face for a beard, and I talked about myself with my parents in the third person. Then the old man would leave the room, and I'd return as regular me, and my parents would tell me what the old man talked about. I could tell my parents were entertained by it.

Universalus: You say you did this in . . . *first* grade? And this character was an old man. Who was *really* you, but wasn't you?

Uniquio: That's right.

Universalus: *And* . . .

Uniquio: And . . . what?

Universalus: And . . . what are we doing, right now . . . ?

Uniquio: Oh! Hey. That never occurred to me. (*Pauses.*) How 'bout that! I guess that's why you're the most expensive psychiatrist in Athens. Oh! And requiring payment in full on the day of appointments. Your receptionist made that very clear.

Universalus: That's Rosie, the Greek goddess of accounts receivable. She's not one of your better-known goddesses, but you don't want to get on her bad side.

Uniquio: Now I can't tell if *you're* kidding.

Universalus: Any more writing experiences from childhood you want to mention?

Uniquio: Not really. Except, well . . . when I was older, I used to play a game, shooting baskets by myself in the driveway. I'd pretend to be all four players in a two-on-two NBA game, and I'd do the play by play and color commentary in my head. Afterward I'd come inside to write up a game summary, like I'd read in the sports page.

Universalus: Did your parents encourage your creative interests?

Uniquio: I don't remember being encouraged or discouraged. They certainly didn't encourage my creative interests in terms of a career path. My parents always wanted me to be a dentist, though I never showed any interest or aptitude in science. When my parents sent me to an orthodontics school to save money on my braces, I ended up having to wear them twice as long as all the other kids. I came to dislike dentistry, generally, and dental school students, especially. I guess my parents liked the idea that it was a financially secure career.

Universalus: Let's talk about your parents, since you brought them up.

Uniquio: My dad's gone now, but he was a great dad. A good family man, always there for us. He wasn't expressive with his feelings, but we knew he loved us, the way he was always there, always present. He liked to tell stories about things that happened to him — funny things, usually. He had a good sense of humor.

Universalus: Was he a creative person?

Uniquio: He wasn't at all interested in anything you'd call 'artistic.' He read the sports page, *Sports Illustrated*, and his Robert Ludlum books. That's about it. The only museum I remember him having any interest in was the Baseball Hall of Fame. He liked to watch TV. Sports, mostly. New York Rangers hockey, especially. He liked comedy shows — *Barney Miller* was his favorite. Oh, and he enjoyed Spanish language variety shows. My brothers and I eventually realized it was to watch the half-naked women dancing around in high heels.

Universalus: Do you think your dad's interest in reading

about sports may have had something to do with why you wrote about your make-believe basketball games?
Uniquio: I never thought of that. I can't remember if I shared it with him, though.
Universalus: Maybe by writing those articles, you were seeking affirmation that it was okay to pursue some kind of writing as a career path. Maybe you even received that affirmation in some way and didn't realize it.
Uniquio: Hm. That's . . . another thing I never thought of before. (*Pauses, shrugs.*) I just remember writing those articles because it was a part of the fun. It was all a way of entertaining myself. (*Pauses again, appears reflective.*) I don't think my dad understood a lot of my interests, but he always seemed to appreciate that I had them.
Universalus: When you think about your dad, what comes to mind?
Uniquio: I always felt better being around him, especially when I got older and didn't see him as much. When he was around, it felt like everything was going to be okay. You could count on him to take care of things. He wasn't the most adventurous guy in the world. Even with food, he had no interest in trying something new. All we ever ate for dinner when I was a kid was meat, a starch, and a vegetable. You wanted to spice up your meal, you had salt, pepper, and butter to do it. We never even had Chinese food. And forget about anything more exotic than that. I wasn't even aware you could get toppings on a pizza until I was in sixth grade. My dad loved plain white bread, and I'd say that accurately reflected his taste for adventure.
Universalus: You've mentioned your dad's sense of humor, that he had a good one.
Uniquio: He did. He got my brothers and me into the old *Batman* TV show, and professional wrestling. He liked the old Woody Allen movies, and Mel Brooks movies. He liked *Airplane*, and *The Naked Gun*. My mom didn't get the

humor in that stuff, but we loved it. None of us liked the *Police Academy* movies the way my dad did, but he thought it was funny how we kidded him about it — he was in on the joke.

Universalus: So you got your enjoyment of humor from your dad.

Uniquio: For sure. (*Pauses.*) I only wish my boys got to know my dad. He would have gotten a 'big kick out of them,' as he would have said. They would have made him laugh. He would have enjoyed seeing me being a dad, dealing with dad things. The idea of my boys and my dad interacting makes me smile, but then it makes me sad it never happened.

Universalus: (*Finishes making a note, and looks up.*) They know him through you!

Uniquio: I guess that's something.

Universalus: It's a lot more than 'something,' son. In the end, it's everything. So how about we talk about your mom now? Feel free to be expansive. Just keep in mind that a play takes up a lot of pages, and there's printing costs to consider, not to mention that a lot of readers don't want to bother with a book that's thicker than a deck of cards.

Uniquio: Sure. Well, the need to express myself, I got from her. My dad kept things to himself, but growing up, we always knew exactly how my mom felt. She's a lot more reserved about family matters, now, but she's still an open book with things like politics, religion, her opinions on certain celebrities. She's told us she thinks American football is 'stupid' a hundred times. I'm not exaggerating. It's a Thanksgiving tradition. My mom *has* to say she thinks football is stupid. She's passionate and expressive about things. I get that from her.

Universalus: It sounds like you were influenced by both parents.

Uniquio: For sure. I'm a lot more like my dad now than I was in my twenties and thirties, happy to stay home with the family. When I was younger, I wanted to get out into the world, participate in what was going on. My mom is like that. She has an adventurous spirit. Although she always chose healthy, positive — *constructive* — new experiences to explore. She still does, with her yoga, and golf, and bowling, and the world travel that she's done. I didn't always explore the most, ah, *constructive* things.

Universalus: What was your mom like when you were growing up?

Uniquio: I'd say 'energetic' is the first word that comes to mind. And 'engaged.' She was always engaged with us, involved with what we were doing. Always the host for the neighborhood kids, taking us to the pool in the summer, being the den mother for Cub Scouts.

Universalus: You said your mom was adventurous. Was she open-minded?

Uniquio: My mom has always been open-minded about people in the abstract. She's always disliked racists, sexists, snobs — any kind of bigot. But she could also be critical of people — especially with our friends and girlfriends; people my dad worked with, certain teachers we had, other family members.

Universalus: How did you respond to her criticism of your friends, your girlfriends?

Uniquio: I came to see it as normal. It bothered me — a lot, sometimes — but I figured that's how everyone's parents were. Maybe that's true, in some ways.

Universalus: Don Miguel Ruiz points out that most everyone is taught to judge, that it's a shared human agreement. We even do it with people we don't know.

Uniquio: Oh yeah, my mom does that. In an emotionally charged way. She'll say she 'hates' people she sees on TV. 'I hate Sylvester Stallone' — that's something I've heard her say. Why, I have no idea. Who *cares* about Sylvester

Stallone? She's never liked guys with macho personas — okay, I get that. But to get so worked up about it!

Universalus: You don't understand why someone would get worked up over nothing?

Uniquio: I know. It's something I see in myself. Same with my brothers. We can all be very judgmental. I'll gladly own that. I can be really bad about it, especially with brief encounters.

Universalus: You define yourself, not the other person, when you judge that person.

Uniquio: I believe that. Now I try to catch myself and stop. Writing this book helped a lot. But I still do it, impulsively. I have to really work at it, with some people and situations. My dad took things in stride, although some people irritated him. He called them 'shit-birds.'

Universalus: It's important to be aware and catch yourself when you're being judgmental, but a writer has a perspective to share, and that perspective needs expression in an honest and forthright way. There's necessarily judgment involved.

Uniquio: You know, it's funny. Years ago, my mom told me — more than a few times, actually — that I should write a children's book. I had always dismissed the idea.

Universalus: And it's exactly what you did. You wrote a children's book, for adults.

Uniquio: And it's also an adult book, for children — for their future. And to hopefully read when they grow up, in the future. I certainly hope my own boys get something out of it, someday. I hope a lot of kids do. That's always been my hope. I was eligible for AARP membership by the time I started writing it, but I finally did it.

Universalus: It's never too late in life to positively change who you are and what you want to do.

Uniquio: No matter what happens with this book, the process of writing it positively changed me — a lot. And I figure if my boys read it someday, and it helps them with their own worldview and path in life, all the work I put into it will be worthwhile. Although my oldest son told me years ago that he's hoping for a beach house out of this.

Universalus: Knowing your intention for the boys to read this, I suppose you'll be leaving out details from your young adulthood.

Uniquio: No one is interested in the disreputable details of my life.

Universalus: People *love* those details. It's not like reality TV is popular because it expands intellectual horizons. Besides, what are you worried about, Mister (*makes air quotes with his fingers*) 'There's No Need to Worry?'

Uniquio: Yeah, and I'm also Mr. Dad.

Universalus: Don't you want your boys to say 'yes' to the great adventure of life?

Uniquio: Well . . . *yes*, of course I do. I just want them both to wear crash helmets and Kevlar body suits for it. At the very least, I want to set a good example for them.

Universalus: Just as any good parent would want to do. Setting a good example is the best and really only protection you can provide. This brings us back to *your* parents. It sounds like you grew up in a home with parents who, for the most part, set a good example for you — in a lot of important ways. Maybe a little over-protective, but they loved you. It's why they did what they did — and didn't do what they didn't do.

Uniquio: All true. Although 'a little over-protective' is understating the situation. They were pretty strict with me, being the oldest. And they were Catholic.

Universalus: Are we talking 'mass twice a year' Catholics or the 'every Sunday' kind?

Uniquio: My parents were 'Saturday night mass' Catholics. Meaning they went every week, but also wanted to get it over with. My dad would time the sermons on his watch

— to him, the shorter the better. After mass, we never talked about the message of a sermon. We only talked about the duration. We'd get in the car and my dad reported on it, down to the minute.

Universalus: Maybe he appreciated the priest getting to the point.

Uniquio: Maybe. Although if Don Rickles had been delivering a sermon at mass, my dad would have been happy to listen to him talk all day. I think he just wanted to put in his time at church and get out, so we could go to Roy Rogers and he could get his Double R Bar burger.

Universalus: Did your dad talk at all about his belief in God?

Uniquio: Not one single word, ever. He showed up at church, made us show up too, and that was it. I had to figure out for myself what it all meant. And it was hard to figure out. A lot about Catholicism didn't make sense — *and* it was boring. Mostly, I found it oppressive. Sometimes, there were nice moments, I suppose. And occasionally, I listened to the sermons, and found some of it helpful. But I dreaded going to church.

Universalus: Not simple, and not fun.

Uniquio: And my brothers and I were usually outside playing, having fun with our friends, when it was time to get ready for church. I remember envying those kids, not having to stop playing . . . I wondered if they pitied us, or were just relieved it wasn't them.

Universalus: What do you remember most about your childhood?

Uniquio: Sitting around the dinner table together — or in the den; the 'TV room,' we called it. Going on vacations, always driving, always to a house near water — usually, the beach. I remember enjoying the big holidays. Christmas, especially, but all of them, really. Halloween, Thanksgiving, Easter, the Fourth of July. I remember going to the pool in

the summer. Playing with the neighborhood kids in the street and in our driveway. Going to summer day camp at our school. Positive stuff, mostly.
Universalus: Sounds pretty nice. I think we established what we need to understand about your starting point. Overall, your parents loved you, engaged you, and set a good example for you — wouldn't you say?
Uniquio: I would. They did. And their positives and negatives informed who I am.
Univeralus: Let's talk about when you left home to go to college.
Uniquio: Life changed a lot. Right away. I mean, it's a different experience, not having your parents around at all, as opposed to having them around, at least at home, all the time. Fairly early on, I formed a group of close friends. We were all outsiders, in our own way. None of us would've fit in well with a group other than our own, I don't think. There were nine of us, counting my one anti-social roommate, who in some ways I related to the most, even though I was the most outgoing of the group. He was into reading and writing and had a great sense of humor. We made each other laugh all the time. He was an English major before he dropped out.
Universalus: Sounds like you formed your own family.
Uniquio: I guess we did. We very much had an 'us against the world' mentality, not unlike my own family sometimes has. We were always making fun of everyone else at school — fraternity guys, faculty members, other kids in our dormitory. The security guards, especially. We tormented those poor guys. Come to think of it, we were pretty judgmental.
Universalus: How did the studies go? Were you making the Dean's list? I mean, one would expect that from someone who's offering up 'towering achievements of and for humanity . . . '
Uniquio: No Dean's list for me. Unless the Dean had a 'naughty' list. At one point I was on social *and* disciplinary

act one ends p. 207

probation. I was never clear on the difference between the two. Although I did avoid academic probation — barely. My freshman year grades in Chemistry and Biology quickly ended my prospects for dental school. I switched to a political science major, which helped my grades, but I had no career aspiration. It was another non-decision from that time of my life that I'd have to live with for the rest of it.

Universalus: Another *non*-decision — how do you mean?

Uniquio: Both times I picked a major, I had a chance to choose what I wanted to do in life, but I didn't. Because I didn't know what I wanted to do. It was the same when choosing what college to attend. I let the school pick me more than I picked the school.

Universalus: Not everyone knows their life's calling at eighteen.

Uniquio: My parents expressed concern I was wasting my education. I had several professors tell me I had ability but was wasting it. I didn't have much self-awareness at the time, but I had enough to realize that they were probably right.

Universalus: You retreated to a comfort zone in college, recreating a family dynamic with your friends, establishing a safe place to judge the world, so you didn't have to look at yourself, and confront the fact that you weren't positively contributing much to that world.

Uniquio: This is more feedback than I ever received from a real therapy session.

Universalus: It was inevitable, once you chose to let go and let flow your writing.

Uniquio: Somehow, I didn't see it coming.

Universalus: Interesting — *and* ironic! So . . . you were a bit of a wee-wee back then. And you had a lot of 'answers' that helped you 'overlook' that you were a wee-wee. But let's look at the positives. Having fun was part of your path to self-discovery — to who you were meant to be, and what you were meant to do.

Uniquio: I suppose. But don't you think we're . . . I don't know, glossing over my shortcomings?

Universalus: Well, we certainly are! But you weren't a bad kid. And you didn't have bad intentions. People liked you — a lot of people loved you. As you point out, we can all be a wee-wee sometimes. Besides, it's easier to move forward when you drop the baggage from the past. Learn from it, but don't let it burden you.

Uniquio: Nietzsche's transition from the camel to the lion . . .

Universalus: True, but probably a little esoteric, don't you think? We all get it, you're a reader. You don't have to be pedantic about it, referencing Nietzsche.

Uniquio: Don't you think using the words 'esoteric' and 'pedantic' could, itself, be considered a little esoteric and pedantic?

Universalus: Fair point! Let's talk about life after college.

Uniquio: Okay, well, my dad made it clear that I wasn't going to Europe to 'find myself' after I graduated. I'm pretty sure he actually said that, even though I never mentioned the idea, or even thought of it as an option. But right after graduation, I pretty much did the opposite, and got a job driving a UPS truck out of Newark, New Jersey.

Universalus: Not quite the appeal of roaming Europe for a few months.

Uniquio: It was pretty much the opposite of that. The union steward told me I had the toughest route in the center, with all the industrial and commercial stops on it. I drove the largest delivery truck in the fleet; it was always full going out in the morning and coming back with afternoon pickups. I had a lot of jobs before then, through high school and college, but I never worked as hard as I did there.

Universalus: Didn't like the hard work?

Uniquio: Actually, I didn't mind the physical labor part of it much at all. It was the stress of meeting schedule deadlines all day long because there was always traffic and backups at delivery sites that were out of my control. And more than that, it was the constant feeling that I was supposed to be doing something else.

Universalus: So, you had a little self-reflection happening?

Uniquio: I felt regret. A lot. On the job, at night, on the weekends — especially Sunday nights. I'd get depressed, just thinking about work. It made it worse, knowing my buddies from school who were computer science or accounting majors were enjoying their cushy jobs in air-conditioned offices with weekly happy hours.

Universalus: Why did you leave? You were unsatisfied, obviously, but people stay in unsatisfying jobs all the time. What prompted the change?

Uniquio: I quit the same week I hit the highest pay rate in the union. It was good money, but I knew I didn't want to make a career there. My dad's pitch to me, to take the job in the first place, was that I could move up into management, make good money, have a good career. That sounded okay; I figured that's what I was supposed to do. Our family friend who helped get me the job there was a big-time manager, and owned a house on Long Beach Island. I wanted that. I still do! But the work environment was unhealthy — even at twenty-two years old, I figured that out.

Universalus: Unhealthy — how so?

Uniquio: A lot of guys who worked there were chain smokers — the supervisors, especially. And they would come out into the parking lot after work and drink a case or two of Budweiser with the drivers before everyone drove home. This was every night, if the weather was decent.

Universalus: How did it go over with your parents when you quit?

Uniquio: They didn't have a problem with it. I think the stories about the chain-smoking supervisors drinking in the parking lot concerned them.

Universalus: What did you do next? I assume your dad still wanted you to work.

Uniquio: He did — and he hooked me up with another blue-collar labor job, working for a tree surgeon. I had to do *something* to earn money. It didn't matter what it was.

Universalus: You were aware that this wasn't something you wanted to do for a living.

Uniquio: Painfully aware. It was a depressing time. I knew people who were in medical school and law school. My girlfriend was a practicing nurse in a major hospital in Philadelphia. And here I was, dragging brush and feeding a wood-chipper, living at home with my parents.

Universalus: Emerson said the person who follows his own natural way is like a ship in a river. 'He runs against obstructions on every side but one; on that side all obstruction is taken away.' The classes you didn't like, the jobs you didn't like, the sense of restrictions you didn't like — they were all obstructions, narrowing your path forward to the center of who you are and what you were meant to do.

Uniquio: You're saying those experiences were . . . guiding me.

Universalus: In a sense, yes, but really you were guiding yourself. It was because you never fully committed to the obligations of a formal education or career that you allowed yourself to be carried forward, toward what you were meant to be and do.

Uniquio: So, to be clear about this . . . you're saying that my attitude toward school and the early part of my career had . . . a purpose. It was a . . . necessary part of the path?

Universalus: You didn't know exactly what you wanted to do, but you were open to finding out. Often, it's the case that people fold themselves into the box they're in and stay there forever. You always looked for a way out. You just didn't realize you were doing it — or why.

Uniquio: Honestly, up until right now . . . I just never . . . this actually makes sense.

Universalus: Well, I *am* the creative intelligence of the universe. Always here, always willing and able to help.

Uniquio: (*Looking down, distracted.*) Right . . . the creative intelligence of the universe. (*Looks up.*) Sometimes I forget and think you're just a concept from my imagination.

Universalus: People go in and out of awareness of 'what is.' Most people are mostly out. Some people are always out. Some people are so far out that they talk to themselves, fall into arguments, and after things get too personal, they refuse to talk to themselves for a week. I've got a well-known actress who does that, you know. (*Shakes head and sighs.*) So . . . how long did you work for the tree surgeon?

Uniquio: Not long. While working there, I got my first professional job, as an environmental policy advocate for a nonprofit organization. Again, I got this job through a contact of my dad's — our town mayor. My dad hooked me up with my first three jobs out of college.

Universalus: Because he was doing his best to help you.

Uniquio: No doubt. But I had to get a master's degree for this new job, in a subject I had no interest in, at all. Public administration. It's what my dad had his degree in, and — well, honestly, it helped open career doors down the road. But by the time I graduated, I knew the job I was in was not what I wanted to do with my life — no more than I wanted to be a supervisor at the package delivery company. But this job was different. There was no pressure to be productive. It felt like I was in on a big scam.

Universalus: You were a salaried full-time lobbyist. You *were* in on a big scam.

Uniquio: It was stress-free, in a way, but I didn't like the networking part of it, trying to get access to people I had no desire to interact with. I really dreaded that part of the job.

Universalus: You're not the schmoozing type?

Uniquio: No. I don't even like the word. It sounds like . . . snails mating.

Universalus: How about hobnob?

Uniquio: What about hobnob?

Universalus: The word. Hobnob. Do you like it?

Uniquio: Not really, no.

Universalus: And you don't like to hobnob. It's the same thing as 'to schmooze.'

Uniquio: Yes, I know. And no, I don't.

Universalus: I think that's a good place to wrap up for today.

Uniquio: I'm not quite sure what we were talking about.

Universalus: Translation, your time is up. We got through the first three stages of your story. Not exactly blockbuster movie material, but also not the most boring one I've ever heard.

Uniquio: Er, uh . . . thanks.

Universalus: Well, look. You could have made it more interesting. You left out a lot of lurid details from your early twenties. People love that stuff.

Uniquio: I can't recall any of that kind of thing. Though I don't think 'lurid' is a word I would use. There has to be a good euphemism for that.

Universalus: I could help you remember at our next session.

Uniquio: Translation, no thanks. Maybe I'll use those experiences — if I can ever remember them — for a comically flawed and otherwise developmentally challenged character in my next book.

Universalus: (*Looks at audience with a wry expression.*) Well! I'm sure we all look forward to that.

act one ends p. 207

Universalus stands up, follows Uniquio to the door, stage left, they shake hands, and Universalus follows him out the door. From offstage, we hear Universalus say, 'Rosie, please let Mister 'The Rock' know that I'll be with him in a moment.'

The stage goes dark; a spotlight appears, center stage, and Loquatio enters from stage right, into the spotlight. He addresses the audience by rapping, accompanied by music.

Loquatio:

By way of introduction, I'm Loquatio.
I'm the chorus to this one-to-one ratio.
I'm breaking down the story of Uniquio.
In the universal steps of the unique hero.

You see, the hero is you; and see, the hero is me.
And we begin our journey in a world that's ordinary.
And when we leave that world, when it's behind us and gone,
Adventure in the unknown is the path that we're on.

Growing up, our hero had it very structured but nice —
And then he left for education, where he learned about vice.
Free of judgment and rules, his older world was shaken.
Life's adventure lay ahead so that he might awaken.

But he didn't have a goal, and so he didn't have a quest —
Life for him was just a party; it was folly and jest.
While his friends were all beginning
their own path to progress
Uniquio was playing — it seemed his life was a mess.

Or at least that's how the surface of his life would appear.
But the boy was on his way to breaking free of his fear.

He was looking for some 'something,'
breaking through his own walls.
Even though it seemed, to those around him,
stumbles and falls.

But even if it seems that you're refusing the call,
It could be that you're moving forward, after all.
Because the work our witless hero had been heavy-handed,
Was exactly where he needed, at the time, to have landed.

That's all I got for now; it's all I got to say —
Time to get back to the story, and our play about play.
I'll be coming back around, I ain't goin' away,
Cuz' it all comes back around — back to our circular way . . .

It's a circular way . . . to our circular way . . .
you know, a circular way . . .

Loquatio continues repeating 'circular way' as he leaves the stage; his voice echoes the message after he is gone, fading to a silence that hovers a moment before the spotlight goes off. Darkness, silence. The curtain drops.

Scene Two: Session Two.

The curtain rises. Universalus, seated, stands to greet Uniquio, who enters his office through the door, stage left. Assuming (hoping) there is applause, Uniquio reacts with a wave and nod to the audience, tipping his chaplet of garland, like a golfer acknowledging a roaring crowd after making a big putt. (Note to producer: Be prepared to play recording of audience applause, if needed.) The two interact briefly with gestures unrelated to conducting a marching band, and they sit down.

Universalus: When we left off last time (*cups hand over mouth to make voice sound like a 1940's radio broadcaster*) our fearless hero was living at home, getting a degree he didn't want, employed in a job he didn't want, working for a boss he didn't want to work for. Where oh where would the misery end? Don't touch that dial! We're about to find out what happens — in the next exciting episode of *Hero in Therapy!* But first, a message from Camel cigarettes. Remember, folks — more doctors smoke Camels than any other brand!

Uniquio: Wow, someone shot *you* out of a cannon today.

Universalus: I was listening to 1940's radio before you got here.

Uniquio: Do you travel through time between sessions?

Universalus: I'm not limited by time — or space. So I guess you could say I travel through it all. The important thing is I never have to take the bus. I noticed you pretending to be a golfer, walking on the stage.

Uniquio: Is there a version of the multiverse where I play on the PGA Tour?

Universalus: There is, indeed! And you're sponsored by Ping, Bridgestone, and the Bigley Piggly Wiggly in Charleston, West Virginia. There's a backstory on that last sponsorship involving a bet with Rory McIlroy. There's also a version of the multiverse where you're the President of the United States. And in another, you have a long beard, wear a bathrobe and rubber boots, and shout biblical commandments at people in Times Square. But let's discuss your life story in this universe. It was just getting interesting . . .

Uniquio: I have no grand illusions, here. Well, maybe I do sometimes . . .

Univeralus: I should hope that you do!

Uniquio: Well, you did a good job summing up my life when we left off. Not a great time.

Universalus: What's great, and not great? It's all a matter of perspective, isn't it? And you were having a good time — a lot of the time! It was the lack of purpose that was getting you down. Did you have a sense, then, that your life was rather pointless?

Uniquio: (*Stiffens, taken aback by the question.*) Pointless? Well, no. I didn't feel it was pointless. Although I guess it kind of was. There wasn't a lot of self-reflection going on then.

Universalus: You were chasing the elusive pixie through the forest, so to speak. And when you do that, you get more lost without realizing it — unless and until you do.

Uniquio: Well . . . getting back to my story . . . the grad school I attended was near the family home, so I moved back in with my parents to save money for tuition. Once I got my degree, I moved to an apartment in Trenton, near the office. No one ever visited me there, except my mom and dad. The city was a social and cultural void on par with a black hole. One of my brothers visited me once. But he wanted to leave early, claiming he had to go home to shine his shoes. He actually said that, with a straight face.

Univeralus: Sometimes being where you *don't* want to be helps you discover where you *do* want to be. Just as sometimes doing what you *don't* want to do helps you find what you *do* want to do. It's the Emerson thing again . . .

Uniquio: Spending time in Trenton was about the last thing I wanted to do. But because of that, I did discover New Hope.

Universalus: New hope . . . how do you mean?

Uniquio: New Hope is a place. It's a small town on the Pennsylvania side of the Delaware River, about twenty minutes north of Trenton. There's a main street area a block or so from the river; pretty idyllic, really, with these welcoming colonial facades stacked up on the wide sidewalks in a way that made you feel engaged just passing by. There were shops and bars and places to eat, with brightly colored doors and signs, and shallow little porches fronting these large paned glass windows you could see into. With the various wares and decorative items displayed inside and outside the shops, you got a sense of, I don't know, everything being . . . connected.

Universalus: Sounds quaint. And quite the detailed recollection for someone who forgets how to run your own dishwasher. So you found New Hope. The place with the mythological name, which you described with unusual — even, dare I say, literary — detail.

Uniquio: I continue to be surprised by the things that you notice.

Universalus: Are you surprised by your surprise? I'm surprised if you're not.

Uniquio: I remember the first time I went there, to see what it was like. Driving up the county road on the Pennsylvania side of the river, it felt like a different world from Trenton. Anyway, during that first trip up there, I decided to go into this little bookstore.

Universalus: Were you reading a lot at that time?

Uniquio: No, that's the thing. I hadn't read a book in years. Maybe a decade or more.

Universalus: You mean other than the ones you read in college and grad school?

Uniquio: I read the minimum to get by in school. I think that may have been the first time I set out to look for a book that I *wanted* to read since I was in the high school library.

Universalus: Do you remember why — what interested you, now, after all that time?

Uniquio: Not really. I just . . . wandered in. I kind of remember an unusually strong impulse, almost like I was being pulled. Maybe I'm projecting, I don't know. But one thing I do know: It ended up changing my life.

Univeralus: You know, there's a lot of hero journey symbolism in what you're describing.

Uniquio: Yeah, that's dawning on me as I'm sharing this. Kind of crazy. Anyway, I gravitated toward the literature section, and browsed around for something familiar. I picked up *Rabbit, Run* by John Updike, and decided to buy it.
Universalus: Why that book?
Uniquio: I remembered Updike's name from a short story collection I had read in high school. The story he wrote was called 'A&P.' It was about a teenage boy who worked at a grocery store. It happened to be where my dad went grocery shopping, across the street from my high school. He went there all the time. It became a family joke, him going there so often. (*Pauses.*) Sorry about that. Went off on a bit of a tangent there.
Universalus: Maybe it was a tangent. Maybe it was something else.
Uniquio: (*Pauses, appears thoughtful a moment.*) Are you seeing something I'm not?
Universalus: Is that a rhetorical question?
Uniquio: Right. So anyway, I bought the Updike book. And I read it. And I decided I wanted to be a writer. Not just any writer — I wanted to be a writer like John Updike.
Universalus: Just like that?
Uniquio: Just like that. After that, I began buying books all the time, reading a lot of literature. I read a lot of different authors from different times and parts of the world; though I kept reading Updike — his novels, and short stories, and eventually even some of his essays. It felt sometimes like he was writing over my head, but the honesty, and the quality, and the distinctive voice in his work — the eloquent way he could describe something on the surface that reflected the human experience beneath it . . . I just remember thinking, wow, this guy is a *writer*. This is what writing's all about. And so I wanted to write like him. I know it sounds ridiculous, but I tried.
Universalus: Voltaire said originality is nothing more than

act one ends p. 207

judicious imitation. People need a starting point before creating their own way, and often the best way is to emulate what you admire. Creativity requires structure, a system through which it can manifest.

Uniquio: In one of the highlights of my life, I got to ask John Updike a question about writing, and he answered it. He was doing a live interview on NPR, and they used my question as the final one in the interview. I didn't get on the air for it, but the interviewer said my name and asked my question.

Universalus: Wow! What did you ask him?

Uniquio: I asked him who his influences were, and when he felt that he had broken free of those influences and found his own voice.

Universalus: That *is* pretty cool. What did he say?

Uniquio: I was so excited that John Updike was answering *my* question on *his* writing that I didn't hear the entire answer. He named three authors who influenced him, but I missed one of the names. The two I did hear were Nabokov and Proust. I want to say the third was Dostoevsky, but I can't say for sure. I do remember Updike saying that he didn't think he had found his voice yet. He said it was an ongoing process. I thought that was an interesting answer, from someone so accomplished. I was kind of surprised by it, but encouraged.

Universalus: Did you change your writing after that, trying to find your own voice?

Uniquio: Maybe, a little. But then, maybe not so much. I kept trying to write in a style that I imagined serious writing should be. With a serious tone, and serious characters, dealing with serious things. I took myself seriously as a writer.

Universalus: At least you were taking something in your life seriously.

Uniquio: I wonder, though, if I wasn't more focused on

'being a writer' than on writing. The idea of being a writer gave me a sense of purpose, and self-importance, and *pride* — none of which I felt, doing the job I was doing. Kind of silly, I guess.

Universalus: No need to judge who you were, or what you did. That's not why we're here. Besides, while a sense of self-importance and pride are generally self-defeating, that sense of purpose you experienced was positive, and important.

Uniquio: (*Shrugs.*) It was around that time that I met a new girlfriend. She was into I guess you'd call them 'artsy' things — alternative music, foreign films, stuff like that. Anyway, she was into literature; different writers than I was reading. And she introduced me to Henry Miller, Anais Nin, Camille Paglia, the Marquis de Sade . . .

Universalus: Some edgy stuff there.

Uniquio: I ended up really loving Henry Miller. I read all of his big novels. And I checked out writers who he talked about, like Knut Hamsen, and Krishnamurti, who I otherwise may not have heard of. It definitely helped broaden my horizons. Although . . . well, do you know the Dirty Harry line, 'A man's gotta know his limitations?'

Universalus: What do you think, I'm able to see everything in the universe except Clint Eastwood movies?

Uniquio: Right. Well, I learned some things about myself, knowing R——. I guess you could say I discovered I was more conventional about some things than I realized.

Universalus: How do you mean?

Uniquio: In terms of my 'social and recreational choices,' put it that way.

Universalus: We can put it any way you like, but what you *really* mean is that you came to realize you were less open about some things than you wanted to admit to yourself then.

Uniquio: Okay, fine. She was a little more 'out there' — or,

I don't know, *wild* — than what made me comfortable sometimes. But I liked her, I found her interesting, and she was very encouraging about my writing. Maybe the first person who ever was.

Universalus: She was, then, perhaps, a muse . . .

Uniquio: I didn't think of her that way at the time, but you're probably right.

Universalus: (*Looks at audience.*) 'Probably,' he says.

Uniquio: We eventually broke up; I honestly forget why.

Universalus: And so you broke it off with your muse . . .

Uniquio: Well, it ended. Again, I don't recall how or why. But sometime after that, R—— called to tell me she was living with a couple of people in a big old house in West Philadelphia; she told me they needed a roommate, and she wanted to know if I was interested. I didn't know the other people, and I wasn't sure I wanted to live in the same house as R——, but I went ahead and did it. I wanted to get out of Trenton, and moving to a big city like Philadelphia interested me a lot.

Univeralus: Sounds like you made an affirmative decision. As opposed to a passive non-decision, like you had been making with your schools, your studies, your jobs . . .

Uniquio: I guess. Although a door had to open first.

Universalus: But you chose to walk through it.

Uniquio: I did. And I was able to experience living in a big city, on my own. It was a different world. There was always somewhere new to explore, something to do. I think the best part was knowing I could get up at any time and go . . . anywhere. It gave me a sense of freedom, and possibilities.

Universalus: So you were paying your bills in an unfulfilling job, enjoying the experience of living in a big city. You lived in two worlds, connected by I-95. I think they did a *Twilight Zone* episode about that. Or a John Waters film. No . . . what am I thinking of?

Uniquio: I have no idea.

Universalus: Anyway. (*Pauses.*) Were you writing then?

Uniquio: Not really. There were a lot of distractions, I guess. And I never felt settled, living in that house. My roommates and I all lived separate lives. We hardly saw each other, and rarely even talked when we did. I was still reading a lot, but I don't recall doing any writing.

Universalus: Does that matter for your writing — feeling settled?

Uniquio: It took me years to realize it, but yes, it absolutely does. I've never been productive writing unless I feel settled with my home life.

Universalus: So life was more interesting, living in the big city. But you weren't writing because you felt unsettled. (*Pauses, nods.*) Okay. I get that.

Uniquio: The social dynamic in the house was . . . odd. The other guy who lived there particularly annoyed me. He was one of those artsy intellectual poser types, but I thought he was a moron. I think that had to do with the fact that he was a moron. And I'd hear gunshots from my room at night. *That* was unsettling. I think I got used to it, although the second time someone broke into my car, I felt vulnerable, living there. That's when I decided to try martial arts. Which wasn't exactly on my radar to pursue, until it was . . .

Universalus: Another venture into the unknown . . .

Uniquio: I had always wanted to be able to defend myself. When I was twelve, *Kung Fu* was my favorite TV show, and I wanted to be like the main character, Kwai Chang Caine — he was like a real-life superhero to me.

Universalus: He did, in fact, have a superpower: He had no ego.

Uniquio: Seeing that in a heroic figure, his humility being such a defining part of his character — that was new to me. *And* he could kick anyone's ass — and did, when needed, which you always like to see in your favorite hero. At least

I do. Anyway, for whatever reason, I made up my mind to try it. This was before the internet, so I found a place in the Yellow Pages. It was just a couple of blocks from our house, walking distance. The neighborhood wasn't great, but I figured I wouldn't need to deal with parking.

Universalus: Ah, yes, the Yellow Pages! For a world without internet . . .

Uniquio: Not to get off track, here, but will the internet save us or destroy us?

Universal: Absolutely. It's happening now.

Uniquio: *What's* happening now?

Universalus: The internet is contributing to saving *and* destroying humanity.

Uniquio: But I'm asking, which one happens?

Universalus: That's up to you. All of you. I will say that social media platforms make it incredibly easy to feed the ego — for those who create content, and those who consume it. It's the main reason why they're so popular. And the destructive intention behind a lot of the content is self-evident. But enough about the future. Let's get back to your past. You decided to try a martial art. Which, properly practiced, promotes humility and diminishes the ego. You saw this in your TV hero.

Uniquio: *Practiced properly*. That's right. Although I didn't realize that when I decided to try it. Which happened suddenly. I walked over one night, watched a class, and signed up on the spot. No research. No sales pitch from anyone. The next night, I was training. Just like that, it became a regular part of my life. A *big* part of my life. It changed my life. In a positive way.

Universalus: That's a big commitment of time and effort to make so suddenly.

Uniquio: Once I started, it was almost easy to stay with it. I mean, the training was hard — the most physically and mentally challenging thing I had ever done — even more than playing soccer, which I did for a lot of years, and put a lot of effort into it. But the decision to stay with it, and keep training, was easy. It never crossed my mind to quit.

Universalus: Why do you think it resonated with you?

Uniquio: I think it was the challenge, and the quality of the experience. I didn't know it for my first six months there, but this turned out to be the dojo of a renowned Japanese karate master named Teruyuki Okazaki.

Universalus: Wow, that's some mentor. This experience helped to ground you.

Uniquio: My mom used to say she thought training saved my life.

Universalus: She's right. It did. You were making progress in life, but you were also a lot more lost than you realized, and so you weren't aware of the importance of the progress. You needed the testing of yourself. And you needed the mentoring. You needed a big change in life, to grow. This was all stuff you understood *innately*, though not consciously.

Uniquio: While I was learning how to defend myself against a physical attack, I was learning to defend against my 'self.' Master Okazaki always said we trained to develop ourselves.

Universalus: Self-defense training. As defense against the self. I like that! So . . . did training help your writing?

Uniquio: Indirectly, I think. It settled me down enough to create a space to meet T——, who became the most important relationship of my life, to that point. She eventually inspired me to write a novel.

Universalus: You wrote a novel?

Uniquio: I never tried to publish it. But I did write one. And T—— was a big reason why I set out to do it. It was her commitment to her own work, and how much of herself she put into it, that motivated me to do the same with writing. T—— had a much better sense of who she was and what she

act one ends p. 207

wanted to be than I did. She had a clear goal and worked hard toward it.

Universalus: That set an example for you.

Uniquio: I think so. I began writing short stories again; and then T—— bought me a word processor for my birthday, and I decided to make use of it by writing a novel.

Universalus: Ah, yes, the word processor! The most short-lived writing tool in human history, between 'typewriter' and 'home computer.' Were you still trying to write like John Updike?

Uniquio: I guess I was, to some degree, but less so than before. I was less conscious about the style of my writing and a lot more focused on the content — on the 'message.'

Universalus: You wanted to impart to the world all your wisdom, even though you were pretty much lost and rudderless.

Uniquio: That sounds about right. I came to realize, or at least believe, that the novel was an effort to justify my worldview — part autobiographical, part fantasy.

Universalus: Not unlike this play.

Uniquio: Except I think the novel was more of a justification for my ego, whereas this play is more of an acknowledgment and . . . I guess a kind of apology for it.

Universalus: I'll buy that.

Uniquio: I should mention that it was around this time that I discovered another big influence, Joseph Campbell. Ironically, the friend who introduced me to Campbell became very religious, and eventually adopted the belief that dinosaur bones were planted by the Devil to fool people into believing science instead of the Bible. He adopted the exact opposite worldview of the Campbell perspective he had opened me to. It was hard to understand. That 'dinosaur bones' conversation was one of the last times we ever talked, I think.

Universalus: People need to believe different things, for different reasons.

Uniquio: Sure. I understand that. And I'm grateful J—— introduced me to Campbell before he needed to adopt beliefs contradicting all facts, evidence, and science. He also introduced me to a guy I would become good friends with — a sculptor who would encourage me with my writing. He was the first person I ever met who I could have conversations with about the creative process. You don't meet a lot of people you can talk to about that stuff. At least I don't meet a lot of them.

Universalus: Everything happens for a reason, they say. Or at least some of them say it. Although I have to say, I don't think they know exactly what it is they're saying when they say it. That said, your sculptor friend was an ally on your hero journey. So, too, was the friend who introduced him to you.

Uniquio: I watched Bill Moyers' series of interviews with Campbell, *The Power of Myth*. I read the transcript, too. And then I started reading some of his other stuff. His ideas changed my worldview.

Universalus: I assume Campbell influenced your thinking about the Catholicism of your childhood.

Uniquio: Yes, well. One of the big things I got from him was learning that an undefinable God could be . . . not just 'defined' in some humanized, limiting way, as an outside force in my life, but actually *experienced*, as a part of me. Campbell's perspective and insights made God more relatable for me.

Universalus: He helped you see things differently.

Uniquio: He helped me see that something can be historically nonfactual but metaphorically true — and that the metaphorical truth, understanding its relation to your own life, was what helped you with life. He pointed out basic similarities between religious stories and teachings, and he

act one ends p. 207

explained them as basic truths that come from the human psyche — the collective unconscious, as Jung put it — to help us relate to what is otherwise unknowable.

Universalus: I've got a soapbox offstage if you want me to roll it out for you now. It's a big wooden box, and it has the word 'soap' on it. Like a Bugs Bunny cartoon . . .

Uniquio: I'm just trying to say that Campbell made sense of religion for me — in general, and the specific one I was raised in. He explained why dogma existed.

Universalus: People want to believe *their* culture's version of God, because of ego. It's the old '*my* culture is better than *your* culture' thing, and so *I'm* better than *you*. It's a very old thing. It still exists today — in a big way. (*Gestures toward the windows.*) Around here, it's a lot of *Zeus* this, and *Zeus* that. Please, with all the Zeus! Give *me* Dr. Seuss!

Uniquio: I like that!

Universalus: Yes, well . . . you wrote it.

Uniquio: Right. You know, I even forget *that*, sometimes. It's easy to get lost in this whole process. With the different . . . I don't know, the different *layers* to it, I guess . . .

Universalus: More layers than you realize. And yet also we are removing them all.

Uniquio: *That*, I don't understand. But I guess I do. Anyway, Campbell explained the limitations of religion, but he also acknowledged that, for some people — not all, but for some — religious belief was the key that unlocked the door to the enlightenment and joy of a true connection to Life itself.

Universalus: That's right. And for some people, religion is an excuse for selfishness. 'How much or how little a belief may be true all amounts to how it opens, or closes, you.'

Uniquio: That's one of my favorite lines from the prologue. Maybe my favorite.

Universalus: Mine, too.

Uniquio: My Catholic upbringing had its positives. Jesus was the ultimate leader by example. He showed us through his actions how to manifest God in our lives — through love. And I have no doubt that the concept of the Holy Trinity helped me understand what I now believe to be true — that God manifests through our physical form of being in our mental and emotional forms of being.

Universalus: As the Being of your being.

Uniquio: I didn't understand the idea of it as a kid, but if you look at the Holy Trinity as a *metaphor*, it makes sense.

Universalus: But as a Catholic kid blessing yourself, you had no idea that you were saying that 'I am a manifestation of God.'

Uniquio: No idea. You did it because everyone else did it at certain points in the mass ritual, and it didn't cross your mind to *not* do it. You figured there'd be some kind of reckoning if you didn't do it. Like it was a kind of voodoo maneuver you performed to avoid trouble.

Universalus: As I recall, you did it *after* you struck out in a Little League game.

Uniquio: I think it's what I thought I saw them do on TV. My coach explained that I was only supposed to bless myself either *before* I got up to the plate, or *after* I got a hit.

Universalus: So Campbell gave you the most powerful tool of all: Perspective.

Uniquio: He helped me develop my faith in the idea that if you open yourself to what's within you, and 'follow your bliss,' then it will take you where — and what — you're meant to be.

Universalus: But even as you became, let's say, 'enlightened' to this idea, you were also well on your way to becoming a colossal wee-wee.

Uniquio: Or maybe I always was one, or had been for a while, and it came out in a way that got to be increasingly self-destructive.

Universalus: Sometimes you have to go through hell to get to heaven.

act one ends p. 207

Uniquio: Did you just quote a Steve Miller Band song?
Universalus: I did.
Uniquio: No William Blake or Walt Whitman quote? I mean . . . Steve Miller?
Universalus: You were being a wee-wee. You want me to polish that up with poetry?
Uniquio: Good point. Okay. Well, with T—— being so involved in her work, and never seeming to mind if I went out without her, I carved out my own life. It was all about me.
Universalus: People very often try to feed the hole inside with something from the outside — looking outside to the near-exclusion of the inside.
Uniquio: I didn't want to look inside. (*Pauses.*) And didn't know that I didn't want to look.
Universalus: That's usually how it works, when things aren't working.
Uniquio: I would leave the apartment on a Saturday morning, and not show up again until late Saturday night. And it was all . . . aimless. I did a lot of wandering around, walking down a street or sitting on a bench because I felt like it. I had to do something, being alive. Why not follow what I was naturally inclined to do? I'd pop into a few bars, inevitably . . .
Universalus: At what point did this cause problems with T——?
Uniquio: I don't know. It wasn't a problem. Or didn't seem to be. And then it was. I'm sure it was something that felt gradual at the time, but it seems it happened suddenly, in retrospect. My parents showed up one weekend because of it.
Universalus: To confront the problem.
Uniquio: There was a confrontation. With my dad. Which I somehow made about my writing. We were both upset with each other, and at one point he said he had always wanted to be a professional baseball player, but gave up his dream, implying it was a practicality or act of selflessness or

something like that. Meanwhile he had never even played high school baseball, so playing for the Yankees wasn't exactly a real option for him.

Universalus: How did you respond to that?

Uniquio: It set me off. I told him not to hold *me* back just because *he* didn't have the talent or put in the work to realize his own dream. Then I walked out. I'm sure it was incredibly painful for everyone involved. But at the time, I didn't care. At all.

Universalus: You were breaking away from an older version of your 'self.' It's often a destructive process, and those closest to you bear the biggest brunt of it.

Uniquio: I wanted understanding for something I didn't understand.

Universalus: What would they know to say? Your dad, especially — a man of few words. You were in the field of the unknown. He was concerned for you. Likely, afraid.

Uniquio: I can see that. And understand it.

Universalus: You were breaking free of your 'nots,' as you might put it now.

Uniquio: I let my relationship with T—— dissolve to nothing after that. We were living together but living separate lives. She moved out, eventually. And I never really saw her again. From there it was a quick spiral downward. Which, of course, I didn't see — for a while, anyway.

Universalus: The irony of being self-absorbed: You don't see yourself.

Uniquio: And so you don't see much at all. You miss . . . a lot.

Universalus: Were you training at the time?

Uniquio: I was training all the time. I can't imagine what would have happened to me without karate. It was my one ballast in life. I was now chain-smoking while writing; and the writing itself . . . I felt connected to it, but it wasn't fun, the way it is now. It wasn't fun because I wasn't doing what I enjoyed most — writing humor.

Universalus: Which you haven't done, at all, for several pages now — but okay, we're getting through your story, and your self-absorption manifested in some self-destructive behavior — the details of which we're downplaying and really ignoring although let's just say you were going in circles, chasing your own tail, so to speak.

Uniquio: Tail-chasing and destructive habitual behaviors — yeah, there was a lot of that.

Universalus: The obsessive pursuit of Circe is a prison of self-destruction.

Uniquio: That's a pretty good metaphor. Some myths put it out there plainly.

Universalus: Really, most of them do. You mentioned you weren't having fun because you weren't writing humor. Which you're not writing now. Which is why no one is having fun reading it. Although some readers are possibly projecting different versions of fun on to this, filling in the blanks on those self-destructive behaviors you alluded to but didn't specify. I'm picturing a character that's a cross between Virgil Starkwell and Hank the Tank.

Uniquio: Really?

Universalus: No, not really. I'm just bringing up lovable and harmless movie characters to smooth over the reader's speculations on what a wee-wee you were.

Uniquio: That was thoughtful of you. But getting back to the humor writing . . .

Universalus: (*Cutting off Uniquio*) Yes — let's, please.

Uniquio: I was about to say, I guess I always knew that humor was what I enjoyed writing most. I had written little things here and there, but it never really occurred to me to make it my focus, until I heard the writer Frank McCourt speak. I saw him at a book tour event. He was probably the most engaging speaker I ever experienced in person — him, and Colin Powell, and then later, my friend, P——, who spoke at his wife's funeral. All three were incredibly powerful, in their own way; and while I'll never remember the specific words spoken, I remember the feeling I had, hearing them. Incredible experiences, listening to all of them. McCourt was light-hearted, though he spoke of dark experiences. It amazed me that he could do that.

Universalus: Perspective allows for humor. Humor allows for perspective.

Uniquio: I could have listened to him talk all night. I bought his book, *Angela's Ashes*; and as I read it, I became aware of how I was taking myself, and my novel's story, *way* too seriously. I mean, this guy had every reason to have a dark worldview. And instead, he saw his childhood with the light, the lightness, of humor.

Universalus: And so, the light went on for you.

Uniquio: More like a thunderbolt hitting me: I always enjoyed reading humor. How did I not realize that before! Ever since I'd read that Woody Allen book at the school library. I always liked the witty writers best, like Oscar Wilde, Mark Twain, Dorothy Parker. And then modern humorists like Dave Barry and David Sedaris, who both make me laugh out loud. I had the most fun reading them. I mean, I got something out of reading authors like Dostoevsky and Thomas Mann, but it wasn't what I'd call fun. Reading humor was fun.

Universalus: And who doesn't like fun!

Uniquio: That's how I came to realize that I needed to write humor. It didn't matter the subject, it just mattered that I wrote in a way to amuse myself. To me, that's the most fun kind of writing, and one of the most fun things for me to do, period. It's joyful.

Universalus: What happened with your self-absorbed and self-important novel?

Uniquio: After I had this revelation — and it really *was* a revelation, even though what dawned on me was incredibly obvious — I set out to rewrite the entire novel as a satire. It took me another two years to rewrite it, I think. And then once I was finished, I hardly tried to publish it. Instead, I started writing short stories, all of them satire. It was the most fun I ever had writing. By far. And I think it turned out to be my best writing. Although, again, I never tried publishing anything — not really.

Universalus: Why not? I mean, I *know* why not, but I'd like to know what you think.

Uniquio: It didn't seem that the small literary magazines that published new writers had much of an interest in humor. I never saw it, anyway. Mostly it seemed the stories they published were about death and disappointment.

Universalus: It's funny how the editors of those magazines don't seem to see the importance of humor. I say funny, but I mean absurd, close-minded, and stupid. Not to be judgmental, but hello! There's a veritable pantheon of great literature that is satire.

Uniquio: It was frustrating. I sent in a few stories, entered a couple of contests you had to pay to enter — what a scam! But after getting turned down those few times, I figured, why bother. The bottom line is I gave up. Maybe I just couldn't deal with the rejection. Although now, after spending more than ten years writing this book, I'm not at all worried about getting this published. I know it will happen somehow. I know *it's happening*.

Universalus: Well, self-publishing is an option now. Anyone can publish a book. But you believe in this, and that's the thing. Even though you already got rejected by a bunch of literary agents before you decided to write the prologue and use it to promote the book.

Uniquio: I do believe in it. More now than ever. I think the thing I still struggle with is that I'm not quite sure I really believe in me.

Universalus: Oh, *for sure*, that's your problem. You still need to let go of all the crap Toni Morrison was talking about, so you can fly. Then you can effortlessly practice what you've been preaching: Self-belief. It's there. You just haven't cleared the way for it to fully manifest. You've made good progress, son, but you need to keep going.

Uniquio: I'm still in my own way.

Universalus: But you *are* finding your way. And *this* is the way. And speaking of the way, we've gotten away from *your* way. We need to get back to your story.

Uniquio: I had enough confidence in my writing to quit my job of thirteen years — the first professional job my dad had helped me get. Looking back on it, I had a pretty easy job I could have stayed in until I retired — with a good pension and lifetime health benefits from the state. But I was unhappy. Discontent. Angry, sometimes.

Universalus: You walked away from the job to get away from those feelings, thinking the job was the cause of them. It wasn't the job. It was you staying in the job.

Uniquio: I think so. And I thought so at the time. So I quit and moved to Los Angeles. My girlfriend at the time suggested we move there to live with her sister, who was out there trying to become an actress. C——'s sister had a two-bedroom condo in North Hollywood, so we had a place to stay, and we just went ahead and did it. We loaded our stuff in a rental truck, I put my car on a trailer, and we moved across the country.

Universalus: You had crossed a major threshold, moving to Philadelphia. And now you did it again, moving further away from home — and everyone you knew and loved.

Uniquio: And I did it with no job lined up, no safety net — and really, not much of a plan. With someone who I had met and moved in with right away — just like that. With no plan.

Universalus: Just like that. And 'just like that' is how you described your decision to walk into the New Hope bookstore; become a writer; move to Philadelphia; start karate training; write a novel; focus on writing humor. All decisions you made 'just like that.' But there was a lot more than 'just that' that went into it.

Uniquio: I still can't get over what I'm learning from this conversation.

Universalus: And just like that, you decided to move in with someone you hardly knew; then quit your job of thirteen years; then moved to California — with no job lined up. You went from being very passive in your teenage years to very decisive in your twenties and thirties. You trusted your instincts. Nearly without inhibition. It probably seemed reckless to your family and friends.

Uniquio: The idea with the California move was for me to somehow find a gig writing comedy for a TV show. Except when I got out there, I learned you had to be a part of a usually big team of writers, and if you somehow got a job, you'd be lucky to get a line or two that made it to final script. I didn't want to do that — not enough to put the effort into making the connections and getting the rejections. My view was — and, really, still is — if you're not creating all or at least most of the work, why bother?

Universalus: Again, with the need to control your circumstance.

Uniquio: One of my favorite things about writing is being fully in charge. There's no debating what I'm going to write, how I'm going to write. No boss self-assured that he knows more than me, telling me what to write. Of course, it would have been helpful to learn about the TV-writing scene *before* quitting my job and moving across the country, but I wasn't big on planning back then, so I had to learn the hard way.

Universalus: Research and planning can certainly help sometimes — especially when making significant life choices. But it seems as if you never did that from the time you had those life choices. And so of course you didn't do it when you quit your job and moved across the country.

Uniquio: I always felt things would work out. Or maybe

it's more accurate to say that I never had a sense that they wouldn't work out. Maybe they're the same.

Universalus: In a sense, they are. So what happened? You were out there, after all — unemployed and living in someone else's home.

Uniquio: I ended up doing a little standup comedy. I figured, since I was out there, I may as well try it. I did it for a while, doing 'open mics' at most of the big comedy clubs in L.A.

Universalus: How did you do, with the standup?

Uniquio: I did okay, I guess. I had some fun, got a couple of laughs. At some point, well, like anything else in life, doing standup required full commitment to be successful, and I realized my heart wasn't into it. Maybe it was where I was in my life — literally, and in terms of my perspective. I never felt at home in L.A. I missed my friends and family. I missed the familiar environment of home — even the weather.

Universalus: I thought people on the East Coast complained a lot about the weather.

Uniquio: We do. We complain about a lot of things. And then we go somewhere else and brag about how great it is back home to people from other parts of the country.

Universalus: I've noticed that. And you do it without any sense of contradiction.

Uniquio: My family was a bit of a microcosm of that whole concept. We could and would get irritated with and complain about each other, but no one from outside the family was able to do that without having all of us against you. We expected the rest of the world to see our value and treat us accordingly. Even if we could all be a gigantic pain in the ass to each other.

Universalus: And your own ego is a bit of a microcosm of that concept, on an individual level. It's the most common human attribute to be self-destructive, and then get defensive when you perceive an outside force negatively impacting your life. Especially when that negativity is expressed in

act one ends p. 207

a form that reflects your own shortcomings. So you realized you missed the East Coast — the family and friends.

Uniquio: I was living in L.A. during the 9/11 attack, and that only added to my anxiety, being away. I also missed having my own place, and health insurance, and a steady income. I never fully appreciated those things until I didn't have them anymore. Now, I would say I shouldn't have worried about all of that, but I did then. It was hard for me to write, without having that foundation. That sense of stability.

Universalus: You stopped writing when you first moved to Philadelphia as well. And you didn't pick it up again until you established a sense of 'home.' You need stability to be creative. Maybe it's because that was what you grew up to know. Maybe it's how you're wired. Maybe it's both.

Uniquio: We should have had this conversation thirty years ago.

Universalus: It would have been a much different conversation.

Uniquio: I guess you're right.

Universalus: Good guess! We're making progress.

Uniquio: By the time my money ran out, the relationship with C—— had run its course as well, so just as suddenly as I had moved to Los Angeles, I moved back East.

Universalus: I think there's a Steve Miller song about doing that as well . . .

Uniquio: I needed income, so I worked at a supermarket deli, and then waited tables, which I'd never done before. I ended up working at the same restaurant my co-workers had taken me to celebrate my resignation, before moving to L.A.

Universalus: Ouch. *That's* humbling.

Uniquio: The 'humbling' devolved into 'humiliating' when a few of my former co-workers came in for lunch to see me one day. It was bad enough, serving them lunch in my waiter's outfit, you know, with the white shirt and black vest and bowtie. But then I spilled someone's lunch all over myself — right in front of everyone. I flipped a tray in a way so that an entire plate of pasta with red sauce hit me in the chest. While wearing my aforementioned white shirt.

Universalus: Sounds like a George Costanza moment.

Uniquio: I wanted a very large rock to hide under. You reflect on your entire life and what you're doing with it in moments like that. At least I did. It was the emotional equivalent of a giant anvil landing on my head and driving me into the ground, leaving behind a big hole with a puff of smoke above it.

Universalus: Yeah . . . that's a Yosemite Sam wallop to the ego, alright. At that moment, it seemed you had failed. Rather spectacularly, I might add! But every success is preceded by what seems to be points of failure along the way. They can be points of inflection, to change direction.

Uniquio: I was back to training, at least. And Master Okazaki gave me a job. I worked at the dojo every day, doing all the writing for the organization, including a transcript of a book for Sensei — a book about the meaning and purpose of karate training. I got to spend hours interviewing him, and then writing the first draft of his book.[10] It was a great experience.

Universalus: Back with your much-needed mentor. All of that had to be good for you.

Uniquio: It was. I never felt better, physically — and because I was working at the dojo, I had to go to Sensei's summer Master Camp. It was an annual camp where you trained under karate masters from Japan and other parts of the world — three times a day. Normally I skipped camp because I didn't want to spend my vacation time training all day and then sleeping in a cabin with a dozen grown

---

[10] *Perfection of Character: Guiding Principles for the Martial Arts and Everyday Life* by Teruyuki Okazaki (2006).

act one ends p. 207

men. I loved karate, but not that much. But because it was my job, I had to be there, and I had to attend every training.
Universalus: Structure can be constructive — when it's not too constrictive.
Uniquio: Structure has always been helpful for me, doing something I care about.
Universalus: The key is finding the right balance. Living with 'all structure' or 'no structure at all' can create . . . imbalance. And that's a problem.
Uniquio: In addition to the training and running errands in between, it was my job to interview the other masters who were there to teach. It was a busy week, but I had a great time. Our cabin was a mix of guys from Philly and Louisiana, which was a lot of fun — a lot of laughs. And the best part was that I met my wife, J——. She was there training with a group from a club in Athens, Ohio.
Universalus: And here we are, in Athens, Greece.
Uniquio: Oh, yeah!
Universalus: Oh, yeah, indeed. Sleepover camp isn't usually ideal for romance, unless you're in the sixth grade. How did things move forward with your wife?
Uniquio: We went to Philly one night for dinner — the city was about 45 minutes from camp. A mutual friend had put in a good word for me with J——, so she agreed to that first date. After that, we stayed in touch, and visited each other, and eventually J—— moved to my place. I was living in a two-story rowhome down the street from the art museum, on 26th Street. By now I had a second job with another nonprofit — mostly working from home, so I could still work at the dojo — and I was able to afford a decent place, in a great neighborhood.
Universalus: It sounds like you had 'made it through' to safety.
Uniquio: I had a steady income, health benefits, an apartment of my own; I was training all the time; and now I had

someone in my life; the last and most important relationship of all.

Universalus: Sounds like you met J—— when you were ready to meet her.

Uniquio: I think so. And I forgot to mention, it wasn't long before that, while I was in a karate tournament in Manhattan, that I experienced something — I mean, I don't know how else to explain it, but it was a very clear message from the universe that you should never be deterred, by anyone or anything, when you make up your mind to do something — especially something to expand your perspective.

Universalus: Here we go with another contrived segue, but I'll bite. So what happened?

Uniquio: One of my friends from Philadelphia had never been to the top of the Empire State Building, so after the Saturday competition was over, we decided to go. It was a cloudy day; and when we arrived, we could see from the ground the building disappearing into the clouds. We figured it would be cool to be up there, in the clouds, even if we couldn't see anything, so we decided to go up anyway. Three times, on the way up, we were told by someone who worked there that we shouldn't bother because there was no visibility. Buying tickets, handing the tickets to someone, and then at the elevator, we were told, literally, 'There's nothing to see here today.'

Universalus: But you went anyway.

Uniquio: We went anyway. And we ended up seeing what was, to me, to this day, the most spectacular sight I have ever seen in my life. Somehow, when we got to the top, the clouds had completely cleared, and we found ourselves beneath a giant rainbow that extended from New Jersey, over Manhattan, into Brooklyn. The rainbow was so large — it was about three-quarters of a full circle; and it had to be *miles* long. I mean, it was unbelievable. I could see it looking in one direction, turn around completely, and see the other

act one ends next p.

side of it. And it remained there; it didn't disappear on us, like rainbows sometimes do. I thought about those people telling us not to bother coming up there, because there was 'nothing to see.'

Universalus: Well, that's certainly a much better way to end the first half of your story than random banter about the words 'schmooze' and 'hobnob.' (*Pauses, smiles.*) And as it is with all endings, really, it's the starting point, for a new beginning.

Uniquio: I had forgotten about that rainbow story. You could see the beginning and the end of it, but I guess I couldn't tell which was which.

Universalus: The universe does communicate to us, important messages, all the time — but we only receive them when we're paying attention. It's why it's important to be open. To be present. Receptive to 'what is.'

Uniquio and Universalus rise, walk to the door, stage left, shake hands, and exit. The stage goes dark, the spotlight falls, and Loquatio enters it from stage right and addresses the audience:

Loquatio:

Our hero found new hope inside a little bookstore,
Discovering a writer as his writing mentor.
And now our writer's writing, life is suddenly exciting —
Helped along by all the muses and
the mentors for his fighting.

He moves into the unknown through
a choice without committee —
Reading, training, learning — living life in the big city.
New people in his life, helped him
create some new connections,

Opening his worldview and expanding his reflections.

But then there's confrontation, and it turns to conflagration
And he finds that self-destruction is a painful education.
Wandering and searching, self-absorbed, he was blind —
To what was there inside of him, he still couldn't find.

Another mentor then alighted when he needed a light,
Helping teach him humor was 'the way' he needed to write.
He found his fun on the inside;
he found no need to go further,
But he still kept seeing life a lot like Goethe's young Werther.

And then he crossed another threshold,
quit his job to go West,
Still uncertain of the purpose of his uncertain quest.
And there he realized, with humility,
that he needed some stability —
He needed a foundation to let go with his ability.

He came back East with nothing,
faced more trials and testing,
But learning home was 'everything'
was worth time investing.
And so the time had come for our good hero's return,
But there was still much left to rediscover and learn.

That's all I got for now; it's all I got to say —
Time to get back to the story, and our play about play.
I'll be coming back around, I ain't goin' away,
Cuz' it all comes back around — back to our circular way . . .

To our circular way . . . it's a circular way . . .
yeah a circular way . . .

Loquatio departs stage and, again, his message continues to echo after he disappears, eventually fading to silence. The stage goes dark.

ACT TWO: RETURNING HOME

The setting remains the same for the second act, only there is a new billboard visible outside through the large office window. It says in bold letters, 'THE END IS NEAR!' But we don't know if it's intended to mean for humanity, or the play. Also there is a new plant on the desk.

Scene Three: Session Three

Curtain rises, and Universalus is watering his new plant. Uniquio enters through the door, stage left, and the two acknowledge each other. Assuming the audience is applauding wildly (or an applause machine was purchased, and it properly functions), both wave in acknowledgment of the loud cheering. Waving continues as they greet each other and move to their chairs, until the applause dies (volume is turned) down; Universalus gestures to Uniquio to sit down, and both are seated.

Universalus: (*Irrespective if the applause was real or canned.*) Wow. What an audience! Good to see you. And by that, I do mean that it's good for *me*, to see *you*. How's it going?
Uniquio: It's going pretty well, I suppose. How's it going with you?
Universalus: Infinitely, transcendently sublime. (*Shrugs.*) The usual.
Uniquio: (*Nods, as if he understands.*) And yet you still find time for sarcasm and silliness.
Universalus: You have to have a little fun while participating in the field of time and space. Otherwise, what's the point? You point that out as a point of your book. (*Peers down at notes in his lap, looks through a couple of pages.*)

When we left off last time, you had made it back to a sort of safety zone in life.

Uniquio: Yeah, I, uh, suppose you could say that once things got——

Universalus: (*Abruptly cuts off Uniquio in mid-sentence and sings into an invisible microphone.*) Uniquio had made . . . it . . . to . . . the . . . safety zone. *Safety* zone . . .

Uniquio: Please tell me that's not the melody to 'Danger Zone' by Kenny Loggins.

Universalus: (*Nods his head up and down, still singing in a sort of high-pitched voice.*) That's right, my guy had made . . . it . . . to . . . the . . . safety zone. *Safety* zone . . .

Uniquio: You know, I thought the semi-normal start to the conversation was a little odd.

Universalus: I gave thought to what you had said, about how you felt as a kid, reading novels, wanting the main character to 'get through' the dangerous situation, the conflict, to a place of safety. It's what makes stories about heroes compelling: They get in dangerous situations, and the audience or reader wants to continue to pay attention, to see if and how they get out of it. You felt that enough as a young reader that you remembered the feeling. It stayed with you and is part of you. It's who you are. Deep down, you *are* a homer.

Uniquio: You mean in the sense that I want to be home. I want to feel settled . . .

Universalus: Well . . . yes. Although you also have a lot in common with Homer.

Uniquio: Something tells me you're not talking about the poet.

Universalus: Well, you do have a lot in common with Homer Simpson. Guileless, with a generally good heart, but prone to thoughtless self-indulgence. Then there's the, ah, let's call them, 'spasms' of impatience. The frequent forgetfulness . . .

Uniquio: (*Interrupts Universalus.*) Okay, I get it.

Universalus: There's a few other things I could mention…

Uniquio: I'm sure you could. Can we move on?

Universalus: Well, in any case, by saying you're a homer, I was referring to your connection to home. You were never far from family when you lived in Philadelphia. You wanted to come home when you were living in Los Angeles — probably, what, a half year into living there? And now, you established 'home' again. You returned to a steady job, a steady relationship. And you realized that it was where you wanted to be in life.

Uniquio: J—— and I got married. We bought a house in New Jersey, near Philly. And I got a job that got my career back on track, working in the governor's office. In *a lot* of ways it was where I wanted to be in life. We had a lot of fun, living in that house. Still, I had the same, I don't know, discontent. It manifested as anger now and then — at work, with family, random experiences in public, and even with J——. She personalized it, which I understand now, but I couldn't back then. To me, it was normal to get upset about something and express it.

Universalus: You got mad, and it was over, and everyone moved on. In *your* mind.

Uniquio: Expressing anger was just something we did in our family. I figure it's some combination of a genetic thing and a learned behavior; my mom, my brothers and me, we were always prone to anger — especially with the people closest to us, our own family. My dad was the only one who didn't get mad. He was generally calm. But when he *did* get angry — which happened now and then — it was hard to be around. We relied on him to not do that.

Universalus: Everyone moved on, you say. But there have been some long-held grudges between family members over the years, with no communication. I think your dad was the only one who wasn't really involved with those long periods of silence between people.

Uniquio: That's true.

Universalus: You had described your dad as a solid presence.

Uniquio: He was. The way he stayed calm about things, compared to the rest of us, was something we all needed. It was right around this time — after J—— and I got married, but before our son was born — that my dad passed away. It happened very suddenly. There was no sign of a health problem. We were told that plaque lining the artery broke off and blocked the flow of blood to his heart, and that was it. He was playing golf with my mom and my middle brother in Florida. It was my parents' wedding anniversary that day, too. My dad loved being with my mom and his sons, and golfing. He was doing what he loved most.

Universalus: You didn't get to say goodbye.

Uniquio: No, not in person. Although a weird thing happened. My youngest brother and I went to Florida to be with our mom and brother. And from the time I learned my dad died, until J—— went off to work the morning after I returned from Florida, I had never been alone. After three straight days of constantly being with someone, I was alone for the first time, in our bedroom, and I started talking to my dad. I apologized, for not being the person he taught me to be, by his own example. I told him I wanted to be more like him.

Universalus: What do you think you meant by that?

Uniquio: I had in mind the calm, steady, reliable presence that he was. The contentment he seemed to have, with himself and his life.

Universalus: In life, especially when you were a younger adult, you tended to see what he was not — compared to what you wanted or expected him to be. You even saw the qualities you just described as signs of something 'limiting' and 'lacking' on his part. You saw him as lacking adventurousness and ambition.

Uniquio: I suppose that's true. (*Pauses, appears thoughtful.*) I've begun to wonder if that's how my own sons see me now — mostly in terms of how they see me fall short.

Universalus: Of course they do. It's the nature of things. Parents teach us how we want to be — and how we don't want to be, through the example of their behavior, which we do or don't adopt as our own. And now, with your father gone, and the loss sinking in, you were facing this — and seeing things differently. You wanted to tell him. So that he knew how you felt.

Uniquio: Well, that's the thing. At some point, talking out loud to him, I got the sense he could hear me. I felt his presence in the room. Then, for some reason, I looked over in the corner, where I had thrown my luggage when I got home the night before. It so happened that I had worn almost the exact same golf hat to fly to Florida as my dad had worn when he died; and I noticed that both hats were facing each other, and it looked as if there were people underneath them, having a conversation. My hat was sitting on the luggage in a way that made it seem as if I were looking up a little — my dad was a little taller than me; and my dad's hat was tilted sideways on another piece of luggage, as if he were listening. It felt like I was observing my dad listening to me. In that moment, I believed he was. I still do.

Universalus: Human existence is an illusion. We don't know what's really happening beyond what we can see. But we get signs, all the time. You can see them, too, if you're open to it.

Uniquio: I saw them. I saw signs of him being around. Less and less, as time went on. But I had a close call or two — and both of our boys did as well, years later, when they were babies. I felt certain that my dad somehow had a hand in preventing a tragedy.

Universalus: You're talking about something that goes beyond the laws of physics.

Uniquio: I know. But . . . it really seemed like invisible hands were involved. When our first son was born, before he could walk, we watched him a couple of times laying on the floor, laughing as if someone were there above him, interacting with him. It just . . . I don't know how to explain it, but it just *felt* like it was my dad there, playing with him.

Universalus: It was soon after your dad passed that your first son was born?

Uniquio: That's right. J—— was pregnant when I took a job in Washington, D.C. We settled in Maryland, had our baby boy, and I got my first management job, in an environmental agency. I did pretty well in it, and got an even bigger job as a result, with a water utility. We bought a big house, and then our second boy was born.

Universalus: You and your family were healthy. You were blessed.

Uniquio: There was a lot I was happy about. And I was happy a lot of the time. But looking back, I'm sure I missed writing.

Universalus: What was the job like?

Uniquio: Parenting children and managing adults is very similar. Sometimes the experience with people is rewarding and even a lot of fun. And other times . . . put it this way: You know how sometimes people say, 'there's two kinds of people in the world,' and then they explain two generalized differences?

Universalus: I say that sometimes.

Uniquio: Oh, really? How do *you* break it down?

Universalus: You go first.

Uniquio: Well, I was about to say that there are people who are primarily motivated by self-interest, and those primarily motivated to advance the greater good.

Universalus: That's not bad. I see it — not unlike the way you describe it in your book — as those who are closed, and those who are open. So there's a lot of gray area . . .

Uniquio: Well, as a manager, you deal with both types of people, and a mix of both — and you have to deal with the problems caused by the people and their egos. Just like you have to deal with your kids' problems and their egos. You start to notice the parallels between grownups and kids, in terms of that basic behavioral source.

Universalus: The question is, always, do you notice the parallels in your own behavior — and the worldview driving it?

Uniquio: Is that a rhetorical question?

Universalus: What do you think?

Uniquio: You're inscrutable sometimes. And I mean that as a euphemism for 'annoying.'

Universalus: So . . . you were busy dealing with little egos at home, big egos at work, and your own ego, of course — *and* you weren't writing. There was no outlet for reflection or expression.

Uniquio: I hardly thought about it. Until one day, I remember sitting at my desk, alone in my office, looking at my computer screen, staring through it, and I remember saying to myself — out loud, 'I guess I'll never be a writer after all.' I felt this sinking feeling; it almost surprised me. I guess I never processed it before. It was a depressing realization. Deflating. But I was resigned to it. I didn't think I'd write again. It was the afternoon, but it was as dark as night outside because of the weather — I remember that, too. Very vividly.

Universalus: Discovering something so important about yourself in the darkness. Surely you see the symbolism there. (*Pauses, tilts head.*) No? Didn't catch that? Yes? Maybe? (*Sees that Uniquio is distracted with his own thoughts.*) Anyone home over there?

Uniquio: (*Looks up, startled.*) Sorry. I zoned out there. I was just thinking . . .
Universalus: Well, you obviously returned to your writing, or we wouldn't be here right now.
Uniquio: Between work, babies at home, a grueling commute through the Beltway every day, I didn't even have time to read, no less to write. And then things started to get more stressful at work because my relationship with my boss was deteriorating.
Universalus: How so?
Uniquio: We had become friends back in New Jersey; we met when I worked in the governor's office. We got along very well, genuinely liked each other, and were fairly like-minded. He had recruited me to follow him to D.C., when he got a big job there. G—— was the reason I moved to D.C. He hired me for one job, and later on, promoted me to two others. I was his proverbial 'right-hand' man, which is how I got into management. He told me I'd be good at it because I could get people to work together without the authority to do it.
Universalus: That all sounds positive. What happened? What changed?
Uniquio: My take on the situation at the time was — and still is, today — that we each became obsessed with our own areas of focus: Me, with how things were working on the inside; him, with how things appeared on the outside. He was building his own brand, as a way to help rebrand the whole utility. But it seemed to me, and others in the organization, that he was focused on his public persona to the exclusion of things that needed attention internally. Maybe he was always that way, but I didn't see it. I saw him as being smart, *savvy* about it. Anyway, we did the Meyers-Briggs personality test with our executive team, and it turned out we had the exact same profile, with one exception: I leaned toward introversion, and he was a strong

extrovert. This one difference meant he had the profile of a politician, and I had the profile of an artist.

Universalus: That can be a volatile interdependent relationship. One is preoccupied with the outside world, the other with the inside world.

Uniquio: I remember telling G—— at the time that everyone is their own worst enemy, but that our personality types were especially problematic own-worst-enemies, and so we needed to watch out for each other. It was my way of trying to open a dialogue about how he wasn't paying attention to internal things, and that people were noticing and upset by it. In my mind, I was trying to be helpful — to *him*. This was someone who had previously impressed me as an accessible and supportive leader. I saw it work for him. But something changed, and it bothered me, and I'm sure he perceived this.

Universalus: You were aware he made sacrifices.

Uniquio: Yes. His children remained in New Jersey when he had taken the previous job to this one. I'm pretty sure they were in their early teens at the time. He left without any plan to live with them again, I don't think. I knew at the time that I couldn't make that kind of sacrifice. I wouldn't.

Universalus: So you knew he gave up a lot for his career.

Uniquio: I did.

Universalus: And his career *was* a political one. And his success in that career got *you* your job. Which, for you, was not political — and you got to go home to your own kids every night.

Uniquio: I understood all of that. I thought about it at the time. Looking back, even with all the things that got ignored, all the negativity from people around me, all the while being convinced that I had his best interest in mind, which I still believe that I did . . . in the end, I know that I personalized things I should have let go.

Universalus: An artist and a politician in a symbiotic relationship can work — up to a point. But when that point is reached, there's a break, and when it happens, the break is complete and usually irrevocable. One will decide the relationship is no longer in their own best interest and cut it off. And the other will somehow be surprised when it happens.

Uniquio: Interesting you mention that. It brings us to my Disney story.

Universalus: That's good to hear. I was trying to get us there.

Uniquio: We took the boys to Disney World, with my mom, for vacation. We had a great time. It was one of those experiences . . . put it this way: I knew it was a special time while it was happening.

Universalus: Disney is big business, and they're all about making money, and so they gouge people with their pricing because they can. But they *do* advance the importance of self-belief. And in that way, they bring tremendous value to society. *Tremendous* value. Government can't provide that. And while religion promotes belief, it's not *self*-belief. It's the opposite — belief is directed outward and onto something that exists somehow separate from what exists within us — the creative force and intelligence that is sustaining, and enlivening, and informing in all ways every person and every living thing in the universe.

Uniquio: You. I mean, ***Universal You***. Which, to me, is you.

Universalus: I'm merely a reference point. A perfectly — *and* purposefully — ridiculous one, at times. Getting back to the point, though, there's a dire need in humanity for self-belief. And for whatever its imperfections, Disney helps to meet that need.

Uniquio: That's a big endorsement. Did you sign a deal? I figure if anyone could get the creative intelligence of the universe under contract, it would be Disney.

Universalus: I put it out there because I'd like to see religion do a better job instilling in people faith in *themselves*.

Also, I'm putting what you're about to share into some context.

Uniquio: I guess I forget you're me, sometimes.

Universalus: *We* are . . . you. (*Pauses.*) You know, Kierkegaard said the self is that which relates to itself, or that in the relation which is relating to itself, so the self is not the relation, but the relation relating to itself.

Uniquio: Is that somehow related to our relationship?

Universalus: I have no idea. But it's fun to say! (*Pauses.*) So, you were in Disney, on vacation with the family . . .

Uniquio: We went to the fireworks show during our last night there and it had an unexpected impact on me, a powerful one. They play music to accompany the fireworks, and it's uplifting if you're in the right mindset. I guess I was, because I was moved . . . I don't know . . .

Universalus: Being in the 'right' mindset means you were open.

Uniquio: For all the running around, and standing around in lines, dealing with the crowds, I appreciated the experience as it was happening. The boys were too young to remember it now. But it was like watching them on Christmas morning, the joy and excitement of it, only it was several days of it. It was pretty cool. I was grateful as it was happening.

Universalus: Gratitude opens you. It's meaning is in the word's sound, right? Gratitude. *Great attitude*. In some ways, gratitude is the greatest attitude of them all. I believe you pointed out that the human brain doesn't process fear while in a state of gratitude. Fear closes you down. And so, gratitude . . . well, as I just said. It opens you.

Uniquio: It opened me to being moved when they played, 'When You Wish Upon a Star.' It made me emotional. I'm not sure why. Talking about it now . . . it's a little embarrassing. I mean, the singer is a cricket with a top hat, and my eyes are getting watery.

Universalus: There's a lot you've shared with me that probably warrants embarrassment. And a whole lot more from your life that you didn't share, that *definitely was* embarrassing. But you had to mention this experience; and there's no need to be embarrassed about it.
Uniquio: Anyway, I was holding one of the boys, and I'm sure that contributed to the emotion of the moment. I remember actually making a wish. It felt like something within and around me was opening up at the same time, almost calling for me to express a wish. So I did.
Universalus: You wished for superpowers. You always wished for those when you were a kid.
Uniquio: Well . . . maybe, in a way, I did. I wished for contentment.
Universalus: The simplest and, so often, the most elusive of treasures.
Uniquio: I realized . . . it *had* to happen. I realized I had to change. It was similar to the feeling I had when I felt my dad listening to me after he passed away. I knew I needed to be a better person. That was my wish — to find contentment, and be a better person.
Universalus: People so often — sadly, *too* often — fail to realize that *true* contentment cannot be realized by acquiring things, power, sensations, appearances. It's only possible by *being* a better person. By doing more, to in some way help others.
Uniquio: Well, it turned out to be a big turning point. Though not at all in the way that I had expected or hoped it would happen.
Universalus: That's often the case. Nearly always.
Uniquio: On my first day back on the job, I was let go. I knew something was up when G—— scheduled a meeting so early in the morning. HR and security were there when I got there, and I knew the drill.

Universalus: This caught you by surprise. So what was the reason given?

Uniquio: There were no explanations. I was told I could either resign, with a financial benefit and a period of health insurance, or I'd be fired as an 'at will' employee.

Universalus: Change was upon you. Just as you had wished for.

Uniquio: I had over 800 people in my reporting line, with a lot of responsibility. Suddenly, I had no one reporting to me, no responsibility, no income. With health benefits going away.

Universalus: What you thought was important was gone.

Uniquio: It felt like one weight was lifted from me, and another was dropped on me.

Universalus: Back into the field of the unknown. In this case, loss of life — as you knew it — was upon you. And as you pointed out, several times, it's painful.

Uniquio: At first, I tried to be optimistic. But I soon realized how hard it was going to be, to get a job that could sustain us. And that was the thing — I had a family to take care of. It was one thing to be out of work as a single guy with no obligations, but I had a wife and two babies depending on me now.

Universalus: I'm sure it was a scary place to be.

Uniquio: I never felt that much fear — at least not for such a sustained period of time. It was constant, and all-consuming. I couldn't sleep at night. It wore me down.

Universalus: The exact opposite of the contentment you had wished for.

Uniquio: It got so bad that I couldn't help the occasional thought that maybe the family would be better off without me. I never seriously thought of taking my own life, but having a decent life insurance policy, I also wasn't sure that being alive was the best thing for my family.

Universalus: That's a bad feeling to have. It's a dark place.

Uniquio: As it was happening, it felt like it would go on forever. We cut back on everything, but our financial situation was bleak. J—— was also looking for a job now, but we both needed to find something. I felt trapped. And guilty, because J—— was worried all the time.
Universalus: Worry blocks out the light, and the possibilities that flow from it. It's a focus on a belief that closes you. But it's understandable, of course — especially in your situation, as you both perceived it at the time.
Uniquio: One night, I was giving the boys a bath. That had always been my job when they were little, and it was one of my favorite things to do. They were too young to realize something was going on, even though I was no longer leaving the house five mornings a week. I remember sitting on the floor, wearing this old white T-shirt, feeling empty. Leaning over the tub, I felt like I was hovering over an abyss, staring down into it. I felt *hopeless*, like a failure; that all that I had failed to do, in school, in my career, had finally caught up to me. And even though I was mad at my boss, and a couple of other people I suspected had conspired to get me out, I blamed myself. I felt, in that moment, that it was all my fault. I let J—— and the boys down . . . they depended on me, and I let them down. By now the emptiness felt overwhelming. The stress was wearing on my body. I'm not sure how else to describe it. I remember thinking, I can't take this anymore . . .
Universalus: For a simple fun book, this feels like a Fellini movie.
Uniquio: What can I say? It was a difficult time.
Universalus: I understand, son. You were at a low point in your mental and emotional states of being. It's a critical point, when one of two things happens: Resurrection, from letting go — or destruction, from holding on.
Uniquio: I felt weighed down in a literal way. Maybe it was more like a feeling of being pulled down. I remember

thinking about how death would have been . . . I don't know, a relief.

Universalus: It was, in a very real way, upon you.

Uniquio: I didn't *want* to feel that way. I asked God for help. I believed in God, but not a 'personal' God, so I wasn't quite sure who or what I was asking.

Universalus: Often, what's needed is to quiet the mind and listen for God to be *heard*.

Uniquio: I knew that I had to let go. But I couldn't do it.

Universalus: It requires knowledge of *how* to do it. And it takes practice, doing it. It requires work to manifest it, to bring it forth — like any human ability.

Uniquio: I didn't understand it that way, at that time.

Universalus: But now, maybe, you were ready to learn.

Uniquio: I knew I needed help, and looked for it by reading. At first, I sought out positive messages online. I'd read quotes and articles about the importance of a positive attitude. It helped a little, doing that. I saved the quotes that helped most in a folder on my cellphone. I wanted to get back to reading books, but wasn't sure what to start with. Then one night I turned on PBS, and I saw this guy, Wayne Dyer, talking about belief. He seemed passionate and sincere in what he was talking about. And the most important thing was that his ideas made sense to me — they resonated. I realized this was someone who could help me. I bought his book, *You'll See It When You Believe It*, and I read it twice, it helped me so much.

Universalus: What was helpful?

Uniquio: He made the case that belief informed outcomes. He helped me believe it to be true. He got into the physics and metaphysics of why. And he pointed out that belief was a choice.

Universalus: *If* you make it a choice. Which requires awareness there *is* a choice.

Uniquio: That's right. After that, I read a book that had been sitting around on a shelf on our bookcase for years. I had picked it up once before, but I didn't really 'get it' at the time, so I set it aside after reading just a few pages. It was Eckhart Tolle's *The Power of Now*.

Universalus: You weren't ready for it before. And now you were.

Uniquio: In the few pages that I *had* read earlier, I remembered him writing about how, in a similar moment of despair in his own life — worse than my own, because he had suffered a full breakdown — he said, 'I can't live with myself' anymore. And it struck him that there was a difference — there was the 'self,' and there was the 'I' that couldn't live with that self anymore. He realized there was this greater awareness within, beyond the ego-based identity he had thought of as the entirety of himself.

Universalus: You remembered that preface . . .

Uniquio: And I realized it was the book I needed to read next.

Universalus: You were, now, open to the power of now . . . just as you were ready to believe in the power of belief.

Uniquio: I've read that book another five times since then. It's a source of comfort for me now. Probably like reading scripture is for some people.

Universalus: These writers helped you. They shared a light with you.

Uniquio: I don't know how I could have gotten through that time without them.

Universalus: At a time when you were ready to hear what they had to say. That's the thing about learning, growing. You have to be ready for the lesson.

Uniquio: In the traditional Japanese way of teaching karate, they never explained much of anything. They only answered questions when you were ready to ask them. And even then, the answer was usually, 'Keep training.'

Universalus: The only way to defend against your 'self' is to *practice*. It's a constant battle.

Uniquio: I kept seeking out other writers who reinforced the basic message that we change our world by changing how we look at it. It reinforced my sense of control. I had learned about it *before* this experience. I had read about it, learned it in the abstract. I had bought into the idea of it. It made sense. But I hadn't internalized it as a belief.

Universalus: The experience of change, of loss, was the transformative factor. You said you felt empty. What better to fill than an empty vessel?

Uniquio: I think the worst part of the experience was the feeling that I didn't have control of my circumstances.

Universalus: You have a strong, innate desire to control your circumstance. And you believed, then, like most people, that your circumstances were the things going on in your life around you. In many ways, you still do. It's an innate perception you'll need to battle your entire life. It's why you can't write without feeling settled; it's why you can't stand waiting, whether it's traffic, or on the golf course, or standing in line somewhere. It's why you don't like being told what to do. It's why you're literally claustrophobic.

Uniquio: I *needed* the realization that I controlled my perspective. I *wanted* to believe it. That was the difference from merely reading about it in a book and briefly thinking, 'that makes sense.' Hopelessness compelled me, in a way, to believe I could do something about it.

Universalus: You wanted to change your circumstances. You were open to the power to do it. You lived your whole life, looking outward for that power. It was inside, all along.

Uniquio: I began actively looking for different messengers, to reinforce and confirm the same message. And that search brought me from metaphysics to physics, because the modern metaphysicians, themselves, pointed it out: This *is* physics! And when I learned that the physicists agreed that the universe changed when you looked at it differently — that was the ultimate confirmation I needed to really embrace the belief. You changed your circumstance, which you couldn't control, with what you could control — your own mind.

Universalus: You had to let go of the one belief to embrace the other, the opposite.

Uniquio: My beliefs changed, and deepened. And, at last, I was able to let go of my fear and all the awful stress that came with it.

Universalus: Because you were aware and believed you had that choice to do it.

Uniquio: It was so incredibly... empowering. To just *choose* to stop worrying — and then... just stopping! Eventually, it became as easy as dropping a piece of mail in the mailbox. It was a 'lightening' experience. I really felt lighter inside.

Universalus: Lightened, by being enlightened . . . who would've guessed?

Uniquio: And once I let go, things *did* change positively. I thought I had lost everything. And now I was finding the peace and contentment I had wished for.

Universalus: There's a lot of cliché wisdom I could throw at you now, but I won't.

Uniquio: I still had to find a job, but the difference was that, now, I *knew* it was happening. And I was patient about it. I learned faith and patience go together.

Universalus: You can't *have* faith without patience. Not your strong suit, patience.

Uniquio: No, it's not.

Universalus: And your impatience manifests when you want to control what's going on around you. Once you figure out the ego, and take steps to overcome it, it will launch sneak attacks. It will get you when you're not looking. And so you need to be more aware of *that*.

Uniquio: I do catch myself, not being patient — it still happens a lot. And when I'm able to catch it, and choose to be patient, I physically feel better, and see circumstances change. It happens in traffic, and golf, and other probably much more important things — although those are two things in my life that seem to constantly present me with the challenge of self-control.

Universalus: And yet you enjoy driving. Your car, and a golf ball.

Uniquio: I really do!

Universalus: You need to look at both experiences, then, as an opportunity to practice patience. Patience *is* openness. And when you're open to life — to Life itself — it provides for you. It's the reason you're seeing things you hadn't seen before with this conversation.

Uniquio: I saw it happen once I was able to let go of my constant worrying. You could say that 'opened me' to the open state of patience. We found a good sum of money in an account from my old job that we didn't even realize we had. And then I met with an old friend, someone I knew from my earlier job in D.C. He hired me as a strategic planning consultant. That first check came exactly when we needed it.

Universalus: Because you were open to it.

Uniquio: And then this book came into being. I set out to make a presentation on the challenge of change, defining the challenge, and explaining how to overcome it. I had learned from experience that it didn't matter how sensible a strategic plan was, how well-resourced it was, the challenge of change was in people changing how people — the leaders, especially — looked at themselves and the way they related to the world around them.

Universalus: Although people in leadership positions don't often see themselves as needing to change.

Uniquio: Oh, for sure. And realizing that, I figured I ought to focus on it. So I drafted an outline of this presentation. I remember sitting at my kitchen table one morning, writing it out by hand on a yellow notepad. At first, I thought it could maybe turn into a white paper.

Universalus: You don't seem like the 'white paper' type to me.

Uniquio: I'm not. Sketching out the ideas I wanted to convey, it occurred to me that I could write a book. I had the time, now. But I quickly realized that there were a million books on change, and the people who wrote them were a lot more credible than me. They had relevant degrees, and experience as renowned leaders. Things I didn't have.

Univeralus: Your ego was giving you reasons why *not* to do it. To avoid failure, and protect itself from the pain of that.

Uniquio: That's right. And it really brought me down. But then it hit me!

Universalus: Sounds like a violent creative process.

Uniquio: It hit me as all the negative thinking began to take over, and I *caught* it — so I was able to let it go! And I remembered: I liked writing humor! So why not do *that.*

Universalus: And you not only chose a different *style* of book, but you took a different angle on its purpose. Usually these books intend and even promise to help people find happiness, career success, financial wealth — something individually oriented. You expanded your scope of purpose well beyond any of that, writing it to help people 'save the world.'

Uniquio: Well . . . someone has to do it.

Universalus: That's exactly right.

Uniquio: The idea kind of took on a life of its own — it just . . . happened. I believed a 'simple' and 'fun' approach would set the book apart. And I believed that I could write it.

Universalus: You wrote the book you wanted to read.

Uniquio: I guess that was a guiding idea.

Universalus: And you never would have started writing this book — you may have never written again! — were it not for you losing your job, and then going through what you went through. You wouldn't have known *what* to write, you wouldn't have had the *drive* to write it, were it not for your experience and what you learned from it.

Uniquio: No. (*Pauses, appears reflective.*) I wouldn't.

Universalus: It's why it's so important to confront, and move past, the fear (*starts singing in that same, sort of high-pitched voice*) while you're moving on the *high*-way . . . to the . . . danger zone! You gotta take the *high*-way through the . . . danger zone!

Uniquio: You know, I never actually liked that song.

Universalus: You *think* you never liked it. But here it is, over and over.

Uniquio: Now I'm not sure I'll ever get it out of my head.

Universalus: (*Bobbing around in his chair like a happy child, resumes singing.*) Danger zone . . . danger — za-watch out when you're flying through the *dane*-jah zone . . . Oh, Lord!

Uniquio: Za-watch! *Za-watch?* You're trying to do lead *and* backup vocals now? And what's with the 'Oh, Lord!' There's no 'Oh, Lord!' in the song.

Universalus: You know, I wanted to sing it earlier, when you were talking about losing your job, but timing matters with humor. Unless you're a dad. In which case you think your humor is funny even and especially when the timing is completely wrong. It's a weird thing.

Uniquio: I can relate to that. And evidently you can, too.

Universalus: I'm glad you can appreciate that, son. So it says here in my notes that you're not going to bore everyone with details on the writing process itself, but that you more or less allowed it to take a life of its own, and so it did. You trusted the process, of opening up, and allowing it to come through, until you knew it was what you wanted it to be.

Uniquio: You have *notes* that tell you what I'm . . . *going* to say?

Universalus: You wrote them.

Uniquio: Was there anything in the notes about still being in the danger zone? Because I was. The consulting job ended after eighteen months, and during that time we were still getting behind financially. J—— got a job fundraising for a local theater, and that helped to keep us afloat, but just barely. I was back to needing a full-time job again.

Universalus: You were in the same place. But in a much different place.

Uniquio: Instead of fear and pessimism, I felt gratitude and optimism.

Universalus: You had, now, everything you needed — your family, your health, a new perspective — and, related to that new perspective, you had the work of your life before you. You were on your way to writing *this* book. And you were aware you had everything. You had contentment — while in the danger zone! And that calm mindset better enabled you to navigate the challenges of that danger zone.

Uniquio: Well, I really want to thank you . . .

Universalus: What for?

Uniquio: For not singing 'Danger Zone' ever again. I'm thanking you in advance.

Universalus: I could break into the chorus of Barry Manilow's 'Looks Like We Made It.'

Uniquio: Please tell me you're kidding.

Universalus: I'd change the lyrics, so there wasn't a romantic connotation.

Uniquio: That won't help. Well, I guess it would. But seriously. Please don't.

Univeralus: If you insist. Anyway, our time is up for today.

Uniquio: Already? (*Seems surprised. Looks around. Points toward stage right.*) According to that clock on your wall, we're ending a little early.

Universalus: It was your edits. You made this shorter, removing some conversation; it was either awkwardly written or made you look bad. Besides, if we had droned on about the bleakness and despair stuff too long, we risked the audience turning to their cellphones to watch AI-generated videos of babies doing standup comedy and house cats fending off charging black bears.

Uniquio: It can be a challenge, spinning bleakness and despair into simple fun.

Universalus: Since we're wrapping up a little early today, maybe you can make it downtown in time to see the Socrates lecture. I heard he's talking about how to seek deeper truth and understanding by questioning the purpose of Kohl's coupons.

Uniquio: Sounds interesting, but I have things to do. I need to, um, shine my shoes.

Universalus: Apparently 'shiny shoes' are a big thing in your family. Although . . . (*points to Uniquio's shoes, then looks at Uniquio*) you're wearing Chuck Taylors.

Uniquio: (*Looks at his Chucks, then at Universalus. Pauses. Maintains deadpan expression.*) I meant to say I need to give myself a haircut.

Uniquio and Universalus rise and walk to the door, stage left. This time, only Uniquio exits after they shake hands; Universalus remains, facing the audience. The lights go down, and a spotlight falls on Universalus. The visual effect resembles the part of Saturday Night Live *when the host introduces the musical guest.*

Universalus: Ladies and gentlemen . . . Loquatio.

He exits, and another spotlight falls on Loquatio, who is standing at center stage.

Loquatio:

Our hero's story gets real, as we approach the ordeal —

Because a family changed it all —
the way he'd think, and he'd feel.
With his own father now gone, his own two sons came along:
He knew with fatherhood, the time was now to right what
was wrong.

Our hero had responsibility,
and now his dreams were no more.
Because he had no time for dreaming,
the way dreams filled him before.
He had it all, but now a part of him was missing and absent.
And sometimes anger filled the void,
the rising up of resentment.

Then our hero got a message, from the land of make believe.
The time was now to change his life —
and life said, 'Go ahead, and leave.'
But then the fear of loss and unknown got so all-consuming
That he couldn't see the seed of possibilities blooming.

And then one day it got too much — at last, he had to let go.
A simple choice, he always had, and yet he never did know.
Belief in Life itself had brought him forward,
into the light —
All the time, right there inside, and yet against it, he'd fight.

So many years, he searched out blindly,
And Life would ask, 'Why can't you find me?'
And then the time had finally come
His own worst enemy, be done.

And so through death and resurrection,
Our hero found his own reflection.
The treasure now in his possession,
The greatest one — a Life connection.

act two ends p. 254

The paradox of life revealed:
To take control, you had to yield.
Through faith and patience we are healed,
We learn this on life's battlefield.

And yet this journey he was on still had a long way to go,
Because his pockets, nearly empty, had a few seeds to sow.
That's when he found, again, his writing;
and he recovered its purpose.
Open your heart and mind, let go,
so you can follow your own bliss.

That's all I got for now; it's all I got to say —
Time to get back to the story, and our play about play.
I'll be coming back around, I ain't goin' away,
Cuz' it all comes back around — back to our circular way . . .

To our circular way . . . to our circular way . . .
to our circular way . . .

Loquatio departs stage and, again, his message continues to echo after he disappears, eventually fading to silence. The stage goes dark.

Scene Four: Session Four

Loquatio returns to the stage from stage right. When he reaches center stage, a spotlight falls on him. A microphone on a wire slowly drops from the ceiling, as it does for an announcer in a heavyweight bout.

Loquatio: Ladies and gentlemen, welcome to our final event of the evening! We're gonna eliminate your confusion, and come to a conclusion, and hope that each contestant can prevail without contusion. (*HEAR: Beginning of the theme song from* 2001: A Space Odyssey, *as smoke rises around the door at stage left.*) First let's introduce someone who truly is 'all that.' Although he's not really 'someone.' Because he's really not anyone. You know him as the creative force and intelligence of the universe, transcending all forms — but here, with us, in human form with those clunky-ass old man shoes and thick-ass glasses! He's the 'Reality King' — he's, really, *everything*. He's the one, the only . . . *Yoooo*-naaaah-*verssss*-uh-luuussss!

Universalus' entrance to the stage is accompanied by flashing lights, pyrotechnics, video, confetti, balloons, etcetera.

Loquatio: Next, let's introduce the hero of our story! (*HEAR:* Entry of the Gladiators, *the theme song for circus clowns, as Loquatio continues to talk over it.*) He's the kind of hero you do *not* want to see having a love scene, attempting his own stunts, or trying to rig something to get out of trouble. Please welcome back, for his final appearance of the night, your 'once in a lifetime' everyday guy, symbol of the hero — and the ego! — in all of us; a man ahead of his time, because he had his midlife crisis in his Twenties; my personal all-time *favorite* writer, without whom I literally wouldn't be here: Yooooo-*neeeek*-eeee-oooohhhhh!

Assuming all the special effects money was spent on Universalus' entrance, have one of the backstage workers trot alongside Uniquio waving a small flashlight in one hand and holding a pinwheel in the other. When Uniquio gets to his chair, Universalus is waiting at his. HEAR: Sound of boxing ring bell. Both sit down at the sound of the bell.

Universalus: So how are we doing today?

Uniquio: Are we going to pretend that whole thing didn't happen?

Universalus: I think that's for the best. Especially for the audience.

Uniquio: I wanted to start this last session with both of us in some kind of ridiculous trap, like Batman and Robin used to find themselves in. You know, on that show from the Sixties.

Universalus: I don't see how that would have made any sense.

Uniquio: It wouldn't. I tried to make sense of it, but it wasn't there.

Universalus: That hasn't always stopped you before . . . the 'not making sense' thing . . .

Uniquio: (*ignores comment*) It's too bad. I was picturing us tied to our chairs beneath two giant magnifying glasses, with the sunlight approaching. We could have played that ominous music they used to play, when Batman and Robin were trapped. That would have been *great*.

Universalus: I don't disagree, but I'm sure the guys from production are glad we're not doing that. It's not like we're working with the budget for a new *Top Gun* movie here. Which reminds me: When we left off last time, you were in the . . . (*pauses; winces visibly, as if trying hard not to sing*) . . . danger zone. The field of the unknown.

Uniquio: It was stressful — for J——, especially. Even though I was confident things were working out, there was no sign of progress. We were barely paying our bills.

Universalus: Maybe you two were under the giant magnifying glasses, metaphorically speaking. Maybe. (*Pauses.*) I need to give that one more thought . . .

Uniquio: I think you're on to something.

Univeralus: We talked earlier about how it's not enough to believe that positive things *will* happen. You have to believe they *are happening*.

Uniquio: Even when things on the surface seem to be going the wrong way, you have to believe that whatever is happening is exactly what needs to happen.

Universalus: It's the 'patience' part of the equation. You know, there's a song that comes to mind. Just say the word. I do a pretty good Axl Rose . . .

Uniquio: I seriously doubt that. No one does a good Axl Rose. *Axl Rose* doesn't do a good Axl Rose anymore. By the way, it just occurred to me, that *you're* the one who's been singing my personal theme song in my head all these years. With the backup vocals, and the orchestral arrangement. You know the one I'm talking about? It's like a Sinatra song. I used to hear it in my head while I was walking to my car after lunch for some reason.

Universalus: It's a *good* song! We really ought to produce it someday. But right now we need to focus on the patience thing. It's important — but difficult.

Uniquio: It is. It *was*. But . . . that was the helpful thing about my mindset. I knew I had to accept not knowing *how* change would happen. I just had to know it was *happening*. You wonder, sometimes, if you're kidding yourself. But you can't let doubt creep in. And when it does, because it *does* happen, you have to fight it.

Universalus: What were you doing every day, if you weren't working?

Uniquio: Mostly, I went to the county library, to look for a job, and work on the manuscript. And look, there were days — moments of days — when I felt like a big loser, being there with all the other people who didn't have a job, for whatever reason. One day, I remember there was this one guy wearing a trapper hat and a ratty old blanket as a cape, walking around and asking everyone, 'Have *you* seen Cookie? I need to talk to Cookie!' You could smell the poor guy from twenty yards away.

act two ends p. 254

Universalus: Was he looking for *a* cookie, or someone named 'Cookie'?
Uniquio: I believe he was looking for someone *named* Cookie; he needed to *talk* to Cookie.
Universalus: Maybe he wanted to talk to *a* cookie.
Uniquio: Does it really matter? Who cares if he wanted to talk to a 'Cookie' or *a* cookie?
Universalus: I guess you're right. So . . . you were struggling to stay positive. Like right now!
Uniquio: I was. I had to fight the impulse to be negative about my situation.
Universalus: (*Sighs.*) I think you'd be surprised by my Axl Rose impression.
Uniquio: So . . . what's up with the singing? I hate to break it to you, but you're terrible.
Universalus: That's on purpose. The imperfection makes me more relatable. More like a normal human being. Aren't you more comfortable, with all *your* imperfections, relating to someone who isn't all genius-y and wisdom-y all the time? I'm flawed, just like you!
Uniquio: I feel like the wisdom-y stuff is a lot more helpful than the singing.
Universalus: So simple fun isn't important, then?
Uniquio: Okay, you got me there.
Universalus: It sounds like you realized what you most needed to achieve was *not* the outcome you wanted in the future. It was the controlling of your attitude in the present moment.
Uniquio: I did. I believed that was *how* I'd achieve the outcome I wanted.
Universalus: It *was* how. But you were also aware that negativity *will* creep in.
Uniquio: I worked at that. It mostly worked. And it got easier and easier.
Universalus: But you probably couldn't convey too much

optimism to J—— at the time. She would have thought you were crazy — or worse, abandoning your responsibility.

Uniquio: The little optimism that I did express about the book I think worried her that I was living in a fantasy world, not properly focusing on the real one. I understood it, so I tried to walk the line of being positive and appearing . . . 'realistic.' Eventually I just stopped talking about it altogether.

Universalus: Well, you *were* in a fantasy world, so to speak. You were creating your own reality. You were literally creating your own belief — you could say, 'living in a land of make-believe.' Which, from an outside perspective, can seem a little kooky — like a person wanting to talk to a cookie. Especially while in the middle of a challenging circumstance with other people depending on you.

Uniquio: Are you saying that me, creating my own reality, was the same as the guy who believed he needed to talk to Cookie?

Universalus: No, it was different because you were creating your reality *knowingly*, by conscious choice. Most self-destructive people develop their realities passively. That goes for people who, let's say, 'normally' self-destruct, as well as those who suffer from a mental illness of some kind who don't, or can't, treat it somehow. What I'm getting at is that you changed your beliefs *actively*, aligned to an outcome, a positive one for you and others, that you chose.

Uniquio: I didn't tell J—— or anyone else in my family, or among my friends, that I knew that things were working out.

Universalus: I'm sure it was a lonely feeling, sometimes, believing what you believed and not feeling like you could really share it.

Uniquio: I've come to believe that being the only person to believe in yourself is part of the challenge of believing in yourself, sometimes.

act two ends p. 254

Universalus: It *is* part of the challenge, to believe in your own dream, knowing that no one else shares your belief. So, how did the job search finally end?

Uniquio: I reconnected with a former colleague, someone I had promoted years earlier, who had recently become the director of the recreation department in the District of Columbia, of all things. It was kind of ironic, in a way, because that's how my dad got his career started. Running a recreation department.

Universalus: Your dad helped you get your first jobs after college. And you got the public administration degree because your dad had one. You also said it seemed your dad provided a 'helping hand' sometimes, after he passed. And now you're saying your dad started his career in recreation, which is where you got an opportunity for employment at this time of needing a job. It seems to me there's a lot of connections there.

Uniquio: So maybe it wasn't a coincidence.

Universalus: Coincidence. What's that, really? I was planning to let you realize this on your own, but you said the 'wisdom-y stuff' helps so I'm just going to put it out there: 'Recreation' is not only the field of your father's career start, but it's arguably *the* major theme of your book — in terms of how you focus on the 're-creation' of reality, and in terms of how you focus on play, which is, of course, another word for recreation.

Uniquio: I never put that together. Maybe this whole thing — what we're doing here (*gestures between himself and Universalus*) — ought to be a new form of therapy: Just have people write out a conversation with themselves, and project wisdom onto one of the conversationalists . . .

Universalus: You've known for a long time that, while writing this, you became more self-aware.

Uniquio: I suppose it's kind of been a 'do-it-yourself' therapy.

Universalus: You *suppose*? The man supposes. So you had this opportunity in . . . recreation.
Uniquio: Yes! Things had lined up nicely. About the same time I got this job offer, my friend, B——, who had hired me to be a consultant in my previous employment, put me in touch with a wonderful lady, very well-connected in the city, who had started her own consulting firm. She offered to include me on a project with a big client, right around the time I got the job offer with the recreation department.
Universalus: So now you had two jobs to choose from.
Uniquio: Well, luckily, I didn't have to choose between them. My new boss, the department's chief of staff, understood I wanted to work as a consultant on the side. He was okay with that because he wanted me to operate as a change consultant in my job. He realized they had a big culture problem, and he wanted me to help him with that. It was a great situation. I was able to use vacation time to work on the consulting gig I'd landed. And I had time to continue writing as well. All three forms of work complemented one another because they were all about helping people change — from different vantage points, I guess you could say.
Universalus: How did it feel, when things came together, after believing everything was working out *without* evidence that it was?
Uniquio: I thought about it all the time. I wasn't surprised, but I was still amazed how 'letting go' brought structure, and support, and opportunity to my life.
Universalus: It was happening — positive outcomes, out of a positive mindset.
Uniquio: And it continued to help. The client for the consulting gig realized I was a substitute for a more experienced and credentialed person who was originally identified as the 'change expert' and she wasn't happy about it.
Universalus: The client wanted to change the change person.

act two ends p. 254

Uniquio: I also soon learned that the entire leadership team was unhappy with the whole engagement because the *real* problem with the culture and need to change was with the person in charge, who hired us. The leadership problem was the CEO of the organization.
Universalus: So the leadership problem, the leader, wanted to change the change person.
Uniquio: I had the feeling no one wanted us there. Eventually, I think B—— and I managed to win over a few people, or at least we were less the object of their objection to the whole thing. But then, I had a full day scheduled to engage every team member, one on one, to help with their own professional development.
Universalus: Including the CEO?
Uniquio: No. In her mind, the problem was with her team, not her.
Universalus: I'm sure her team members loved that.
Uniquio: B—— confirmed to me that they were not happy about it.
Universalus: And maybe they went back to projecting that resentment onto you.
Uniquio: I tried to prepare myself, to not personalize it, if they ended up being resistant to our engagement. I understood it, really — it would be a way for them to exert some control over a situation they didn't want to be in and probably felt otherwise powerless to avoid. Still, I wasn't looking forward to those one-on-one conversations. I mean, who wants to talk with people who don't want to talk with you?
Universalus: People who lack self-awareness don't mind at all. It's one of the reasons they say ignorance is bliss. Ignorant people are ignorant of their ignorance. They talk about what they want to talk about without pretending to care what other people have to say.
Uniquio: I've worked with people like that.

Universalus: I know, it's why we mentioned it. It feels cathartic, getting in those digs. But really it just exposes your own shortcomings, and how you need to grow past them.

Uniquio: Well, that stings. But I know you're right.

Universalus: So you were going to have conversations with a bunch of people who didn't want to have a conversation with you. *One on one* conversations, no less. Hm!

Uniquio: I remember taking the train into the city, thinking about the long day ahead, talking with people who didn't want to be there. Seven of them. In a row. For an hour each.

Universalus: And you had no experience doing this kind of thing.

Uniquio: None.

Universalus: Perfect! What an opportunity . . .

Uniquio: I tried to prepare. I had questions written out to ask them. And I tried to be positive about it. It was when I was focusing on that, on being positive, that I realized that I needed to ask them questions to get them talking about things they wanted to talk about. By now, I was thinking about simple fun a lot, because that was the working title of the book at the time. So I figured the questions should be simple — and fun! — to answer.

Universalus: Practicing what you were preaching.

Uniquio: It's surprising how easy it is to forget to do what you *believe* works.

Universalus: The challenge isn't so much remembering new ways of thinking, as much as it is catching old habitual thought patterns that contradict those new ways of thinking, and then purposefully letting them go. Unlearning the old is harder than learning the new.

Uniquio: We have the same problem as dogs. But we like to think only the dogs have it.

Universalus: Rather than dwell on what could go wrong, you opened yourself to a new way.

act two ends p. 254

Uniquio: Right. And I figured there's three things everyone likes to talk about: What's most important to them, what they love doing most, and what they're the best at.

Univeralus: You're figuring all of this out on the train into the city.

Uniquio: Yeah, it was a last-minute thing. I think I sensed a conventional approach wasn't going to work.

Univeralus: You know, a train symbolizes progress on a spiritual journey.

Uniquio: (*Pauses to reflect a moment.*) Well, I *did* end up having a discovery of sorts. Something that no doubt got me to where I am, and still helps me to this day. Something I still practice, and is still helping. Did you——? Never mind.

Universalus: The 'omniscience thing' can be handy. Especially in this line of work.

Uniquio: Yeah. (*Pauses.*) Well. Hm! By the time I got to the metro station, I made up my mind that I was only going to ask those three questions, to get people talking about things they wanted to talk about, and let the conversation go however it naturally went from there. The plan was open-ended. I guess there was some faith involved . . .

Universalus: Did you have a backup plan? Maybe pulling the fire alarm during a bathroom break? Or you could have done that thing you mentioned earlier in the book, shuffling backward out of the room and acting like you didn't know what your feet were doing . . .

Uniquio: No, I just had Plan A. My new Plan A. I kept building on it right up until the first person arrived to talk. I thought about this book I'd been reading, about what really motivates people, and how important it was to have a sense of purpose connected to what you're doing, connected to something bigger than yourself . . .

Universalus: Like, saving the world . . .

Uniquio: Broadly, yes. So I added to the last question, to ask, 'What do you do best, to make the world a better place?'

I figured I could help these people see their professional objectives a little differently by discussing their answers to that question — along with the other two.

Universalus: How did it go?

Uniquio: It was amazing. Honestly, I could hardly believe how well things went.

Universalus: That's ironic. But not unusual. It can be hard to believe when the belief — in yourself, especially — manifests in some way that you don't expect.

Uniquio: They actually *enjoyed* talking with me. Just asking those simple questions, about things important to them, and then listening, mindfully, just really paying attention to their answers, to convey my interest in theirs . . . it visibly built their trust and won them over. That had been the plan. And it worked.

Universalus: I have to give it you kid, that was a good plan. Pretty . . . pretty good.

Uniquio: There was another aspect to it. I came up with this idea at the end of the train ride. I had dismissed it as first, but something was telling me I had to follow through with it.

Universalus: That was me. I was telling you. And I made a point of providing you the idea while you were still on the train. So that you would decide to follow through while you were waiting for your first client. So that we could make this connection now.

Uniquio: I feel like you're adding another dimension to this whole thing.

Universalus: I am. (*Pauses, smiles.*) That, I am.

Uniquio: (*Shakes head, turns to audience, gestures to Universalus.*) Can you believe this guy?

Univeralus: That's the question.

Uniquio: Anyway . . . so, I figured — or, rather, I was (*rolls eyes, makes finger quotes*) 'inspired with the idea by the creative intelligence of the universe' — that by encouraging each person to come up with their own 'I am' mantra, based on the answers to those three questions, it would help them manifest what they wanted to do in life. I would actually be helping them in a way I believed would help them — through belief.

Universalus: Imagine that!

Uniquio: And you know the old saying — that the best way to learn is to teach. It occurred to me, hey, I ought to have my own message to myself, my own chosen belief, to put in my mind.

Universalus: Like a mantra — a seed to see what one wants to see.

Uniquio: I like that!

Universalus: You're patting yourself on the back.

Uniquio: It's still easy to forget what we're doing here, somehow. You added a new dimension. It's confusing.

Universalus: So you were going to clearly define *your* chosen belief.

Uniquio: I had a little time to get settled before my first meeting, so I took the time to come up with my own . . . chosen belief. I answered those questions — for myself. It was easy to do. What was most important to me in the world? My family, and providing for them, in every way. What did I love doing the most in the world? Other than being a dad, it was writing. Which also happens to be what I believed I do best, to help make the world a better place.

Universalus: And your view of success?

Uniquio: I viewed success as helping people throughout the world. I combined those answers into two sentences, and I had it. Oh, and I made the statement in the present tense, to affirm that it's *happening*. Not *going* to happen. That it *is* happening.

Univeralus: And you said that you were going to add at the end, 'I am that, I am.'

Uniquio: That's right. And I also decided I was going to share with everyone my own chosen belief, hoping it would help to build trust — you know, sharing something personal.

Universalus: You know, sharing that kind of thing could have gone horribly wrong. You were dealing with a potentially hostile audience. The whole mantra thing can seem weird to people, not to mention a little 'cornball.' You were making yourself vulnerable to ridicule.

Uniquio: I know. But somehow, I knew it was going to go well. And it did. I mean, everyone was varying degrees of skeptical at first, but by the end, they were all engaged and even seemed to enjoy the conversation.

Universalus: Wait a second, now. What did you tell them? About your own belief . . .

Uniquio: What I shared that day, and have continued to say just about every night, ever since then, is that 'I am a successful writer who helps people throughout the world; and through my work, I bring to my family presence, love, well-being, and abundance. I am that, I am.'

Universalus: Okay, not bad. I mean, it beats 'I'm good enough, I'm smart enough, and doggone it, people like me.'

Uniquio: You were taking credit for me coming up with this about five minutes ago.

Univeralus: C'mon, you *know* I was kidding. People need to purposefully create the belief in their minds that aligns to the positive outcomes they desire. And with so much negativity and self-doubt generated by ego, you've got to plant that seed and nurture it.

Uniquio: It's funny. Not your Stuart Smalley joke — although it was okay. I mean the way people reacted to the question about what was most important in the world to them. As if they hadn't thought about it before. But they were easily able to answer the question.

Universalus: And that opened the door to constructive conversation.

act two ends p. 254

Uniquio: A couple of people even seemed to have their own revelation.

Universalus: And planting your 'see what you want to see seed' ended up helping you. All because you were trying to help other people.

Uniquio: The thing is, I didn't *really* believe my chosen belief at first. But I kept planting the seed every night in my mind. And over time, the belief took hold and became real. And then the belief became reality. While still writing this book, I brought more presence, love, well-being, and abundance to my family. I don't know if they noticed, and probably, they didn't.

Univeralus: When you're a dad, the tendency is for the rest of the family to focus on what you do wrong. It goes with the territory. And that can be helpful, if you look at it the right way.

Uniquio: But I know it happened. And those things all happened *before* I finished writing the book. I hope to continue to bring more of those things into reality, every day.

Universalus: Sounds like things were going well. For the third time in our story, here, you made it back to the safety zone. That is, you returned to the *perception* of a safety zone. The perceived circumstances you associate with a safety zone.

Uniquio: An important distinction.

Universalus: But things *were* coming together. You were manifesting your belief. You had two jobs now — and were bringing your writing into your work.

Uniquio: I felt like I made a positive impact at the recreation department, too. One person, a colleague I became friends with, painted a watercolor of Albert Einstein for me, because she knew Einstein was an important part of this book; and another person — someone who I didn't even know very well — gave me a 25th anniversary edition of *The*

Alchemist. I was really flattered by both of those gestures. It meant a lot to me.

Universalus: So you were in a good place, literally and figuratively.

Uniquio: But I had to muck it all up somehow. I can't say it was a bad decision, really. J—— and I thought it might be the best for us in the long-term. Now, of course, I believe that it *was* for the best, but it wasn't in the way we thought it would be.

Universalus: Did you say you had to . . . *muck* it up? With an 'm'?

Uniquio: It was an 'm,' but it did eventually seem like an 'f.' Not long after this all happened, I got recruited for a job in Pittsburgh, and we decided I should take it. It seemed like a good career opportunity at the time, but once I got there, I found out that the job itself, and the politics surrounding it, was all-consuming.

Universalus: Cliché alert: The grass wasn't greener . . .

Uniquio: No, it was not. Plus I was traveling back and forth to Maryland for a couple of months before the family moved out to live there with me. I wasn't writing much; progress with the book barely limped along.

Universalus: So you had faith in the book, but not enough to hedge your bets and walk away from a more conventional career opportunity.

Uniquio: I know. I realized that. But I also have no doubt, now, that it was what had to happen, to get us to where we are today. We loved the city and our neighborhood in Highland Park, but the house we rented had a lot of problems — it was falling apart, there were no kitchen counters, windows were falling out, there was no heat on the third floor. We even had a ghost. By the way, can you explain those?

Universalus: There's a number of things that can cause rotting window frames.

act two ends p. 254

Uniquio: No, I mean ghosts. We heard one knocking from inside our little guy's bedroom closet. It went on all night, for several nights, until we unlatched the door — and then we never heard it again. Prior to that, S—— said he saw someone sitting in the corner of his room sometimes. He called it, 'Freaky.' My other boy, B——, said he saw a shadow walk up the steps.

Universalus: That kind of stuff freaks me out.

Uniquio: No kidding. It freaked *me* out. What's *that* all about?

Universalus: We're not here to explain ghosts. They're not explainable. A lot about life isn't. Getting back to Pittsburgh . . .

Uniquio: Okay, fine. Well. The school the boys attended had problems, too — our little guy complained it felt like a prison, which I understood completely, given the iron bars on the windows and the iron fencing penning in the narrow, paved area for kids to play. That's not to mention what they experienced on the bus. We're talking elementary school felonies, here.

Universalus: They got to see firsthand how rough it can be for some kids.

Uniquio: I think they avoided the direct bullying, mostly, but yeah, they saw it. Which is something else I just don't understand. It's harder to understand than ghosts, really. Why all the suffering in life? Why does it have to be? Especially for innocent children.

Universalus: Because it is.

Uniquio: *That's* your answer?

Universalus: It is.

Uniquio: Well . . . it *is* a *very* unsatisfying answer.

Universalus: The people who cause all the suffering are doing it because it's a projection of their own worldview. You talk about the value of suffering in your own life. You just did.

Uniquio: That's because it was self-inflicted suffering. I was creating the pain in my own life. That's different than the suffering of innocent people. People who have suffering inflicted on them by others. I don't see how any good can come out of that.
Universalus: No, you don't. You're looking for a dogmatic answer to life, and that's not why we're here, is it? So let's get back to Pittsburgh.
Uniquio: (*Pauses, frowns, sighs, unsatisfied.*) Hm. Well, we talked about the house, the schools . . . and then there was the job. It was just one unnecessary problem after another, dealing with all the politics. It was like working in the governor's office in New Jersey — incompetent people in important positions who had no idea what they were doing, but being absolutely certain that they did because they had political influence.
Universalus: So you were in a less-than-ideal situation in Pittsburgh.
Uniquio: Well, we weren't there long, because a recruiter found me, and we had an opportunity to take a corporate job in West Virginia, and we did it. Everything turned around for us — we found a great house and neighborhood; a great school for the boys; and the job went really well. It wasn't without its challenges, by any means. But there was stability, which is something the whole family needed.
Universalus: And it's what you needed, to write.
Uniquio: That's right. And I finished it. I got into a regimen of waking up early every day to work on it. At first it was all the weekends and days off; then I added in early weekday mornings until it was every day. Of course the pandemic came along, which on the one hand made my job a lot busier, but it also somehow made it easier to write before work started. I could get up at five am or so, write until eight, and then get to my job.
Universalus: No big problems to deal with?

Uniquio: There are always problems to deal with. Did I mention the pandemic? But it didn't seem like there were always problems because I chose not to focus on them, or what I perceived to *be* problems, and the 'what ifs' of worrying about them.

Universalus: All that was left to do was share what you learned.

Uniquio: By the time I was in the homestretch of writing this, I was appreciating everything in my life a lot more. I felt contentment, mostly. Although I still struggle mightily with patience. Still, I was very happy with where we were in life. I still am. I'm grateful.

Universalus: What you wished for. Upon a star, if I recall — with music, and fireworks.

Uniquio: Crazy, isn't it?

Universalus: It's the opposite of crazy.

Uniquio: Life was fun. I picked up golf again, with my older boy being very involved in it, and I've found a lot of joy in that, playing with him, and friends, friends from work, J—— and our little guy, when I can get them out there. I play alone sometimes too, and I enjoy it.

Universalus: As addictions go, golf is a pretty good one. It's you against you. Like karate. And writing. And being a human being.

Uniquio: I had already put those connections together on my own.

Universalus: Well look at you, self-analyzing like a big boy!

Uniquio: Now that I'm nearly done writing the book, the process of getting published begins. But even as I'm, now, making final edits, I've already made connections to make it happen.

Universalus: As expected. And it's happening. In fact, it happened. Look, there (*gestures to the book on the table.*) You did it. It got published.

Uniquio: So are we done, here?

Universalus: I think so. So what have we learned?
Uniquio: Maybe I like the song 'Danger Zone' more than I thought or cared to admit.
Universalus: That's right. Anything else?
Uniquio: I remind you of Homer Simpson. Which means I remind . . . *me* of Homer Simpson. Or maybe Homer Simpson reminds me of myself.
Universalus: That's almost Kierkegaardian. Almost. What else?
Uniquio: There's a circle of life, for every person. And how you live within — or beyond — that circle depends on how you look at it. Do you live as a prisoner within your own, limited worldview, or do you live as a free person, beyond it?
Universalus: So . . . you'll allow your boys to do whatever they want?
Uniquio: What? Whatever they *want*? No! I mean, I can't do that . . .
Universalus: Say again?
Uniquio: I have to keep them safe, and healthy — and channel their powers for good.
Universalus: That's right. You can't transcend the boundary of a circle unless there is a boundary of a circle to transcend. A parent should help create the child's circle, their boundary, and then help the child to transcend it.
Uniquio: Help them find what they love to do, to make the world a better place.
Universalus: And then let go.
Uniquio: (*Sighs.*) Yeah. And then let go. They're well on their way to going. I can see it. I'm going to miss them when they move out. A lot.
Universalus: But you would agree that, when they do move on, it *will* be a positive change for you — as long as *your* 'Big A' Answer to life is 'Yes.'
Uniquio: Well, yes. Sure. Accept the suffering that goes with a sense of loss . . .

act two ends p. 254

Universalus: Acknowledge it. Observe it. Accept it. And then let it go — to make way for the feeling of gratitude that you were able to help prepare them for their own journeys. It's all you can do.
Uniquio: Yeah . . . it's all pretty simple. (*Pauses.*) But still, it's going to be hard. It's that constant battle, to choose one's attitude . . .
Universalus: The battle *is* constant. And it's the battle of human life — to bring forth Life itself. (*Pauses and smiles.*) I'm glad we had this talk.
Uniquio: I am, too. It needed to happen. I learned a lot.
Universalus: Well, we've been relating in some way ever since you came into this world, although hopefully this helped you to open up, and get some things out in the open.
Uniquio: I'm an introverted extrovert, so I have mixed feelings about sharing so much. Mostly, I'm uncomfortable with it.
Universalus: Oh, c'mon! What are you worried about?
Uniquio: Well, some will judge. Instead of actively directing their open-minded attention to what is, people passively engage their close-minded diversions from, self-serving perversions of, and flat-out hostile aversions to what is. But there's no point in worrying about it.
Universalus: *Everyone* will judge. It is what it is.
Uniquio: 'It is what it is.' You know, I never liked that phrase. And yet it is . . . what it is.
Universalus: That, it is.
Uniquio: And in a way, I guess *that's* what this has been all about.
Universalus: It is.

Uniquio and Universalus sit quietly for a moment, stand up, and then do that awkward thing where one of them extends a hand to shake while the other tries a fist bump, and then the other one goes for the fist bump while the original fist-bumper tries to shake hands; they simultaneously wave off the whole failed attempted exchange, and walk to the door, stage left — where, this time, they embrace, and wave to the audience, before departing for the final time. Loquatio returns to rap about the final part of the journey. The stage lights remain on.

Loquatio:

It's the fourth and final quarter of our circular journey,
With the danger of our hero running out of his money.
He doesn't want to find himself, again, in that position,
And the answer is his writing; it's inside his composition.

Letting go — of the society, the piety, anxiety —
He found the light of simple answers, like a new sobriety.
Inside it had been hidden, as if stolen by a thief,
The life of love he wanted, self-created through belief.

There yet remained one test, one final sacrifice.
But was he ready now, prepared to pay the price?
Could he say 'no' to the judging, and the fear — and desire?
Could he say 'yes' to what is, and so to keep rising higher?

You gotta' bring forth Life, or you're gonna be destroyed —
The life that you're, now, living's meant to be enjoyed.
You gotta' let go of ego, let it suffer and die:
Only then you'll be released,
and with your wings, you can fly

This is the boon of resurrection —
Lightness guiding your direction.
Allow the Life you are to be.
A simple task, and you'll be free.

act two ends next p.

Our hero to his home returned,
With wisdom learned, awareness earned.
The book is done, he's more aware,
And all that's left to do is share.

That's all I got for now; it's all I got to say —
And that's the end of the story, and our play about play.

I won't be coming back around, cuz now I'm goin' away,
But it all comes back around — back to our circular way . . .
To our circular way . . . to our circular way . . .
To our circular way . . . to our circular way . . .

Loquatio leaves stage, tips his white and red striped hat as he walks off.

PART FIVE

The Prophecy

There's 'nothing' to see here!

Man is the center of a circle without circumference, except the one he creates for himself.
-Mahatma Gandhi

Same goes for Woman!
(Circling back to an earlier clarification.)
-Universalus

At last, you have learned about *everything*. And perhaps learned a thing or two! Because that was the point: To explain how life works, so to help make it better for you. When you simply have fun *and* aren't being a wee-wee, you're open to Life and it flows through you freely. But when you're unopen to opening more, then you reduce Life to some 'thing' you ignore.

To further our point, we defined the big problem, which is you — and the 'me' in the world that you see. By projecting your fears and desires and judgments, you self-create what is your worst enemy. That bad apple, ego, first lures and then traps you inside your false, self-centered reality. Though wisdom and science, together, have taught us: The way to break free is to simply 'be.'

But simply 'being' is not at all simple. It's an ongoing battle to make life your own. It requires a journey — a hero's adventure! — on a path that's well-traveled, but traveled alone. You *are* ***unique*** you — *and* you are ***Universal***! The two are as one (fun!) whenever you play. With mind and heart flowing, ability going, you say 'yes' to life and to Life you make way.

We saw this play out in our play about play, in our hero's own story of his way to *the way*. And wasn't it funny, all of what was uncovered? By opening up, his own path was discovered! Yes, it's true, he did not see (though clearly right there) his own father beside him, from out of nowhere. But with presence and love going into the play, he shared with his Pop all that he had to say.

Past prologue, point, problem, path, play about play — we have come to the end, time to be on our way.

But wait! It's the reader:

'Now then, tell us — what's next? For something is missing from the end of this text! Do you see anything on our human frontier? For ourselves and each other: Where does life go from here?'

Oh, uh . . . yeah. Hm! Okay. (*Pauses, reflects, uncertainty, awareness of the uncertainty, awareness the reader is waiting, wonders what the reader is thinking, visceral experience akin to panic arises, but it's not too bad (though enough to notice) until sudden pangs of worry about dying overtake him (God knows why) immediately followed by existential dread at the thought of being there when death happens, awareness this thinking is ridiculous and unhelpful, remembers not to worry, engages in the usual mental sparring until the worrying subsides, notices lingering upper body tension, remembers to let it go, purposeful relaxation (that feels better!), remembers the reader, then the question; then it dawns on the writer.*) Oh! I see . . . something about everything to send you on your way. Yes, of course . . . nothing to it. (*Another pause, this time a brief one.*) How 'bout this:

Around in more circles we're all bound to go. Will you rise or fall? Know your Answer to know. Remember your madness. Remember to be. Remember to choose what and how all you see. Remember to play your own song for this dance, for belief *be*-comes *life*. *You divine circumstance.*

And then we have rays of light — really, one great light within which individual beams of light, evenly spaced apart and clearly lined by Nature, as if to make a point — burst forth from the bottom of the page. So magnificent, so astonishing, so *inspiring* is the radiance, it makes you think of angels singing. (If you can't see its radiance, it may be because the page is the exact same color white as the light, or more likely because we don't have that kind of technology for paper just yet, which the publisher confirmed.)

Whoa! Lo, and behold! It is our prophecy!
From which all can profit, by Being set free:
Bring forth **P**resence — and **L**ove — and **A**bility
— and '**Y**es' is your Answer to Life and to Be.
Yes, **PLAY** *is the way*. And we hope you agree.
Your own 'Big A' Answer to life is the key.
You see, *everything* is about how you see.
(And that, my good reader, is the last word from me.)

Presence in mind . . . Love in heart . . . Ability in body . . . Yes in choice . . .

PLAY

is
the
way!

HALLOWED HEATHEN

Raised in Maplewood, New Jersey, C.J. Carew began writing during his early adult life living in Philadelphia, where he wrote a few short stories and, eventually, a novel that remain unpublished (and are perhaps unpublishable).

He discovered his affinity for satire while writing a collection of (also) unpublished (though perhaps publishable) short stories after an encounter with author Frank McCourt. Life, marriage, and children interrupted Carew's writing for nearly ten years, until a job loss presented what became an opportunity to write **LIFE STANDS EXPLAINED**.

He continues to write while living with his wife and two sons in West Virginia.

www.ingramcontent.com/pod-product-compliance
Ingram Content Group UK Ltd.
Pitfield, Milton Keynes, MK11 3LW, UK
UKHW040604210726
13854UKWH00009B/2422

9 798900 757018